What is the **BREAKTHROUGH ZONE?**

Breakthrough Zone is about how to create breakthroughs for people who work in large organisations where so much of the energy is committed to keeping things going the way they are.

It is simply that to invent new futures you need a new way to be innovative.

In this book **Mac Andrews** and **Roy Langmaid** provide managers with a step-by-step journey that will enable employees to become more innovative, with the end result of creating exciting new products, brand extensions and services.

Breakthrough Zone comes complete with checklists and tools to resource this journey: how to execute it, manage it and draw results from it.

Mac Andrews and **Roy Langmaid** have worked together transforming brands and businesses for 8 years. Their work with big brands spans the globe from AMP in Australia, Singapore Airlines, Holiday Inn EMEA, Saudi Arabian Airlines and VISA in San Francisco to Unilever throughout Europe as well as a list of British companies that includes B.A., Granada, Carphone Warehouse, BT and BUPA. Those experiences formed the basis for this book.

Mac, co-founder of the Institute for Creativity, UK, is a highly experienced specialist in creativity, insight and learning and their applications inside businesses large and small. He now operates with The Brand Works Ltd using customer insight to grow and develop brands, their products, services and cultures - he can be contacted by email at mac.andrews@thebrandworks.com

Roy is the originator of the Breakthrough method. He works for Promise, a consultancy based in London and New York, which specialises in helping organisations to keep their customers at the centre of their thinking. He may be contacted at rlangmaid@promisecorp.com

The Breakthrough Zone

THE BREAKTHROUGH ZONE

Harnessing Consumer Creativity
for Business Innovation

Mac Andrews
and
Roy Langmaid

John Wiley & Sons, Ltd

Email (for orders and customer service enquiries): cs-books@wiley.co.uk
Visit our Home Page on www.wileyeurope.com or www.wiley.com

Other Wiley Editorial Offices

John Wiley & Sons Inc., 111 River Street, Hoboken, NJ 07030, USA

Jossey-Bass, 989 Market Street, San Francisco, CA 94103-1741, USA

Wiley-VCH Verlag GmbH, Boschstr. 12, D-69469 Weinheim, Germany

John Wiley & Sons Australia Ltd, 33 Park Road, Milton, Queensland 4064, Australia

John Wiley & Sons (Asia) Pte Ltd, 2 Clementi Loop #02-01, Jin Xing Distripark, Singapore 129809

John Wiley & Sons Canada Ltd, 22 Worcester Road, Etobicoke, Ontario, Canada M9W 1L1

Wiley also publishes its books in a variety of electronic formats. Some content that appears in print may not be available in
electronic books.

Library of Congress Cataloging-in-Publication Data

Andrews, Mac.
  The breakthrough zone / by Mac Andrews & Roy Langmaid.
    p. cm.
Includes bibliographical references and index.
  ISBN 0-470-85539-8 (Cloth : alk. paper)
  1. Organizational change. 2. New products. 3. Consumer satisfaction. 4. Customer relations. 5. Creative ability in
business. I. Langmaid, Roy, 1946- II. Title.
  HD58.8.A713 2003
  658.4′062--dc22

                                                                                            2003019774

British Library Cataloguing in Publication Data

A catalogue record for this book is available from the British Library

ISBN 0-470-85539-8

Typeset in 11/14 pt Palatino by Sparks Computer Solutions Ltd, Oxford – http://www.sparks.co.uk
Printed and bound in Great Britain by TJ International, Padstow, Cornwall PL28 8RW
This book is printed on acid-free paper responsibly manufactured from sustainable forestry
in which at least two trees are planted for each one used for paper production.

Contents

Foreword

If your business depends on keeping your products and services fresh and relevant to customers then this book is for you. If, too, you rely on staff to play a part in the delivery of these same products to your customer, you will also find a great deal of use for the book.

I first met Roy Langmaid and Mac Andrews in 1999 when I was Chief Executive of the then Granada Group. During that year they helped our senior executives get a first hand experience of our own businesses in a most original and exciting fashion. These same executives, myself included, visited another operation within our company as customers. So a TV boss went to an hotel, hotel executives visited TV studios as part of a public audience, people from our head office rented TV sets and the rental people travelled the motorways and stopped off at our service outlets. This meant that they went as bona fide customers, for they were not known outside of their own businesses.

More than that, they gave up considerable time to do this and took their families with them. This ensured that the impressions we got were not constrained by the natural wishes of an executive to be supportive of colleagues. The wives and children in particular pulled no punches.

They helped us to go further, too, with our learning from this exercise. Not only did we experience our businesses at first hand, but when we got together afterwards we brought our partners along too and the whole group developed 'live' reconstructions of their experiences and invited the actual business owners to visit. It was a day of creativity, fun, openness and a great deal of learning for everyone involved. We were able to go straight from these experiences to generating product, service and management improvements to bring our customers better products.

I have long felt that we must put the customer at the centre of everything we do. And that many of us do not place customers high enough on our daily agenda. We have a great many layers and filters that keep us safe from face-to-face encounters with our customers. We collect their opinions and preferences through surveys and focus groups; and while these provide an excellent set of data for our operations, they don't really let you walk a mile in their shoes. Roy and Mac do. Should these shoes have holes in them you will feel the discomfort on the soles of your own feet and this will give you an insight into the faults in the customer experience that can prompt corrective action immediately.

Some time later we had a great new idea that needed the enthusiastic support of a large group of staff. This was in one of our businesses where the core product offering had not kept pace with customer needs – TV rental. Roy and Mac devised and ran a programme that had more than a thousand staff pitched into understanding and working with the new product, each with a great degree of individual freedom to bring their own personality to the process. You could see on this programme that learning with these guys is fun and that everyone got a chance to make their own contribution to the mix. This business was struggling with some very adverse market conditions and it was mightily refreshing to see staff enthusiasm picking up and taking off again.

The book is full of practical ideas and suggestions; but more than that it contains some passionate and timely arguments for the importance of creative, personal and fair relationships in our business community.

Charles Allen, Chairman, Granada Television

Acknowledgements

We would like to thank all the people who have pioneered this work with us and their organizations in 17 countries around the globe. Without their courage and trust, the insights that we have endeavoured to share in this book would have no authority at all. Through their generous partnership with us, and beyond the normal parameters of accepted practice, we have gained access to privileged information about ourselves, clients and customers to the ultimate benefit of us all – and in all domains of our lives.

We also want to thank our families, Nicky and Gabriel, Roy's partner and son, and Kim, Tom, Abby, and Jessica, Mac's wife and children, for their inspiration, love and daily lessons in all the things that matter most about people and living.

1 | On Innovation and How to Use This Book

As we celebrated the millennium it seemed that the world had gone innovation crazy. 'Innovate or die' had been the rule for the preceding few years. Just a few months later we were living through the downturn caused by one of the biggest innovation misjudgements of all time – the overvaluation and excessive optimism generated by the Internet boom. At the time of writing we are still living through the effects of this downturn and, just as at the millennium it seemed as if nothing could go wrong, now it seems as if nothing will go right.

In that purple period leading up to the year 2000, innovation was the order of the day. People were being ordered to invent, being seconded onto innovation teams, brainstorming like there was no tomorrow. On the whole, we found people who at some level were a little bit lost, doing their best to 'think out of the box', generate new ideas, etc. Innovation at this level for the average manager is a pretty tall order. There is so little certainty, so few means genuinely to tell the 'dud' from the 'great' idea. True innovation, however small, affects the whole business. It is risky, difficult, and requires that the person has some idea of what to do and how to do it. Not only that, it presumes that the person *wants* to innovate.

Since the downturn the call to innovate has had a hollow ring. Economic uncertainties have made us vulnerable. Certainty is hard to come by these days. How do you know for certain what innovation is not only relevant to your market but also relevant to your brand? How can you pioneer breakthroughs being sure of anything? Might it not be better to just keep doing what you

1

know best? So many people bet so much on the 'New Economy' and then the bubble burst.

In addition to the concerns raised by uncertainty there is always a great deal of internal unrest provoked by innovation programmes because they can rebalance the whole business. They might enlarge someone's empire while diminishing someone else's. They might mean shelving someone's pet project or diverting resources from one department to another. Thus even though staff have no direct involvement in such a programme, they may be wary of it.

There is also a missing dimension to most innovation programmes. What if you could explore and incorporate customer insights as you develop your ideas? Rather than generating a stack of flip charts and then

Breakthroughs demand much more substantial information than superficial survey tools are able to provide.

trying to decide which might succeed, wouldn't it be smart to have customers to guide you in this creativity? What we have noticed over the years of working with big organizations is that they very rarely consult their customers in ways that support true breakthrough thinking. *They rarely invite customers into their creative process at the deepest level.* Admittedly there is some market research activity based around the ideas process, but most of it is of a conventional nature. Survey data and the outputs from focus groups are the standard tools, and both these are inherently based on opinions and preferences. All of our opinions are contingent on the day-to-day situations that we find ourselves in. They vary as the weather, or as the attitude to innovation does. This seems especially true of products that are everyday or do not seem to affect us at any deeper level. A choice of toothpaste or washing powder might seem superficial, unimportant. Indeed, switching between brands in this sort of market has become commonplace. But is that because of the lack of importance of the brand, or because manufacturers in these markets have fallen over each other trying to exploit, steal or borrow any glimpse of originality in their areas so that all claims to our loyalty have become devalued by insincerity or overuse? Breakthroughs demand much more substantial information than superficial survey tools are able to provide. There is importance both to toothpaste and washing powder, but you have to go about discovering it by using different tools.

Look at how the sales of computers went from meteoric growth to stagnation almost overnight. Who could have predicted it? Yet if you were involved in the PC industry you only had to come out from behind your desk and witness first-time buyers struggling to operate their PCs at anything like peak performance to realize that the industry was failing to manage and support its promises.

In our view, breakthroughs require us to get under the surface and make contact with people's deeper desires and wishes. Of course I want to be a man with plenty of RAM, but I don't want to look like an idiot because I can't send my child's first picture to the printer in front of my expectant family. Moreover, such is the embarrassment and shame attached to such failures that I am not going to be the first one in a focus group to admit that my performance was floppy, if you will excuse the pun. When you look at all the self-confident crowing in computer magazines it would be akin to admitting that you can't change a plug on the iron.

This book seeks to provide some answers to the questions of how to create breakthroughs and innovate successfully. We are writing it in the sure knowledge that just as the world turns, sooner rather than later we will all turn our eyes back to the value of innovation.

Powerful brands are based on enduring customer needs and desires: unless they satisfy these they are on a high road to obsolescence. *Uncertainty about what will sell generally originates inside the increasing distance between the customer on the outside and staff on the inside of organizations.* How can you possibly feel certain about appetites from which you have distanced yourself? Customer Relationship Management, one of the latest corporate fads, provides few if any answers. It is largely an attempt to appear to be treating customers personally, whilst trying to sell them more. It is essentially a sales tool and customers fully understand this. Many of them are offended and irritated by the pretence. Reducing customers to statistics and data renders them two-dimensional along with our understanding of them. It might seem cost-effective, but we would argue that CRM does customers no service whatsoever. It certainly cannot lead to breakthrough innovation except by accident. How do *you* feel when rung up at home in the evening by someone who has got your name from a list? How do you feel when wading through the mass of unsolicited mail that finds its way to you addressed in an impersonally personal fashion? How does it feel when people who don't know you from Adam profess personal connections? Fake, phoney, intrusive and shiver-making are the words that occur to us. So even if your CRM programme does generate some sales, how much damage is it doing to your long-term reputation and relationships? How long before you, too, become another toothpaste?

There is only one reliable path to customers' hearts and minds that we have found – COMMUNICATION BASED IN TRUST. Without trust, customers will not respond honestly when confronted by questions about their needs and desires. To the average person their deeper needs and desires are some of their most closely held secrets. Inquire about them and people will play safe. Let's face it, some of our desires and needs might feel quite shameful or embarrassing to us. This is so with customers too. Therefore, special environments are necessary to make such conversations possible. Such forums – in which customers can learn about their own desires and needs, and then share their learning with host companies – are what we specialize in creating and facilitating.

We call a forum like this the 'Breakthrough Zone'. It is the most reliable source of true customer-based insight that we have found in 35 years of working with groups. This book outlines the most efficient and effective route for anyone to take in order to create breakthrough innovation from the creation of initial insights right through to final implementation.

Without trust, customers will not respond honestly when confronted by questions about their needs and desires.

The Breakthrough Zone is the central arena in our journey of discovery. Viewed as part of our process it is sandwiched between two other elements in the innovation process:

- preparing for the Breakthrough Zone (gathering resources);
- in the Breakthrough Zone (creative research with customers); and
- after the Breakthrough Zone (insight creation, project invention and implementation).

Throughout the book we have attempted an outline of the process that is systematic, as far as is possible. There is a recognizable pattern to the book that will allow you to consult it in a predictable fashion or take a more casual 'dip' into it for information or ideas. In general, each chapter will have two parts. First, what to do, when and why, and second, where appropriate, a resources list. Some chapters will require you to take in more principles than others.

We have found that the bigger the project and the more there is at stake then the more questions people will have. Furthermore, as new ideas take shape there will be a need for explanation, rationalization and justification. We have endeavoured to give you the knowledge you will require to be able to create your own answers to questions by fully explaining the process as we go. If there are any questions where we have not provided the information you need to create an answer, then please let us know.

Each of these types of information has been kept separate for convenience. Each is indicated by its own icon.

Icon 1 – what, when and why   Icon 2 – what you need   Icon 3 – advanced practice

As you read it you will easily get the hang of recognizing exactly which section you're in and whether or not you need it.

Each chapter will begin with a few simple principles to set the context. Then it will tell you what to do, when and why.

It will then inform you what you will need in terms of resources (room types and bookings, physical resources, film crew hire and briefing, type of facilitators and skills etc.).

There are several chapters that deal with more personal practices that will build some new skills that will enhance your results. We have separated these out by giving them a third icon.

This book is based on years of experience with customers and clients. We believe that the chance to build on their experiences is absolutely invaluable to anyone who is charged with responsibility for developing or renovating products, services, brand positionings or designs. In the case of the clients, each of them has worked with us on sizeable breakthrough projects in large organizations. They have been generous enough to share their experiences retrospectively in order to provide us with the best learning available in this field. All of our principles have been thoroughly tested in the real world – not just by us. What we are writing is a synthesis of our experience, and most importantly their feedback to us about what has worked and what has not.

We have found that all too often innovators are sent out alone. Split-off into Skunkworks or Innovation Teams, they take all of the organization's hopes for the future with them into some off-site bonanza of flip charts and magic pens. They may rapidly become an object of resentment and derision to those left behind in the organization to do the daily work, who perhaps feel that their own prescience or intelligence was not good enough to get them invited to take part. To help cope with this divisive component of innovation work we have built a communication strategy that ensures the project sponsors are kept both well informed and in the seat of their authority. Permission to continue the project is given step by step. The process is full of checks and balances. The process design protects your budgets by not committing all your financial resources to final implementation until a series of activities has been completed that has proved or disproved the feasibility of the innovation in question. There are also systematic consultations with colleagues and other members of the organization to ask for their input and suggestions along the way.

Above all, the process keeps the most important authority of all in the centre of any innovation programme: THE CUSTOMER.

If you want innovators, you will have to be innovative about how you manage them. Anyone at any level in your organization who reads and inwardly digests this book will become a powerful influence for the kind of innovation that will keep your business ahead in whatever market you exist.

Enjoy this book and prosper.

2 | Building Your Case

Step one – before you start … STOP

State **T**he **O**bjective **P**roblem/**S**helve **T**he **O**pportunity **P**anic

You might find it strange that we are beginning here. Surely innovation is usually driven by the appearance of an opportunity in the marketplace? Of course this is true. However, responding to opportunities in the marketplace creates problems. Any call to change does. Being swept away by the excitement of the opportunity often leads to premature implementation of poorly crafted solutions. The race to solutions is all too common.

Organizations tend to express problems in terms of solutions …

> 'The problem is that if we just changed the way we trained and recruited customer service personnel then …'

Tucked away in an obscure corner of upbeat and optimistic briefing documents we often find hidden what we call the 'objective problem'. This is the spin-free, unmarketed and simple fact that outlines the problem.

> 'Our market share is declining and our shareholders are losing confidence.
> 'With no change we will be insolvent in six months.'

Objective problems are unsophisticated and hard facts. 'My wife doesn't love me any more' is a simple and hard fact-based summation of a clear problem.

In corporate terms a hard fact-based summation of a clear problem might be:

- 'our sales are declining by 35% per year'; or
- 'our training programmes do not deliver the results we want'; or
- 'our customers see through our proposition and don't believe us any more'; or
- 'we don't know what to do to put us ahead of the competitors.'

When we do not take the time to bottom out the problem, we tend to start organizing premature solutions to what appear to be problems but are in fact merely symptoms. Suppressing symptoms might temporarily make us feel more comfortable, but the disease is unchecked. It will pop up everywhere.

We have learnt that nobody generally knows what the problem is for several reasons, and even if they do, they do not dwell on it for long:

- hardly anyone will ever say the words 'I don't know' in business;
- problems are dispiriting, depressing and cause anxiety;
- when we are anxious at work we want the cause of the anxiety to go away;
- the knowledge is obscured by generating premature solutions to stop us being anxious;
- the word 'problem' is replaced by 'opportunity';
- until we *know* that we don't know we can't find out – all our energy goes into sustaining a pretence that we do.

Individuals tend to think that they know what the problem is, but it is interesting to see how difficult it is to get people to agree. When did you last put the world to rights with one of your parents or family? What about with your husband or wife – how do you both get on when you discuss 'the problem'? Many such discussions descend into argument. Everyone will have their pet point of view. Look at Prime Minister's Questions for example. Communities are never short of a variety of views, many of them conflicting.

Yet until the disease is diagnosed as a simple fact, the treatment will be symptom suppression. Suppressing symptoms weakens the health of the entire body allowing the disease to spread further. This is what we suggest you do instead.

This first step involves some active research. This is the research that starts with you. It requires you to answer three questions fully.

- *What is the fundamental objective problem?* No spin.
- *What is the simplest way of stating it?* (What we call our 'STOP Statement'.)
- *What is the corporate impact?* (Where is it showing up and how? What are the overt and hidden symptoms? Be as detailed as you can be.) These will ultimately be where you place your measures for success of any project that comes from the implementation process. Draw a Corporate Impact Map – this is a drawn model of your business with each department identified in its own box (see Fig. 2.1). In a central box write the primary function of your business. This we also call the 'primary task'.

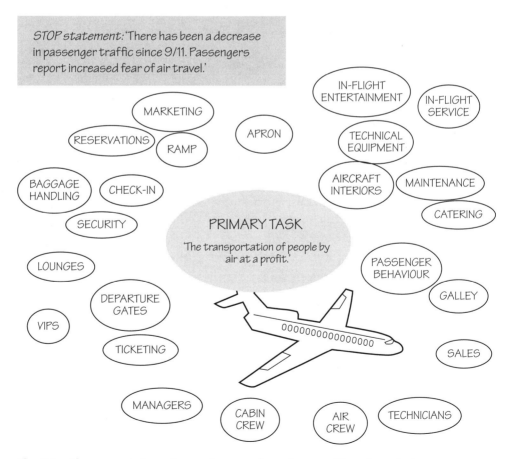

Fig. 2.1 The corporate impact map, step one: elements around the primary task.

What is the main thing you do? Next arrange the departments and/or operations or functions around the primary task (see Fig. 2.2). What do you think the impact of the problem or opportunity is on each of these departments/functions (see Fig. 2.3)? Whether or not you have answers does not matter – the next step will take care of that!

Take some time with our diagrams and enter what you think the impact is likely to be on an airline experiencing this objective problem. Add one item for every department before you move on.

Don't buy anything yet! Don't buy your own spin! Don't buy blame ('if only the MD would listen to us then …')! Don't buy *any* solutions!

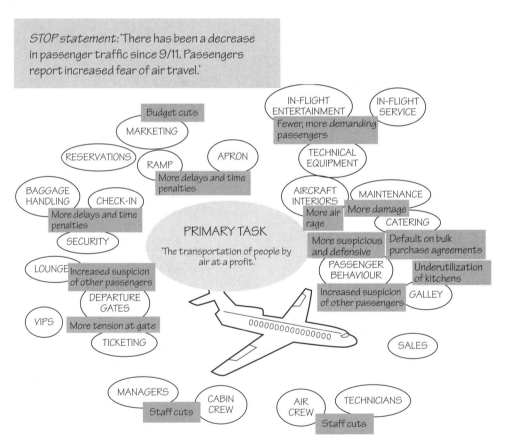

Fig. 2.2   The corporate impact map, step two: mapping the impact.

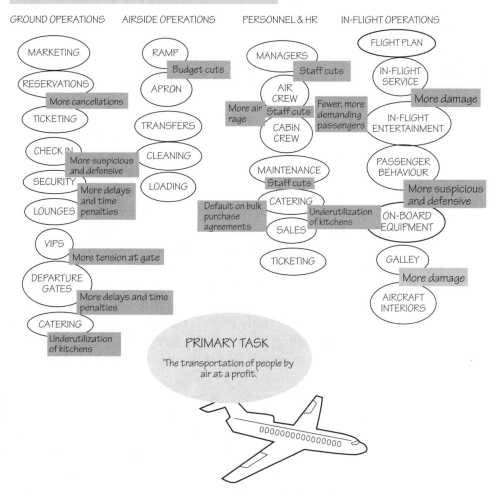

Fig. 2.3 The corporate impact map, step three: impacts operationalized by function.

Step one – resources

At this early stage you need nothing more than your own wits and your fa-vourite thinking aids.

Step two – people, power and purpose

There are three things that an innovator requires: *people, power and purpose.* In all the creative endeavours that we have witnessed, relationships are always the source of results. It may be that you are the only person that sees the opportunity for innovation. In that case it is really essential that you enrol as many people as possible into a shared view of the situation. No one ever achieved anything of note alone.

The British culture encourages an ambivalent attitude towards power. Within organizations, power is really the most sought-after commodity, even though very few people will ever admit it. Everything from trying to get longer lunch breaks to winning million-pound budgets is about power – the difference is scale. Making any difference at all requires raw power. How an individual uses power defines them. Powerful people are able to empower others to lasting effect.

Powerful people are able to empower others to lasting effect.

If you think that you have very little power in your organization, then it is time to start seeking it. Every action that we advocate in this book is designed to help you acquire more power. It also contains all the guidance that you need in order to use that power well. Not only that, it is designed to protect your more senior colleagues from feeling in anyway threatened by your power. If you are already at the top of your company, the process we are recommending protects your interests too.

Without purpose there can be no direction. All too often we find teams whose members are all pulling in different directions, even though on the surface they appear to be committed to a common goal. Defining the purpose is the first step to creating firm foundations for the future of your innovation project. This will require some research, because your view of the problem or opportunity will be just that – *yours.* Throughout your organization people will view it differently whether you like it or not. Finding out how they view it will accomplish two things. Firstly it will enable you to define the problem or opportunity in terms that are meaningful *for everyone,* and secondly, listening to people will begin the difficult process of enrolling your team. Preaching the meaning of data and your own point of view will almost inevitably distance people. Everybody is selling a point of view either overtly or surreptitiously. There is something to harvest from everybody's point of view; which brings us to our first principle of enrolment – inclusion. It is vital to enrol as many people as possible in your initiative and the way you include folk is by listening to them.

So, *people*, *power*, and *purpose* are all interdependent resources. Expanding any one of these resources will immediately expand the others. So let's get moving.

Every problem has a history. Every department that is suffering symptoms caused by the problem has been staffed by people who have moved on and taken their expertise with them. People move on faster and faster these days and often everything they have developed in experience, history and wisdom goes with them. The people who have replaced them will have a lot to say too. It's time to have coffee with some of these people.

Here is your to-do list.

- *Listen to stakeholders (and ex-stakeholders)!* A stakeholder is anyone who is affected by the STOP Statement as you have written it. Remember that CUSTOMERS are probably stakeholders too! How might you listen to them – not just through the CRM and MR data – really speak to some!
- *Is what they tell you affecting your STOP Statement?*
  - *Don't* buy waffle. (Avoidance strategies.)
  - *Don't* buy blame. (Especially 'If' statements.)
  - *Don't* buy solutions. (Fear motivated rescue packages!)
  - *DO* listen for the objective problem.
- *Thank them all for-helping you – they will help create your team when the project hots up! Take care of them.*

Step two – resources

Many people set off for interviews with a tape recorder, forgetting that in order to get anything from the tapes they will have to listen to them. This takes as long as the interviews and is unnecessary. Listening is the best thing you can do. Things will strike you as you listen. The more people you listen to, the more themes will emerge. Take a notebook with you but do not have this be a substitute for listening. It is best to use your notebook after each session to record the main points and the impact that it had on you. Keep notes brief – trust your listening to tell you what is important.

All you need is your ears, your ability to let things land and questions to ask.

Open questions are best on the whole:

- 'What do you think about …?'
- 'What do you think is the real problem with …?'
- 'What do you think are the most important aspects of …?'

Stop talking at that point and listen, even if you think they're talking rubbish. They will be feeding you jewels; above all they are enrolling themselves in your project!

Step three – distilling your STOP Statement

Distilling your STOP Statement into its most accurate and simple form is now what you must do. The shorter and more concise your STOP Statement is, the more effective it will be. Start with a summary of everything that you have heard. Make sure that all the points of view you heard are represented in what you write. Your job is now to edit it to its most concise and accurate form.

With each version of your statement keep asking yourself *'Is this a symptom of something deeper?'* When the answer is *'I don't know'* or *'No'* then you have the best statement of the problem you are likely to get. This is now the most powerful piece of data in your world, and it is the *only* piece of data that you need at this point.

Remember that it will be a hard fact-based statement. Most people will find it intolerable and will start to race around trying to reframe it as an opportunity. There will be opportunities galore – but don't go there yet.

You will also have a significant set of facts regarding the corporate impact of the problem. This is the second most important piece of data you have. The cost of the problem being this way is the most compelling motivator to your finding a sponsor. It is helpful – if you have not already done so – to build a Corporate Impact Map. This is a useful tool throughout the entire process.

The higher up the organization your sponsor is, and the more overt their sponsorship, the easier will be the whole project. How you get to this person or people must be considered carefully within the context of your line management system and your communications hierarchy.

Some organizations are quite free about upward communication and some are most certainly not! The best you can do is to share your intelligence with whomever it is that you report to. You will have accomplished, at this point, a significant piece of work. It may be stolen off you and claimed by your boss, if he or she is that sort of person. Unless you have only just arrived, you will be used to this behaviour already. It is the sincerest form of flattery as well as being a guarantee of your indispensability. Cream usually rises to the top, so bide your time and keep true to this process – your time will almost certainly come. Even though an insecure boss may take credit for your discoveries, his or her broadcasts will make awareness of the problem wider. It is likely that fairly soon questions about what to do about it will find their way to you.

You have done some listening around your company, and listening is the best and most powerful enrolment tool in your armoury. You will have already forged some links with people through listening to them. Many of those stake-holders are already on board at one level or another. Their speaking to you has included them in your STOP Statement. This internal customer contact will also have rounded off your expertise. You are an obvious candidate to take this forward, unless someone's personal agenda is somehow ensnared – e.g. your boss is so clearly the cause of the problem that he or she wants no documentary evidence that they've blown it and has you sent to Siberia!

You might already have access to a research and development budget, but you will almost certainly want the ear of someone with a direct influence on the purse strings because the investment starts to increase considerably if this project is to go any further.

You have a brief summary of the objective problem, you have a Corporate Impact Map, you have some people on board – you have a case. Sell it to some-one with power they can support you with and access to money.

3 | Resourcing the Breakthrough Zone

Step four – the perfect set-up for success

 Our work in the Breakthrough Zone forms the central and most important part of the whole process. It is within the Breakthrough Zone that the way forward will be created.

The STOP Statement and the Corporate Impact Map are the only data you need at this point. Yes, really, this is the case.

The STOP Statement clearly communicates the problem that is driving the inquiry. The Corporate Impact Map indicates the effect the problem is having on the whole business as far as you can ascertain at this point.

Your sponsor has the authority and budget to allow you to continue. He/she is your source of power. From hereon in this book we will refer to the sponsor as your Internal Investor. They are investing some of their power and resources in your endeavours and will expect a return on their investment. Those who have power to divest want an increase in their power as a return. Thinking of them as an investor helps maintain consciousness of this fact. You are an instrument for successful investment – that is the way it is.

No one has the answers yet. Any illusion that you know what the answers will be is counter-productive. Within your community there will be thousands of ideas and quick fixes all of which could descend at any moment to confuse and cloud the way forward. You cannot stop to pick up real gold nuggets if your arms are already full of fool's gold! Being the one person who can remain clear at this point is extremely important. Being uncluttered at this point is extremely advantageous.

The Breakthrough Zone is a creative immersion event involving a significant number of people from the business who represent a relevantly cross-functional team, as well as a substantial number of customers. In some cases organizations we have worked with have included their advertising agency, designers, and any suppliers whose services to the company might be enhanced by their participation.

The whole Breakthrough Zone event takes six days in total, three days Breakthrough Training for the company Breakthrough Team, and two days, usually over a weekend, spending time with customers. There is a one-day Insight Workshop which follows the customer event. Notice, if you will, any resistance that is already arising within you to committing that much time to anything, especially an untried or unknown technique. That resistance, although perfectly natural, says something about the limits of where we are prepared to go and for how long in search of breakthroughs!

The basis for the Breakthrough Zone is creativity. There will be very little time spent canvassing opinions. The purpose of the Breakthrough Zone is to go where other forms of research are unable to go. A large group of 15 to 30 people from your company will be involved in a learning exercise where the learning will be about individual and collective needs and desires within the marketplace in which you operate. You're going to ask people to discover their deeper motivations, desires and aspirations, and then to share them with you. From this learning we will later be creating the insights that will provide the context for any decisions we make relative to new products, services, etc.

There will not be a discussion guide. There will, however, be topics for creative exploration. People are generally at a loss for words to express what motivates them. Most of us are at the mercy of our motives – our largely pre-conscious drivers. Because they are so difficult to talk about, many of the processes that we use in the Breakthrough Zone do not require language. They deliberately employ simple creative techniques that people can master immediately and use to express themselves without words. They enable people to surprise themselves with what they discover about their inner drives and motives.

We will deal with this in more detail later in the book. Suffice it to say for now that you are about to invite people to a remarkable and enjoyable event. What you need for the Breakthrough Zone are the necessary limits and none of the unnecessary constraints. You are going 'blue sky', but with focus!

We have introduced the term 'Breakthrough Zone' as if it were a place. In many ways it is; a special zone where an extraordinary encounter between members of your organization and your customers takes place. Look for a moment at Fig. 3.1.

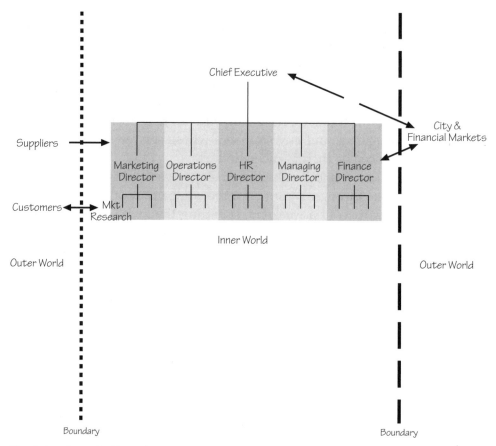

Fig. 3.1   The typical boundaries in a modern organization.

As you can see, there are boundaries or borders on either side of the organization: on the left between the company and its customers and on the right between the company and its owners or shareholders. We have tried to show that the barrier on the left is much less permeable than the one on the right. Later, when we explore the influences on corporate culture, we will discuss this more.

Data only passes through this left hand barrier in very limited and structured ways. It is all filtered by a gatekeeper too, the market research function. You will see in Fig. 3.2 how the Breakthrough Zone is a place that dissolves or bridges this barrier and immerses a cross-functional team from the organization in an event where there are customers. Think about it for a moment; how often do relatively senior cross-functional teams from your company meet with customers without a formal agenda to engage in creative activities together? If you had some friends or people you depended on in everyday life, how well would you know them if you never really spent time together doing new things?

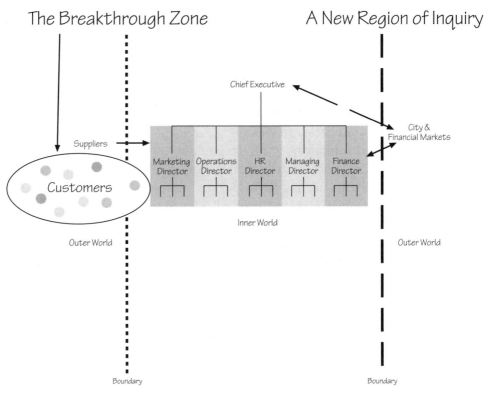

Fig. 3.2 Where the Breakthrough Zone occurs.

Assuming that you have won the authority and budget to proceed, the next step is to *create your Breakthrough Team*.

People are going to be asked to give up three days of time in the office as well as a whole weekend, not to mention some follow-up days. The invitation will have to be irresistible.

You will know by now who has shown the most interest in the problem that you have surfaced. Make sure that these people are invited. In the resources section you will find an example of a compelling invitation. You can use and adapt this as a template for your own invitation.

You will be inviting them initially to a three day Breakthrough Training to take place in the week prior to the Breakthrough Zone Event. Those invitees should be made up of stakeholder representatives, as well as your Internal Investor or their trusted representative. The Breakthrough Zone Event will have a powerful impact on everyone present – and you want the same impact to be available to the people that hold the purse strings and have access to the most powerful relationships in the organization.

The Breakthrough Training is where you will build your core team and expose them to the simplicity of the STOP Statement and the Corporate Impact Map. You will practise some creative exercises that will be used in the Breakthrough Zone Event and to prepare everyone to be able to put aside their expertise, opinions and pet ideas about what the organization 'should do'. You will be preparing them to participate with the customer guests as equals. That means that rather than being experts when they meet the customers, the Breakthrough Team members become customers too. They get to participate, not stand back and watch.

You want everyone to be equal in their ignorance of the solutions. There is nothing more inviting than someone admitting that they do not know what to do next and asking for help. This allows everyone to be inside the process at an experiential level with nobody standing back as if they have 'the answers'. Experiential data is what we seek. Being open to this requires preparation. This Breakthrough Training will take three days together, away from the office and with mobile phones switched off! You will need a good facilitator.

We will revisit this in more detail later.

Right now here is your to-do list.

- Select stakeholders to invite to the Breakthrough Training and the Breakthrough Zone Event. Make sure your team is cross-functional and contains both potential allies and enemies of your project.
- Where possible ask them to invite customers with whom they have a relationship (good or bad).
- Create selection criteria to guide the recruiters picking customers to join the Breakthrough Zone.
- Find dates for the event leaving time for people's diaries to be clear, but not so far ahead as to be forgettable.
- Find venues that are away from the workplace, comfortable and roomy, and that can tolerate noisy events! The noise element is extremely significant, in our early days we often had complaints.
- Hire and brief a film company for the Breakthrough Zone Event only.
- Cost the process.

It is crucial for you to invite the Internal Investor, and if they cannot attend, that you ask them to send someone they trust who can report to them after the event.

To give people the best chance of finding space in their diaries, you must send your invitation out of as soon as you can.

We have found, even in organizations that have repeated this process, that running a two-hour briefing session 5–10 days before the Breakthrough Training helps to keep people on board, maintain their commitment and gives them a chance to ask any final questions they might have. By the time you have read this book you will be well equipped to create just such a presentation.

Step four – resources

1   Here is the example text for a typical of Breakthrough Zone invitation to company members.

> We need your help.
>
> We are about to try to solve our problem of low sales in the market place. This is the core issue facing us all right now. To do this we want to assemble a widely representative cross-functional team from our business to be agents of change.
>
> These agents will engage in a special form of action research with customers and from this programme we will develop the strategies and activities that we need.
>
> This type of programme has worked for others all around the world. It has inspired new products, advertising, brand positioning and sales. It is a breakthrough approach and quite unconventional. Having said that, it is not dangerous and people have a wonderful and beneficial experience in this work.
>
> As action research it will involve us in doing many of the things that we usually pay others to do! We will meet customers and work with them on creative projects. Who better than our own people to understand the possibilities and their consequences for us?
>
> There is quite a large time commitment, three days off-site, a weekend event with customers followed by a final day's Insight Workshop.
>
> Please join us in the most important project to drive our business forward. Spaces are limited and the dates for the event are_____.

2   You will now need an accurate set of figures in order to cost out the entire Breakthrough Zone process. This will enable you to enter your costs and calculate the final totals as you go.

3   You will need to brief facilitators. Before you hire your favourite trainers read Chapter 4, 'How to Facilitate a Breakthrough Zone Event' carefully. We recommend that you take this opportunity to look for people who are experienced in building teams and facilitating insights through the use of creative activities, for example dramatic techniques, art, using modelling and construction materials etc. Use the information there as a template for your brief. The Breakthrough Zone is a special environment and requires special handling.

4   Book venues as soon as possible. The requirements are very specific and are as follows.

- *Both* events should be off-site.
- Ideally the team days should be spent as a three-day residential. Although this is not essential, it makes a significant difference to the overall process.
- The working space dimensions must afford people a minimum of two square metres per person. Note that this is a minimum – the bigger the space, the better.
- The space needs to have natural light.
- Keep tables to a minimum – merely those necessary to put supplies on – none to sit behind!
- One chair per person.
- One flip chart for every six people plus one for the facilitator.
- Plenty of notepaper and pens – where the pens disappear to is one of life's great mysteries (we have a theory that odd socks and golf balls end up there too!).
- Name badges for everyone with the name they want to be called written in 72 point font so they can be read at a distance.
- Lunch should be available (buffet style is quicker) within easy reach of the room. We have found that keeping the food on the menu light (i.e. salads, fish and fowl, rather than red meat dishes with rich sauces) helps people remain more energetic for longer during the afternoon.
- Keep any alcohol off the menu at lunchtime!
- Food preferences need to be catered for.

Both the Breakthrough Training and the Breakthrough Zone Event will require the same facilities. However, there are special considerations for the venue housing the Breakthrough Zone Event with the customers. You will need to arrange:

- somewhere for people to hang their coats and stow their belongings;
- a place for smokers to satisfy their needs without disapproval;
- a registration desk outside the room where the event will take place;
- a technical area with a sound recording desk, and enough ceiling height for lighting to be installed for filming;
- sufficient power outlets for the film equipment; and

- sufficient and inexpensive car parking facilities.

Remember that you will be a large number of people who must get completely through lunch in one hour. That will have implications on serving stations, style of service, menus and the location of the dining area with respect to the main activity room. In some venues the restaurant/cafeteria is half a mile from the workroom and this can cause all sorts of difficulties; people get lost, there is confusion between your group and others using the venue, the restaurant staff are overwhelmed by everyone arriving at once. Make sure you have made your needs clear to the venue manager and that you walk through the process before the event begins. Smokers will want to know where they can smoke. Waiter service at tables is never a good idea. It takes too long.

5   Select and brief recruiters. Normal market research recruiters are quite capable of providing you with the sample of people that you need. What you must do is help them to fully understand that this is different from anything else that they have recruited for in the past. We recommend that you dispense with terms like 'respondents' and replace them with more personal words like 'guests'. They will need:

- An invitation script. Here is an example of one.

Hello xxxxxx.

Forgive me for disturbing you but I'm calling on behalf of 'Flea In Your Ear Telecoms' to ask if you'd be interested in helping us with an international creative project. Please may I tell you something about it?

This is not a sales call; in fact if you are interested we'd like to offer a valuable incentive to those who take part. We need your help and are delighted to pay for it!

We want to involve some of our important customers in helping us design our new International Holographic Conferencing service, due for launch in 2006. We feel that our business subscribers know better than anyone what is needed and how this can be best used and implemented. To do this we're holding a series of weekend workshops around the world where a selected group of subscribers and FIYET staff will work together to come up with some special designs and ideas for the future.

The workshop in your region will be held on _____(dates) at_____(location). Each day we will work from 9.30 to 17.30. We'll be happy to accommodate you overnight, feed and refresh you to ensure your comfort throughout the workshops.

We know you are a busy person and we very would much appreciate your help. We would like to offer you the following rewards for those who will give up a precious weekend to take part:

- An overnight stay for you and your partner on the Saturday of the workshop at_____(venue name).
- A dinner hosted by FIYET on the evening of the Saturday. A month's free rental and calls on your existing call plan.

If you are interested I'll be happy to tell you more about the workshop.

- You will also need a written invitation to be sent out directly from the company signed ideally by your Internal Investor. Here is an example:

Draft letter from the Internal Investor to potential participants

Dear xxx

On behalf of Cajun Airways, I would like to thank you for agreeing to participate in our weekend workshop. Your input in this program is of utmost value to us, and we sincerely appreciate your time and effort in helping us create the flight experience of the future.

As you know, we are due to take on new routes to the West Indies in 2006. At this point, the flight experience, service routine, in-flight entertainments and aircraft layout have not been decided and we would like to take this opportunity to invite you to assist us in making it the best in the business. Listening to feedback from our customers has been a cornerstone of our success and this will be a genuine opportunity for everyone to make a real creative input into something that is of interest to us all.

To do this we have arranged a weekend workshop on XX and XX XXX at (location – full address and telephone number) from 9.30am till 5.30pm each day. At the workshop, there will be a group of xxx people, made up of frequent fliers and Cajun Airways staff.

The workshop will contain a number of individual and group games and activities, all of which will build the group's resources and creativity. We will do some role-playing, prototyping of interiors and presentation of our work to the group. Your participation and creativity in all the sessions will be required over the two days. Although it might seem like an intensive workshop, I guarantee you will enjoy yourself with this once-in-a-lifetime experience.

> The workshop will be coordinated by a team from an agency based in London. They are specialists in conducting creative workshops, which help to generate best possible ideas for designs of the future.
>
> If you would like to attend, they will contact you to enquire if you need accommodation arrangements. In the meantime, please feel free to contact XXX at XXXXXX if you have any queries.
>
> Once again, thank you for your continued support of Cajun Airways. We look forward meeting you to help us invent the future of flying to the Caribbean!

The logistics of setting up both the team training and the Breakthrough Zone can sometimes seem overwhelming. Just take it one step at a time.

What is the Breakthrough Zone?

Virtually no one in any significant position in any company spends any time in an open and liberated forum with their customers. Rather, the opposite is true, we have invented a whole set of procedures that give senior people interpretations of customers through sets of data about customers' opinions or preferences. This creates two-dimensional impressions of customers, and assumptions borne from them are unreliable. Much of this is done to provide comfort and reassurance to the senior executives that the company is in touch with the customers' hearts and minds.

In our experience this kind of reassurance contains a good proportion of nonsense. How can you know people you have never met? Look at how wrong assumptions based on 'evidence' about people's attitudes towards you can be. How many people are queuing up for WAP technology in your high street? Who could have predicted the urban tribe's love affair with SUVs?

For the past ten years, we have been developing and running total immersion experiences with consumers for the likes of British Airways, Holiday Inn, Singapore Airlines, and BUPA. In their best-seller, *The Experience Economy*[1], the authors develop their argument that, in the case of both goods and services, customers are no longer looking simply for *things*. What people seek are experiences. Here are some examples of *experientialized* products:

- computer games;
- Starbuck's, Café Rouge, McDonald's;
- children and pets;
- Christmas, summer holidays and weekends;
- Disney;
- British Airways Club World;

- themed restaurants from Pizza Hut to Yo! Sushi;
- theme parks;
- BUPA Healthchecks;
- extreme sports/kit;
- most clothing;
- most food; and
- bikes, cars, motor bikes, boats, scooters and other forms of conveyance.

The difference between an experience and a purchase is that *the experience is embodied*. It happens to the whole of you, body, mind and spirit. Manufacturers of products and services should focus on the experience that customers have while using their products. An experience is an event, it is not a piece of data. It is formed from a mixture of content and context, which is influenced by events in people's inner world as well as the outer.

Researching experiences

How can we construct events to share with our customers where we get to participate in experiences together; then to share the impact of these experiences?

It is very difficult because all of our preferred customer contact processes are reductionist in their approach. What do we mean by that?

Essentially, companies are large groups of people wishing to make contact with an even larger group, the potential community of customers. To do this, companies break both communities down into small chunks in various types of samples, measure these, and then generalize from these measurements. They virtually never work spontaneously with large groups. Even the so-called ethnographic approaches like in-home observation and accompanied shopping retain this element of 'us' looking at 'them'.

> We all spend a lot of time as consumers and often ignore this part of ourselves when in our professional persona.

The truth is that we are all 'them'. We all spend a lot of time as consumers and often ignore this part of ourselves when in our professional persona.

There is something magical in the experience of a large group; something which gets lost when you break it down into smaller chunks. Psychological research shows that a large group brings up deeper and more primitive feelings than smaller groups.

You only have to look at a football crowd. People are uninhibited, spontaneous and as fully expressed as children are. What would we give to have this aspect of men (or women) in our focus groups, talking about our brands?

Furthermore, we can see other interesting phenomena in this crowd. Things seem to spread by contagion; they ripple from one part to another, like a brand spreading by word of mouth. The crowd seems very suggestible; things started in one place are taken up in another. But not everything is agreement; sometimes a chant in one area is met by a counter-chant or riposte from somewhere else. Like competitive brands, warring in the market place for share of voice.

The crowd also seems sure of its invincibility. Yet a few moments later it is vulnerable, cast down by a missed opportunity or a coup from the opposing side. It is very emotionally charged. We have parallel experiences in our company communities, one moment the cellphone networks were cock-a-hoop about the 3G phones, now they are not so sure that their technology is desirable.

A large group, like the football crowd, has great desire to win: there are, too, countless subsidiary desires, to make the others look foolish, for our hero to score, to be fitter, stronger, faster, smarter. All human desire and social comparison is there, flowing like a tide back and forth. In this large group there are many moments of surprise, insight and discovery.

A large number of people work in the companies we know and so in this way companies are crowds too. As are the general public that they serve. Yet they never meet as large groups, only as individuals through surveys or in small carefully chosen numbers in focus groups. In other words small samples of one entity bump into small samples of the other in carefully constructed forums.

In the diagrams below we contrast the typical research or consumer inquiry with the large group process that we want you to be able to conduct for your business. It is our aim to provide for our clients an experience of immersion with their customers and then to make sense of it.

In the first four diagrams you will see the conventional quantitative or qualitative process for consumer inquiries. In the fifth you can see a visual of our method.

Figure 3.3 represents the undifferentiated crowd. This is both the most exciting and the most terrifying group. We do not know them, nor they us. The kind of questions people ask themselves in such a group are 'What are their intentions? Who can I trust? Who is like me?'

We look for external signs of compatibility, age, dress, hairstyle, sex.

Are we attracted to those unlike us, or merely fearful of them?

Should we speak up or say nothing? What's the best strategy?

If we do nothing, how will we feel?

Figure 3.4 shows the differentiated or structured crowd. This is what an organization is. In order to fulfil its business objectives, the organization has recognized that structures for efficiency, specialization and consistency are best.

Fig. 3.3   The undifferentiated crowd.

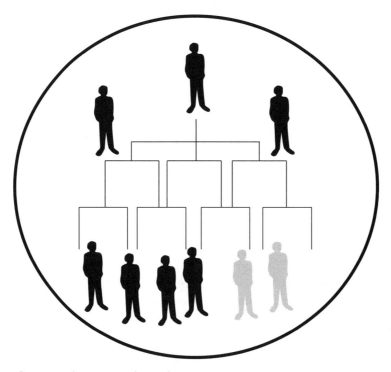

Fig. 3.4   The structured crowd – an organization.

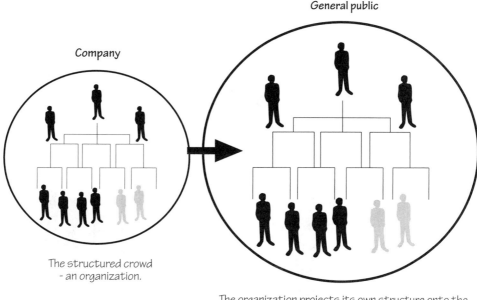

General public

Company

The structured crowd
- an organization.

The organization projects its own structure onto the
general population through the use of surveys,
segmentation and stereotyping, and
sees itself mirrored there.

Fig. 3.5   Seeing ourselves in the world around us.

Unsurprisingly, the organization then looks for mirrors of its own structure in the undifferentiated population and starts to impose a version of its own structure on the world around it. This can be seen in Fig. 3.5.

Through the mechanism of projection, the organization structures and measures the general population in a way that reflects its internal structure. This 'validates' the organization's view of itself and the community. Then, these supposedly matching structures are sampled to find 'representatives' of various categories. This is the way conventional consumer research works (Fig. 3.6).

This is the way our approach works.

In an immersion process, between 50 and 500 people from the organization and the general population meet and spend one or two days together. This is the Breakthrough Zone (Fig. 3.7).

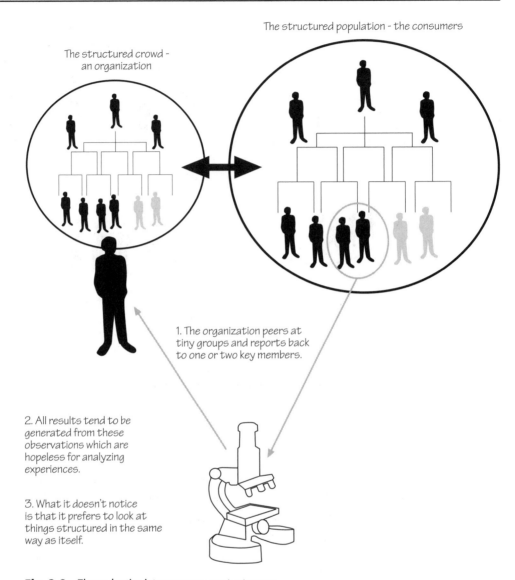

Fig. 3.6   The reductionist consumer contact game.

How can such large groups possibly work?

Most researchers and authors agree that once a group gets more than eight to ten members, a new set of dynamics takes over. First and foremost, eight or ten is about the most number of people we can communicate with simultaneously at any one time. It is the most we can encompass in our awareness. As soon as you have more people than that, some will move beyond the edge of our awareness and we have no clues or evidence about what they are thinking.

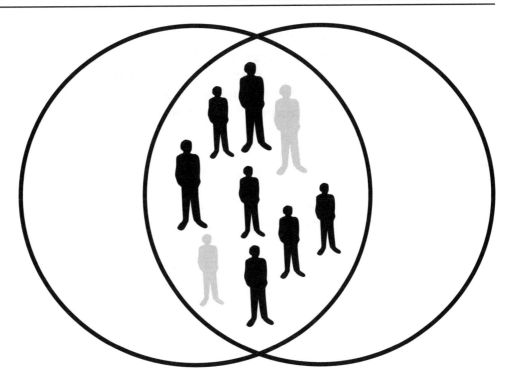

In the Breakthrough Zone between 50 and 1000
people from the organization and the general population
meet and spend one or two days together.

Fig. 3.7   The Breakthrough Zone.

If we are in their presence yet they are outside of our immediate sphere, these other members of the group could be potential allies, enemies, colleagues, rivals or strangers. Thus, we are likely to have many thoughts and feelings about them.

This will lead both to projections and introspection about what is going on: what do they feel about you and you about them?

In this way within the large group our mental processes become fully alive and charged with feelings in a way that they are not in a small group.

This is why we say that such a group is bound to bring more primitive and powerful emotions to the surface where they can be experienced, reported on and explored. Since much of modern marketing relies upon projection for its value – for example the potential customer for a new car is helped by the advertising to envision himself as the owner – it is vital for our understanding of what drives people to gain insight into their projections and motivations.

The large group is simply buzzing with projections and fantasies, and quickly becomes the perfect medium for exploring otherwise inaccessible drives, desires and needs.

We have heard it said over and over again by grateful clients who have participated in these experiences that: 'I didn't realize that I would get a whole new perspective on the fundamental things that drive our brand. Many of these realizations were completely new to me and others were powerful reminders of things we have forgotten in our hurry to move on.'

Note

1   Pine II, B.J. & Gilmore, James H. (1999) *The Experience Economy*, Harvard Business School Press, Boston, MA.

4 | How to Facilitate a Breakthrough Zone Event

How to facilitate the Breakthrough Zone

In the moment-to-moment experience of living it is obvious that we are all unconscious of everything that is not in our conscious awareness. There is stuff that we are unable to call into consciousness at all because we have always been unaware of it. However, this stuff motivates us in all sorts of ways. Follow me with a camera and record what I do and you will have a marvellous record of what I do when being followed by cameras, but you will still have no certainty whatsoever about what is driving me from my unconscious when the camera has gone. Ask me about what it was that drove me to do what I did, and I will still be unconscious of what it was. I am then likely to make something up out of the menu of things that I am consciously aware of to provide you – and myself – with an answer. Much research has shown that we are prone to inventing 'causes' or explanations in order to reduce the anxiety that is generated by inexplicable behaviour. These answers are fool's gold! They are merely rearrangements of currently available data posing as something new.

Recording and observing what people do has worth, as does soliciting opinions and preferences. The problem is that even very ordered people can be unpredictable in what they do, and the deeper and more fundamental their motivation or desire, the more likely it is to be out of sight. As psychologists have been pointing out for years, there are some fairly primitive and antisocial drives in all of us for things like power, sex or comfort.

33

If we are in search of deep drives and motives, somehow we must invite things held in the unconscious into conscious awareness. To do this we have to make it the common currency of the inquiry. This chapter introduces you to the background principles that will work in the Breakthrough Zone to guarantee that we unearth real gold.

We need to create community, where glimpses through the gateways to our deepest wishes are celebrated rather than rebuked.

We asked ourselves a very simple question: 'What conditions and group dynamics would best facilitate the emergence of previously unexpressed thoughts and feelings?'

The simple answer was 'a safe environment'.

To create a safe environment requires special skills. For the members of the group to perform at their best for you, they must have their basic dependency needs met by a primary carer i.e. the facilitator(s) who must be the best 'parent(s)' in the room.

This vital piece of information should also inform how you choose your facilitator(s). If you don't feel safe around the facilitator it is unlikely that the group will.

There are six groups of dependency needs:

- security needs,
- relational needs,
- reward needs,
- stimulatory needs,
- permissive needs, and
- completion needs.

Security needs

These include a space to call my own (my chair, my desk). Somewhere to escape to, knowing where the toilets are, somewhere to keep my valuables safe, ways to keep warm enough, a place and time for food and drinks, knowing how to get out of the room if a fire should occur. But there are more subtle and less objective needs included under this heading. For many years of working with groups we could not fathom the complete list. Recently one of us had a conversation with one of our children:

> Mac: 'What are grown ups for, Abbie?'
> Abbie, aged 5: 'They're there to make sure that children are fair to each other.'

We have long held that good leadership is substantially to do with good parenting. Both of us know that there have often been occasions when we have been participants on courses and have felt that there was no one in charge who could hold the boundaries in order to protect us from the abuse of someone else. Now, one might say that we should all be able to do that for ourselves. However, in a Breakthrough Zone we want people to be free to be creative without having to be distracted by the need to protect themselves. Whoever leads the process must have enough parenting ability to ensure that the necessary boundaries are enforced.

When groups get together for the first time, they are scared, and scared people operate survival strategies. The more scared they are, the more committed they are to the effectiveness of their survival strategy. We all know the phrase 'survival of the fittest'. When terrified, people will go to many lengths to have their strategy succeed, and believe us, we can all fight dirty!

Someone in the room must be the arbiter of fairness, the keeper of the boundaries, and the enforcer of the rules. The problem is, what are the rules? Surely if we are going to be open and honest then we should have no rules. Rules cramp everyone; they limit the possibility, don't they?

Rules can be used for anything. They can be used to facilitate and excuse abuse, or they can be used to create a degree of predictability. They can be used to control people, but they can also be used to liberate them. Finding the appropriate set of rules is fraught with problems – look at political frameworks, all of them looking for a version of Utopia, and all of them with a web of rules and regulations. None of them is perfect.

For people to feel as safe as we want them to there must be some predictability, so that if they let themselves go into a process, they can be sure of protection from the more damaging whims of you and the others. This element of predictability reassures group members that they are being held safely.

People also fear being abused. Abuse is a big word. We have learned to associate it with reports of adults perpetrating sexual acts on children or men forcing themselves on women against their will. These are incidences of abuse, no doubt, but how do we define it so that less dramatic and everyday occurrences of abuse might be recognized?

We are indebted to John Bradshaw,[1] one of the world's leading experts on shame and addiction for this idea. He distinguishes abuse as 'Using someone for my needs without their full knowledge and consent'.

This definition is so complete that if we wore it responsibly when facilitating a group, we would be sure to get the job done. But do not deceive yourself that this is easy. Abuse as defined by Bradshaw is accepted as normal practice everywhere. Here are some common examples.

- We work in company after company where 'taking the micky' is almost the only kind of feedback there is. Although often witty, it is really a way of cutting someone else's head off to make you appear taller. It almost always leaves someone, the target of the wit, with a niggling doubt about themselves. It has no place in the creative environment.

- Often when people hear this they think that the creative environment must be a dull and humourless place. On the contrary, there are so many non-abusive forms of humour that become available when we let go of mockery and these enrich the process without any cost to anyone. Children detest being laughed at and made the butt of jokes. Adults just learn to live with it, some to respond to it, and others to dish it out. Whatever your orientation in this regard, mockery does not contribute to safety.

- Another abuse is excluding some details and parts of the agenda that you think might cause people to refuse to participate. Often it is excused as being unnecessary, or because it would 'confuse them'. This, too, amounts to getting people involved under false pretences.

- Most people who have attended focus groups will be familiar with the experience of sitting behind a one-way mirror whilst the people on the other side are being subjected to denigration and ridicule out of their earshot. We are sure no one has ever consented to participate in a focus group in the full and certain knowledge that *this* would happen!

- Another example is the covering up of your own mistakes by deflecting responsibility or blame onto someone else.

- Another abuse of status is to enrol the group into suppressing someone whose ideas you disagree with, thus isolating them, ultimately discrediting both them and their point of view. As a facilitator you need to be seeking ideas you don't agree with as keenly as those you do.

- To use someone as a target for your anger or frustration that things aren't going the way you expected is also abusive.

If someone does any of these things to you in a group it is essential that as a facilitator you can role-model polite and enabling ways of pointing out what is happening. As you do so you can inform the person doing it that the behaviour is counter-productive to the job in hand, and that you require it to stop. It is important that you do not become an abuser in return. Most people do not premeditate abusive behaviour. They can be informed gently and in a non-blaming way. They can be assured that normally no one would react openly about such things happening, but in this environment we need to take care of each other's finer feelings.

As a preparation exercise for facilitating at this level it is a good idea to spot ten abusive incidents every day, either where you are the abuser or the abused. Notice how you are left feeling. As the protagonist you will probably get a short lived moment of power followed by an empty feeling, and as the victim you will feel a level of humiliation followed by a degree of anger. You might also just greet both experiences by being numb; in which case, ask yourself what you would be feeling if you were not numb. Then answer your question.

As a facilitator, moderator, group leader, whatever you want to call the role, it is essential to learn how to enforce boundaries that relate to possible and probable abuses. This is not easy because in group activities it is not easy to work at the boundaries, it feels much safer in the middle somewhere. Be sure that any facilitator you hire to do this job can hold boundaries effectively.

You are the person set up to be the role model/parent of the group. If you cannot hold the boundaries then who will? Without a potential enforcer the group are left to apply their own values and defences.

Here is a security needs summary and checklist.

- Make people aware of the surroundings and where they can deal with their physical needs, i.e. toilets and fresh air, etc.
- Ensure that there is refreshment available, and they know when they can eat and drink.
- Explain the fire drill and point out exits.
- Facilitate them claiming a place that can be theirs – territory is a vital dependency need to all members of the animal kingdom.
- Let them know how safe their personal belongings are – if they are at risk let them know to keep them with them.
- Let people know what they can rely on ethically from you, and what your ethical expectations are of them.
- Share your own fears about not being taken care of when you are a participant in a group, and use these as a context for explaining how such ethical boundaries are important.
- Deal with ethical breaches without condemnation. Normalize them in the context of everyday life, and explain how the breach of ethics affects them adversely. By reassuring people of their normality, you relieve them from the burden of having to either defend themselves or feel ashamed.
- If the ethical breach happens to you, be honest about the impact it has had on you without blame. Let them know that you are sure

they did not intend to have the adverse effect. Enrol them into taking care of you and others.

- Do not abandon the group, or any individual within it. A good group leader does not leave until the agreed time has arrived.

Relational needs

The big group needs to experience the level of relatedness between each individual that will get the job done. You too are part of the relationship structure. You are an equal to each and all of them.

Through our years of working with people we have noticed that we can divide relationships into three broad categories.

Professional relationships

These are functional relationships, mainly dispassionate, or with passions concealed. Professional relationships create results within the limits of a transaction at the level of product or service. The successful exchange is satisfying and largely predictable. They get things done, dusted and paid for at best efficiently, at worst inefficiently and inappropriately to the contract – i.e. *un*professionally.

Many organizations use what they know about people to increase their professional relationship with people. People become data not persons. Business has much expertise in this sort of relationship.

Personal relationships

These are relationships where what is important to each of the people involved is shared openly. Personal relationships create results through transactions based in the realm of what is important to people beyond the constraints of the functional product or service, or the professional transaction. They have an emotional impact on the participants, inspire loyalty, delight, and feelings of being cared for or nurtured in some way. Most business has very little expertise here. Many people in general have very little expertise here.

Personal relationship is exemplified between friends who share everything about themselves and still remain friends. Such relationships flourish through mutual acceptance of each other, allowance of differences and trust.

Private relationships

These are relationships in which information about ourselves and the world we keep to ourselves, or only share with significant others. Generally speaking it is a forum for information that has a powerful emotional effect on those involved. Private is secret, kept back, even lied about in professional relationships – doctors double the alcohol intake we admit to because they know we lie when asked about it! Our private results are shared only with a few others, if any, and sometimes even kept from conscious recognition by ourselves! Needs, hungers, disowned parts of ourselves, unacceptable thoughts and fantasies and primitive drives are all held privately.

Many so-called 'private' people have blanket privacy without any necessary clarity as to why. They just do not reveal anything about themselves, with the exception, of course, of the very interesting fact that they do not reveal anything about themselves!

Private is where hidden agendas are kept, the one we know is there but can't quite identify.

Privately held information *cannot be accessed reliably from within the professional relationship, only from the personal.* Inside personal relationships almost anything can get said … with ease, even private information. The best counsellors and therapists create a deeply personal relationship inside which very private information can be shared. There is much to be learned from this world.

The business of customer research is often – if not always – in the private arena, as most choices and appetites are run from the deepest of private places, the unconscious mind. Because of this, the candidates for research are actually unable and resistant to truthfully accessing this knowledge. It rests somewhere unavailable to them. Trying to access this information from a professional relationship is impossible.

To get anything from the unconscious it must be brought through preconsciousness into conscious awareness. It then has to be met by the person whose information it is, accepted by them, and then fitted into their world in a way that they are happy with. At any moment in this process they can become so anxious about what it is they are meeting and hurriedly dissociate from it, sending it back from whence it came.

What we have noticed is that personal relationships, once created, expand the possibility of learning together, and private information soon gets shared. As the private information sees the light of day, new perspectives become available. Successful personal relationship always and inevitably leads to the formation of private relationship.

If the leader is not able to be in personal relationship with the group, with a will to share relevant private information about themselves, then the group will remain guarded, except where there are compulsively 'boundary busting' talkers involved. These are people who are motivated to test who will accept them and who will reject them. They usually do this by reckless self-revelation. The pay-off for them is they control how the group rejects them. A leader who is not able to be in personal relationship with such a person will be unable to give them the acceptance they require, whilst affirming the boundaries that will keep everyone safe and enabling them to become a productive part of the group.

Creating personal relationship depends on three essential steps.

Step one

Seeing the person who is there. This might seem obvious, but we very often do not see the person who is there; we see the person who we think is there. These are two completely different people. One is a construction of our imagination as a preparation to protect ourselves from a past experience that we do not want to repeat, and the other is merely the person who is actually there. It is a normal defence mechanism that we all have and use to prevent the recurrence of unfavourable past experiences.

Our heads are full of opinions and thoughts about other people. The moment we meet them we spend an intense few moments trying to work out whether or not they are dangerous in some way to us. This leads to a nervous opening to our encounters in which we run some of our most loved social formulae. In the Breakthrough Zone we need to get beyond this sort of thing very quickly.

Most facilitators who lack depth or experience tend to believe that they can sort people into types within the first 30 minutes of working with them. 'I can spot dominant types from a mile off.' This kind of belief puts immediate constraints on those very people; they will be construed through the facilitator's expectations. These result from the facilitator's own nervous defences and are not a finely honed psychic gift. It merely protects them from anything unexpected occurring.

> In the Breakthrough Zone we actively want the unexpected to occur.

In the Breakthrough Zone we actively want the unexpected to occur.

Seeing the person who is in front of you demands that you separate the facts about the person from your opinions about them, and your instant set of analytical judgements about them too. Seeing the person in front of you means allowing them to be there long enough for something about them to have an impact on you.

This requires looking at them with all of the other stuff that goes on in your head about them disengaged. There is always a background commentary playing in our minds, but in this situation you need not to enrol in the internal opinion-based messages you get. To make contact with the person you must first let go of controlling the interaction. Just look!

It takes practice, so practise as often as you can. Listen to what you tell yourself about people and learn to let it go. The more you do this, the more people will reveal themselves to you. We guarantee this.

Step two

We have noticed that relationships can often be defined by what you choose to put into them. To create trust, you must be willing to entrust something *of value* to you into someone else's keeping. If it is of no value, then no trust will be required anyway.

The value of any relationship is dictated by the value of what you put into it. If you put shallow stuff in, you get a shallow relationship. If you put stuff that is important about you in, then you get a relationship that contains what is important about you.

A personal relationship is built around what is important to and about you. If you are there to conduct an inquiry into, for example, personal hygiene, share something important about *you* that is relevant. Make sure that it is a step towards where you want the group to go in their own self-revelation. Be the permission giver. Here is something we said in one such enquiry:

> 'Talking about personal hygiene I am reminded of times when close friends have told me that I have a bogey hanging out of my nose and I have no idea how long it might have been there. I then go into an over-whelm of paranoia about who might have seen it and what they might think about me.' (General laughter.)
> 'I suspect that most of my personal hygiene habits are designed to avoid being caught out. I have a fear of being seen as incompetent, and part of me believes that if I smell bad, or people see me as uncouth in my basic personal grooming, that this is exactly what they will believe.'

This short quotation exemplifies the process of self-revelation, including the entrusting of important information on a personal or private level, and sharing the learning that is to be found in the self-observation.

When you share yourself, you become a role model of what can be shared. You create trust by entrusting something of importance to the others in the group. You start the process of calling information from the unconscious mind of the other people in the room, into the preconscious mind from where the continued sharing of the group will pull increasing amounts of information into conscious awareness. From there it can be incorporated into projective and creative vehicles, and eventually anchored into language.

Step three

Reassure people that what they share is valuable, whatever the level they choose to share is. Acknowledge them for personal qualities that appear through their speaking. See and tell them that you see their courage, their honesty, authenticity, resilience. Do not lie to them, just look for the qualities in them that work and appear through what they are willing to invest in this relationship.

If you do not let them know that their level of sharing is okay, welcome and valuable, if what they are sharing is new to them, they will soon become ashamed. Never forget how vulnerable people become when they are being spontaneous.

Watch out that you do not start to compete with members of the group. Get good at praising them for the talent that you feel they threaten in you. If your intellect starts to look inferior in your own eyes, acknowledge their intellect for its contribution – honestly! This is the quickest cure that we know, and you will feel much better for it.

Enrol the group in offering words of acceptance and approval. When they know that they do certain things well, they are likely to repeat them. This will contribute to a culture of safety and acknowledgement that will support the entire project.

If you do not acknowledge what people are contributing for its worth, they will all too soon start to criticize themselves and others for their openness. Suddenly feeling exposed and unacknowledged they will sense shame or vulnerability, and self-criticism will quickly bring about their shutting down. Micky-taking will take over, and individuals in the group will very quickly be at odds with each other.

Acknowledgement is the primary tool for successfully maintaining personal relationship. With it you are guaranteed to increase the permission for people to go further in their honesty, and extend access to material held in preconscious awareness. As the permission expands, so too does the creative opportunity. More and more private material will become available.

People invited to join a group need also to have a personal relationship with the agenda. From the invitation they must be able to glean how they relate to the topics being examined. They need to be enrolled into it, excited by it and curious about it. They will get that from the facilitator's level of curiosity and excitement.

Once they are there they need to be resourced for the subject of your inquiry and the methods that you are going to use to surface the outputs that you require. Here is something a participant said about their uncertainty and competence; you can be pretty sure that most groups will contain this feeling as you start out.

> 'When I join groups that are dedicated to learning something, I not only find myself worried by the other people in the group, and the facilitator, but also wonder what hidden agenda there might be. I want to know what to expect, what kind of things I'll be expected to do, and I worry

that we could be asked to do things that I am completely unable to do. Then my fantasy grows that I will be exposed as useless, and that nobody will tell me – I will be tolerated as I am seen to contribute absolutely zilch!'

In all our innovation programmes we fully inform people about the kind of experiential processes we will do, we let people know that we want them to dig deeply into themselves, and that when they find things they had not realized before, we want them to share their new knowledge. We let them know that sometimes these new realizations can change the way you see everything. We inform them that we will look after everyone through the process, and that we will not ask anyone to do anything that we are not willing to do ourselves.

If participants constantly have to worry about what happens next and are not being told about how others are using them and what they revealed, it will not be long before they are back on the defensive and playing safe.

We take time to play games that loosen up the parts of people we want them to use in the next exercise. We let them know that this is what we are doing. This way we restore their relationship with their inner tools for the job.

Finally, it is essential to forewarn you that in a permissive environment where people feel safe, they might express anything. People get moved to tears from time to time. This is normal. However, you may see the critical parent that they have inside them start to comment on the feeling they have let out. Often people will say things like 'Oh God, I'm being so stupid', or 'I'm sorry', or even try to run from the room.

It is absolutely crucial that you give them permission to feel what they are feeling, and that you normalize it quickly. By normalizing it, we mean that you actively communicate your approval for their feeling, that you thank them for trusting you with it, and that you reassure them that what they are feeling is entirely normal. When children cry, adults often criticize them for it, or ask them why they are crying. 'Why?' is a question to the thinking mind about a feeling that originates in the emotional mind. It is virtually impossible to answer it whilst in the throes of the emotion.

People often say things like 'Please don't cry.' Really they are saying 'You are exciting feelings in me that I do not want, so stop it so that I can feel better.' Sometimes this kind of plea is accompanied by running for tissues, lots of hugging, treating the person as if they are an emergency case. Should it occur in one of your events then gently call the 'helpers' off, and point out that the person is doing really well at expressing how they feel.

Anger is similar. When people are passionate sometimes they get angry about things. Perhaps only anger can provide the fuel to correct injustice. As a society we have confused anger, which is a feeling, with punishment, which is a choice of action. We have them so bound up with each other that some people only have to feel angry for a nanosecond before they are looking for someone to punish. Punishment can take many forms – being 'right', blaming, name calling, making derogatory comments and, worst of all, threatening violence or being violent. All of these will destroy the trust in the creative environment, and developing expertise in handling this is essential.

Anger is an emotion that we have a rather frightened and defensive reaction to. When people become angry in our processes, it is because they are realizing something. We have noticed that if we listen to what they have to say without judging them, very often a door opens to an insight into the topic in hand. Let's face it, any brand or product that can excite passions like that in their customers is onto something worth close scrutiny!

We have never encountered violence in our groups. Violence or threats of violence however must always lead to the exclusion of the perpetrator without exception. Violence and threats of it are illegal. Not only that but they instantly destroy trust, our most precious commodity in the Breakthrough Zone.

Here is a relational needs checklist.

- Create personal relationship. This requires that you see people as they are – as apart from your judgements about who they are.
- Play games that allow them to see the people they are with – as they are.
- Entrust something about you that is important within the context of your agenda. To create trust you have to entrust something to people. Give them the opportunity to do the same with each other.
- Acknowledge what works about people. Be the messenger for the qualities you see in them that enhance the process and encourage them to do the same by your example. Thank them for being courageous, funny, wise, honest, authentic. As they believe what you tell them they can start to use these qualities more and more. If you find this distasteful then we leave you with a question – *how does it protect you to deny people knowledge of what works about them and how it can possibly benefit them?* And, by the way, acknowledgement is never patronizing when sincerely given.
- Let people have all the information they need to know all of the agendas. If a game requires that you need to keep some information back, let them know that you are doing this and ask them to trust you. They will be delighted. If you have a hidden agenda they will smell it, however good a liar you may be. Deal with all doubts.
- If you want them to do something unusual, then tell them how your own fear gets in the way and what it tells you. Show them

how to do it by doing it first. Play games that put them in touch with the internal resources they will need to use to deliver on your requests.

- Acknowledge them individually at every opportunity, especially anyone that you have decided that you do not like! Let them all be 'better' than you at anything and everything.
- If someone hogs the limelight at the expense of others stay on their side, thank them for being so willing to take the initiative, and then enrol them into encouraging others to do the same, ask them for their help.
- Walk in their shoes whenever you change the game, or they complain, express their needs, get upset, etc.
- Stay present with them, come what may. And stay on their side. And always remember – a good friend does not leave until the agreed time has arrived!

Reward and recognition needs

Reward and recognition are two vital survival needs of all people. Have you ever noticed that when people feel powerless to create reward in their lives because of poverty or deprivation, they almost always have a vivid picture of rewards they will get in the afterlife? Many of the poorest cultures in the world have created religious or philosophical beliefs that contain paradise in an afterlife. Whether or not there is an afterlife is not the concern of this book, however, one thing is for sure: people are starving for rewards, and we are not talking solely about money, although that has its place too.

We were asked in 1998 to discover why it was that nurses had begun to shun private-sector nursing opportunities and were either leaving the profession or returning to the National Health Service. The nurses that we met were some of the angriest people we can remember being with. We inquired into and listened to their complaints – money came up, lack of facilities came up, and disappointed expectations also arose. These were all the easy things for them to talk about – they were the acceptable complaints, well practised, the already known stuff. As we listened to them, we were struck how none of the reasons for their complaints felt causal, however valid they might have been.

What gradually exposed itself as the glue that held all these complaints together, the real unexpressed and disowned need that could not be spoken and that these surface complaints were substitute expressions for, was that their primary source of reward had become unavailable to them. Through the implementation of more and more bureaucracy, nurses now had to do so much paper-based administration that time spent with patients had been cut to a minimum. Any nurse found talking to a patient was treated as if she was doing nothing and redeployed to administrative tasks.

The buzz for the average nurse was seeing the results of their care for patients manifesting in the increased wellness of the patient.[2] We heard stories of how they had been stopped from holding elderly patients' hands while they underwent the stress of having their cataracts removed under local anaesthetic. The suppression of their desire to comfort and witness the effect of that care was robbing them of the satisfaction they most craved.

They could not articulate this as they were not conscious of it themselves until they were in the right environment for it to emerge. Nurses throughout history have worked in the most appalling conditions – war-torn regions, makeshift field hospitals, ghettos – and thrived on it. Money is easy to blame, but it is seldom if ever the whole solution. Let people get the nourishment that they entered their vocation to feed on, and you will watch their genius arise over and over again in the pursuit of it. People who are not rewarded start to complain. Hungry people get tetchy.

People on the whole are living in bad faith with their visceral appetites. The people who arrive to work with us, just like everyone else that we meet, are starving for reward and recognition. We make it our business to feed them at every opportunity. We might be the only people in their world who they encounter who are willing to do this for them.

The first evidence of recognition is the use of someone's name – the name they want to be called!

Names are important. Sometimes names are misspelt when they reach us.

We always check that if people have badges that their name is spelt the way they like it, and that we pronounce their names properly.

When using processes which are unusual for people, or in which they have to dig deeper into themselves to get a result, praise them for their willingness, their courage, for doing whatever it took for them to accomplish this feat.

Reward people with applause. It is a ritual that represents appreciation. If the accepted ritual were to dance naked around gooseberry bushes, then we would be recommending that instead. Thankfully it is not. Applause is much easier to do. Applause is meaningful, and these people are putting themselves at risk for you.

Reward and recognize people with gratitude for what they are doing. We do not know who it was who said, 'He who thanks everyone thanks no one', but it is spot on. Thank people descriptively. By that we mean let each person know when you thank them precisely which bit of your gratitude belongs to them.

'Thank you so much for your enthusiasm. It has inspired everyone.'
'You haven't said much, but when you've spoken it's been well worth the wait.'

'Thank you for getting your group organized – it helped the group genius to shine.'

When one of us was on a course two years ago to train in psychometrics, the tutor said, 'Thank you for your contributions in the room. Every time you speak the whole group grows.' This kind of praise is a never to be forgotten experience.

When people have delivered for you, let them know what will happen to their input, and the difference that it will make. Let them know where to look for the difference they have made. Arrange to e-mail them about the outcome of their work.

At the end of every Breakthrough Zone event, people invariably express the desire to see their insights change the world. This is a great trophy to give people. Be aware too that their expectations need to be managed. Do not believe that they will forget so whatever you promise, make sure you deliver.

Pay them money too. Let them know how much, when and how they will be paid. Make it easy for them to get their money, and ensure that they do not have to ask you for it. If you promise other perks, make sure that someone is empowered to deliver them. Even free samples of products are received with real gratitude. If people are promised something and you do not deliver, it throws them into doubt about the validity of everything else you have said.

Here is a reward and recognition needs checklist.

- Never underestimate how important non-financially-based rewards are.
- Use people's names. Ensure that you are seen to try to pronounce their name correctly even if it is difficult for you. Then, if you get it wrong they know that you care enough to make the effort.
- Use applause, however embarrassed you might feel. Applause is worth having. If you have problems giving it you could probably do with some yourself!
- Notice what it takes for you to dig as deeply as you are asking them to. Then praise and thank them for it.
- When you praise or thank people, be precise about what it is you are grateful about or praising them for. We call this 'descriptive thanks' and 'descriptive praise'. That way they know why it belongs to them.
- Make paying them simple and reliable. Make sure that you deliver any perks that you promise. Ensure that they do not have to ask for either.
- Give them access to the real-world implementation of their work. Let them share in the pride for the results.

Stimulatory needs

When endeavouring to excite people into action on any topic that is unfamiliar, or more in-depth than they are commonly used to, they need to be able to engage with the subject matter at a spontaneous level. This requires that they be excited by the subject matter, that they have their own desire behind the project. This fact alone makes this set of needs the most crucial and problematical to meet because we have all spent a lifetime suppressing our natural excitement. You must reconnect with yours if you are to work with groups at this level. We recommend that anyone wishing to work with groups in this way undergoes training in 'being with' whatever is stimulated. *What you cannot be with in yourself you will find impossible to be with in others.*

By 'being with' we mean 'staying in relationship with' whatever happens, no matter what it might be. In some of our Breakthrough Zone events the subject of death has come up – unless you are able to have such a conversation yourself then you will inevitably try to close it down in some way. Being able to facilitate such awkward and difficult subjects, as well as people's emotional reactions to them, requires that you can 'be with' such topic areas and individual group members' responses.

Moreover as a facilitator you will go to great (unconscious) lengths to avoid stimulating anything that you are running from or afraid of. Look at the discussion of applause or abuse above. We will return to deal with this point directly later in this section.

We have shown that normal people like ourselves are busy trying to ensure that this excited energy is kept well under control. In children, however, this energy is readily available. When someone knocks at the door of our house, our children get very excited about it, whereas we are just as likely to groan inwardly and wonder who it might be trespassing on our doorstep! This excited energy displayed by the children is what the Swiss psychologist, Carl Gustav Jung, called *libido* or *libidinous energy*; while the other type is a prime example of defensive energy. Libido has come to be connected by the layman with sexuality alone (no pun intended) which limits the scope and meaning of the word. It seems that we are variously either drawn towards making contact with people or drawn away from contact. Our libidinous energy draws us towards contact and our defensive energy withholds our libidinous energy and thus we draw away. Much research has confirmed that we as a species are inherently contact-seeking i.e. we are attracted to contacting other human beings. Contact, however, as we have already discussed, becomes too risky to pursue openly. Try talking to strangers in the street and you will experience it yourself.

We want this libidinous energy from each person engaged in the topic of our inquiries. Unless it is involved, we can be sure that the same people will soon be withdrawing, and the only energy available will be defensive energy.

Apart from security, recognition, reward and relationship with each other, and the topic, participants also need to feel inspired. What inspires each individual varies. Some of us switch off when conversation spills into football. If you know nothing about the game, the teams, the leagues, who cost what and plays in which position, you will know how this feels. After a moment of wishing that you could join in too, you will probably withdraw inside yourself and defend your growing sense of isolation with derogatory points of view about the people who are busily swapping their 'expertise'.

Here is just such an inner dialogue from one of the authors.

> 'I tell myself that I have better things to do with my time than jumping on that particular bandwagon, that it's for sheep, and anyway the game leads to violence and I can't really see the point because there isn't one.
>
> 'My haven then becomes a secret, rather self-satisfied smug feeling of superiority. I might even at this point summon up some sarcastic put-down about the sport just to remind them that I am there. However, conversely, I will sit enthralled for five days watching a cricket test match, only getting out of my chair to maintain my bodily functions.'

Notice how your energy is relative to what you've just read. Notice what you are telling yourself. It may be that you agree, and your libidinous energy is flowing towards the person expressing this last point of view. It may be that you are a football lover, and that is where your libidinous energy is directed and cricket is 'boring' to you. Make a note about what you are saying to yourself about the person quoted and their point of view. It might be that you love both sports or neither of them. The point is, notice what has happened to your energy.

Many of the areas that we get asked to generate 'consumer insight' about start off feeling like the football example to us – we wish for a moment that we could care but we soon get inside our own defences. This is what happens to people, it is normal behaviour. Our job, however, and our primary source of satisfaction comes from our total immersion in the topic. We have to change our state of inspiration by choosing a different attitude.

Begin following the process we outline by informing yourself about the topic. Look for people in your internal group who have a passion for the business they are in and then look at the whole thing through their eyes. Imagine what it would be like to be them. This will provide you with gateways into your own excitement about the topic – let yourself feel it. This is analogous to an actor who projects himself into a role. If there is no one from your side who is passionate about the business, then you will have to generate your excitement yourself. From inside this experience you can then begin a journey of discovery. Anything less than this becomes an academic or objective experience, looking *at* the issue from a distance, using only your rational faculties. All you can produce from here are rational hypotheses, rather than experiential insights.

In a group, the members will ordinarily be unable to shift themselves, even if they are willing to. To be at the threshold of one's abilities is always to risk exposing oneself as incompetent. They will need someone to latch onto. They need to catch the passion and involvement from the person they most see as representing the job to be done, and that person is you. If you are not authentically inside the topic, if you have not engaged your own libidinous energy with it, you have not got a hope in Hades of generating it within your group.

They then need to be sure that it is OK to step beyond our competence together, and stumble around until someone trips over something worth noticing.

You as the champion of the process and/or the facilitator are the primary stimulus for the guests in the room. If you are stimulated, and can communicate meaningfully about the inquiry directly from your stimulated self, you will inevitably start to engage them with the subject matter.

We worked for a short while with a company that manufactured fragrances. We thought it was interesting, and were pragmatically involved until we met one of their managers, David Pybus, who immersed us in their business as if it were magic. He took us around the plant, and showed us the tinctures and essences. He smelt them with his whole body, and handed them to us to do the same. He handled them as if they were priceless artefacts, and we felt nervous and excited to be entrusted with them in our hands. He introduced us to the people who blended these rare and exotic ingredients telling us that they were 'alchemists'. Everything about fragrances excited him. And as he showed us badger pouches, and various herbs and barks, explaining the musical science of composing the symphonies that fragrances are, we got more and more enthralled. He opened the door to the heart of their business for us. It made the job we were there to do much easier to accomplish.

In an inquiry the most valuable asset you have is curiosity. Curiosity is evidence of two things – that you do not know the answers, and that you are compelled to find something out. Curiosity is a great opening to any invitation because, if you do not know, then the people you are inviting to join you do not have to pretend that they do know. They can 'not know' alongside you until something reveals itself to someone. Then you can share it.

Owning up to not knowing is tremendously enrolling. There is a pioneer in most people. If you raise your status by pretending that you know it all anyway, they will put their pioneer away and defend themselves. Ask yourself this: when was the last time you admitted that you did not know something? The belief that we know the answer shuts out the possibility for new learning. The more we live, the more we realize that we do not really know very much at all! Our children ask us the deepest questions about existence, things that great minds have been working on since time began, like 'what happens after we die?' Both of us want to be completely honest with them, and the only truthful answer is that we just don't know. Creative environments only thrive when there is a collective unknowing, a *naïveté*, a permissive environment in which we observe the moments that impact on us rather than recycling things that are already known. If you have an explanation for everything then what's the point? Try owning up to the fact that just like the rest of the world, you are making it up as you go along.

If you go on treasure hunts with kids on the beach, you don't have to know what you are going to find before you begin. You don't even have to know what you've found when you pick stuff up and bring it back. You can get very excited about it, nonetheless.

Talking from your libidinous energy, your passion, your fascination, from what strikes you viscerally about a topic, does not have to be loud. We have watched very quiet people express their passion quietly, and the net result was an inspired roomful of listeners.

Any of you that had a teacher who loved their subject and included you in their love of it will have experienced something that had a lasting impact on you. Your relationship with that subject was almost certainly shifted forever. You may even have made that subject a central part of your life.

Turning yourself on is likely to turn others on too. This kind of creative environment is sexy, and we use the word deliberately. Libidinous energy is exciting to the body, the mind and the spirit. This is why having ethical boundaries is pretty important. People in their full flow start to look extremely beautiful whatever their body shape might be. Do not start seducing people. Remember our definition of abuse!

Sometimes we seem to get the whole thing 'wrong' and the room goes dead. There is no point trying to soldier through at this point. Something powerful is happening to the group and there is no point pretending that it is not happening. Firstly the drop in energy might be significant. If you are talking about a piece of packaging design and the room goes cold, what does that say about the design concept? You may not know, but you can be sure the group does. If you get your curiosity involved in the drop in energy, you can then get them curious too. Then you have an excited group wondering how they all got turned off. It just takes someone to observe how they feel, and see if the rest of the group feels that way too.

We too have spent so many years facilitating groups of switched-off people, trying to push them into enthusiasm and failing miserably. It is easiest to blame yourself for this, believing that your job is to keep everyone entertained, and thinking that if you admit to people that the energy is low, they might see you as some kind of fraud!

It is much better to use the lack of enthusiasm as a topic. We might say to a group:

> 'You don't seem to be enjoying this. I wonder what's going on. What are you noticing? Can you remember when it happened or what caused it?'

It might seem crazy, but we have watched people get very excited bottoming out what caused them to get bored!

Never forget that people need breaks. When a group has played together and co-operated in the production of a creative output they need a break. Creative output is rather like having an orgasm. Its completion and revelation to an audience requires a crescendo of focussed energy and, unless you are blessed with the gift of multiple orgasm, you will know that you need some recovery time before embarking on the journey towards another. Some people like to have a cigarette, or a cup of tea, a snooze. Build breaks around the creative climaxes. Each new endeavour needs foreplay. We use this analogy because it is relevant. It is not meant to offend. We are sculptors of libido. Try putting that on your curriculum vitae!

Now, let us deal with the most serious issues relating to this section on people's stimulatory needs. If you want to be the facilitator of the Breakthrough Zone, then before working with people at an emotional level it is essential that you do some work on your own emotional fitness. As an ethical rule we suggest that you never invite people to go anywhere that you are not yourself willing and able to go.

We live in a society that has trained its offspring to avoid expressing emotions openly. The stiff upper lip is still our most readily recognized national characteristic. As children we were taught how valued or valueless our emotions were by our parents' and teachers' reactions to them. Commonly, our expression of emotion was treated intolerantly. As a result, many of us have put our passions away in life – let alone at work – and learned to keep them secret. This is so for many of the people who participate in our innovation programmes.

Inevitably, when we contact our libido we experience an energy that we have at least in part hidden or put away. The age we were when we put it away was the age at which we were practised in its expression. Our ability to express it has not matured with the rest of our personality. We will have to begin again where we left off. This is why expressing our emotions often leaves us feeling small and childlike. We are often struck by how often people regress in their behaviour and posture to very early years when they begin to experience their emotions again. This is a journey into areas of human experience that is not available in most inquiries. It requires excellent parenting.

The capacity to feel and be with our own joy is affected by our capacity to feel and be with our own anger and sadness too. Holding one in abeyance directly affects the other. When we curb the expression of one emotion it always has an affect on our expression of other feelings too. Most people have learned to live in a 'safe' but narrow band of human expression that leaves them able to hide from the feelings that lie beyond these limits. The Ancient Greeks understood this well. Their theatre was designed for audiences to witness these hidden or 'put away' parts of themselves through the rituals of their plays. They understood the concept of catharsis; in fact it was Aristotle who originated it. They knew that through the invocation of fear and pity on stage, the audience could purge it in themselves. Theatre for Greek society was a form of purifying therapy. In modern psychotherapy the word catharsis is used to describe the bringing of repressed experiences into consciousness. This is often followed by the subject's inclusion of those experiences into their everyday sense of identity. When such repressed experiences emerge into consciousness there is often a release of held or 'put away' emotion into expression. People might cry the sadness that they have withheld. It is not unusual that someone carrying a lot of suppressed emotion might suddenly feel furiously angry for no apparent reason.

During our work with private healthcare we encountered people who had closed down on their feelings of powerlessness to get anything effective done on behalf of elderly sick parents. Alone, they had been unable to allow themselves to experience the feelings that they could not fully explain in language. In the safety of our process, they were not only able to feel and express fully what they had been through, but also to experience in the mirror of our reactions to them that their feelings were justified, worthwhile and evidence of their love for their parents. On top of all that, they had contributed to a discussion that might lead to a world where their experience would be less common.

For facilitators, knowing how to be great parents to people in vulnerable and uncertain states is the key. This has to be learnt. We run courses that tackle these issues as the necessary skills cannot be learnt from a book. With the necessary skills the whole process can feel beneficial to people who participate, and they need never experience it as 'therapy'. The brief for the project creates the legitimizing context for the group's discoveries, indicates the value of the discoveries to everyone, and anchors the purpose for everyone concerned. Always stick to it. We are not there to do therapy. Be clear that the context for this work is a commercial one. If it happens that an insight which is commercially viable also makes for a better world, so much the better.

If we are to find out what motivates people to attach and detach themselves – and their lives – to and from certain products or brands, then we must be willing to follow them into the part of themselves that contains their most powerful drivers. They themselves are detached from this part of their psyche, but it drives them nonetheless. They are unable to explain this part of themselves because they have no conscious relationship with it. When we are brought back into conscious relationship with these vital and visceral parts of our inner world, there is an irresistible emotional reaction which occurs. Because we are unfamiliar with this connection, it is new to us; our habitual thought processes have no points of reference for the experience, and thus cannot effectively rationalize it away. This moment of reconnection is vital, for to be rejected at this point will be potentially as traumatic to us as the original experience was. Any sign of disapproval will certainly be evidence that they were right to put it all away in the first place and that they should never bring it out again.

There are at least a hundred ways to abandon people without actually physically leaving them. To fulfil a duty of care to our participants we have to be there in mind, body and emotions. Only in this way can we hold our participants as they encounter unexpected experiences and support them by sharing and endorsing their discoveries. This is an essential set of skills. Without it we can only lead people away from where we really need to go, and run scared when anyone is expressing powerful emotions we do not recognize in ourselves.

For stimulatory needs here is a summary and checklist.

- Find a way to be excited by your topic. If you are not, then no one else will be.
- Learn to communicate from passion and curiosity. This is easier if you practise the art of saying 'I don't know' when people ask you questions. It takes a while to get used to it, but it really changes the way people communicate with you. Your world will open up in a different way.
- Stay tuned to the energy in the group. If you are bored, irritated, sad, sleepy, then check to see if you are the only one.
- Create breaks in the programme that reflect the climaxes.
- Recognize when you have 'left' and bring your attention back.
- Find a way to value everything that is expressed. Work at recognizing and approving of people's emotional reactions to things. Do this for yourself as well.

If you find yourself excited by taking your expertise further then we recommend that you undergo training in working with your own and others' emotions. Acting classes are a start; psychotherapy or counselling training is also extremely useful. Our own leadership courses deal with these issues directly and are the best preparation for this work that we know. You can contact us about these if you are interested.

Permissive needs

Our lives are full of rules.

> 'Always take your coat off indoors, otherwise you won't feel the benefit of it when you go back out.'

When children feel too full up to finish their food, how many people hear the thought, 'Think of the starving millions'? Or that 'nice girls don't get angry'? And that 'big boys don't cry'?

> 'People should … shouldn't … mustn't …'
> 'You just don't do things like that!'

Behind most rules is a 'don't imperative': 'don't keep your coat on indoors', 'don't waste food'.

Our minds do very interesting things with 'don't imperatives'.

As you read this, *don't think of a big red bus* – you know, one with the open platform bit at the back, where the conductor stands and there's a pole you can hang onto, just by the hole where you put prams and things, *don't think of one of those*, with the bell that goes ding-ding, *don't think of one*. Hey presto, what does the mind do but conjure one up!

Schools have rules, families have rules, and so do communities, societies, clubs, countries etc. We have been doused in rules for ever!

However, creativity thrives on breaking rules.

When working with groups, we often deliberately and overtly suspend normal rules of politeness, using games that give people permission to break their own rules. The energy that gets released is extraordinary. People of all ages become much freer, they get excited and we can then direct the excitement to the brief.

Permission to break the rules starts with your willingness to go first. What are the interpersonal rules that are in the way? Asking people to suspend their rules also requires that you give them permission to refuse your request. Permission to refuse also leaves room for them to accept. We rarely get a refusal. Refusals are often a sign that the scope of the rule breaking is 'too much too quickly'. The process might require some practice in the form of games and icebreakers. Use smaller steps to relax people towards the level of interaction that you require.

The creative environment needs few rules. It does need some though. We come back here to our overriding ethic of non-abuse. As the group facilitator you must be an example, and arbiter of this most crucial of regulations. Never use someone for your own needs without their full knowledge and consent. Do not create processes for people to go through that they have not been informed about and given the chance to refuse to participate in. If you must do something to surprise them, then ask them if they will trust you to run a process with a surprise in it. Never construct a confidence trick: your group will feel betrayed even if they are unwilling to tell you. You will have successfully created a rebellious and closed-down group.

Permission does not presuppose consent. Permission outlines the space available to people within clear parameters. Permission must also go hand in hand with all the information necessary for people to consent. Permission might also require outlining things that are not permitted. If you see anyone straying into the realms of the unacceptable, this needs to be spotted and used as a resource for reinforcement of the boundaries as early as possible. This can be used to fuse the group more soundly, and increase the feeling of safety. When it is not spotted and dealt with, it creates fear and limitation. There have been many programmes and courses run in the corporate world and in the public arena that have demanded a reckless level of commitment and agreement from participants, with subtle penalties for those who do not comply. To us this is unacceptable. It is also counterproductive. We find that people crave the safety that we create. They flourish within it. When they experience positive regard from both facilitators and the group with gentle and non-punishing enforcement of ethics, people have the time of their lives.

People need to know that they are okay to express themselves in a world that hitherto has taught them the opposite. It is our duty to keep them safe when we invite them to break those rules. We need a great deal of reassurance when we change our habitual modes of communication. Keep reassuring people as they go.

For permissive needs here is a summary and checklist.

- The creative environment needs rules to be broken where they are in the way of free expression.
- The creative environment needs rules to be observed that take care of people's vulnerability as they express themselves.
- Breaches of the second set of rules must be exposed in a non-punishing way, otherwise trust breaks down fast.
- Never allow someone to create at the expense of someone else who is in the room.

- Remember that your giving permission does not oblige people to accept it. Refusals indicate that the size of your request may need some 'stepping stones'. Build in some games to get people to where you want them to go safely.
- Ensure that you communicate clearly what is not permitted, so that people can feel safe at the hands of others, but also so that people can feel safe from what they might do to others.
- You are the parent of the group when the situation demands it. Do not condemn the person who breaks the rules, point out the disadvantages of their choice to break them. We believe people are great; it is their *choices* that sometimes are not.

Completion needs

People in the groups run to our recipe get very close to each other indeed. They allow each other into deeply personal learning experiences. They play together and they give rise to new ideas and forms that have never existed before. They explore their vulnerabilities and they have fun together. The atmosphere rapidly becomes extremely intimate. For some people it might be the most intimate experience of their lives to date.

How you end such a group is essential so that they may go into their lives again without being troubled by disappointment because they have changed their perspectives while other people in their lives probably have not.

We have found that the most important way to end a Breakthrough Zone event of this nature is to give everyone a chance to complete it his or her way. We give them time to think about what they need to say or do to 'tie a bow on it'. We then give them some time to express what it is they need to say. Often people want us to arrange a follow up where they get to input on the next stages that issue from the work we have done together. This is rarely if ever feasible, and we let them know honestly whether or not this will happen. We never leave people with 'maybe'. Likewise, as mentioned before, we set up a mechanism for them to hear about what outcomes issue from the work through the client company.

Often during an ending session a 'killer insight' suddenly appears. Someone, in finishing up, suddenly draws the strands of their experience together and expresses a gem.

We let people know that we are grateful for whatever they have put into the work with us, and where we can we give individual descriptive praise. We let them know what will happen with their creative output, assuring them that it will be put to good use and what that use will be.

Finally, we perform one last process together to say goodbye and mark the end. We have had a candle-lighting ceremony where groups devise a wish for the work and each group sends a representative to the front of the room to light a candle and speak the wish. This might seem corny to some, but do not mistake your fear of sentimentality as being more valid than our human need for rituals and dignified symbols of ending.

You do not have to be elaborate. The process can be as simple as standing in a circle and applauding each other.

We need completion so that we can let go and move on. Always make sure that you send people away having had the opportunity to complete.

This is the single item on the completion needs checklist.

- Always make sure that you send people away having had the opportunity to complete.

A final word in summary.

We have brought this section on facilitation skills to you early in the book because the success of all the events in the next chapters depends upon this style of work. You will not get deep insight unless you make it safe to go deep.

Working with people anywhere is a responsibility. Inviting people to discover things with you is a huge thing to ask. It is reckless and irresponsible to be unprepared. If you want to be the facilitator, then make sure you are prepared with the necessary skills and the distinctions we have outlined. Are you willing to be an example in everything you ask of them? If you are hiring a facilitator, make sure that they are skilled and willing in this way.

Notes

1   Bradshaw, John (1991) *Family Secrets: What You Don't Know Can Hurt You*, *Healing the Shame That Binds You* (and other books), Piatkus, London.
2   Andrews, Mac & Langmaid, Roy (1999) 'Understanding Nurses', BUPA, London. This was a study we conducted for BUPA in 1999 to discover why nurses were returning to the NHS having migrated into private nursing.

5 | Training the Breakthrough Team

Step five – the Breakthrough Training

The Breakthrough Team is the group of company employees and members of relevant agencies who will develop the innovations. Usually, there are between 15 and 30 members of such teams. It is important that all of them make a commitment to attend the team training, the Breakthrough Zone and the Insight Workshop.

Let us assume that you have successfully assembled everybody in the venue of your choice for the Breakthrough Training. What will you do with them? In this chapter we will outline the most important ideas and the principles behind them that will reap the rewards you seek.

Before we start, let us state two main objectives for the training:

1 To give the staff group early exposure to the kind of experiences they will meet in the Breakthrough Zone.

2 To distinguish and go to work on some of the standard blocking mechanisms of the company's culture. This is vital work because breakthroughs interrupt the status quo and will be seen by elements of the culture as disruptive. At the very least they will cause some anxiety and this will tend to push people to respond in a conservative manner.

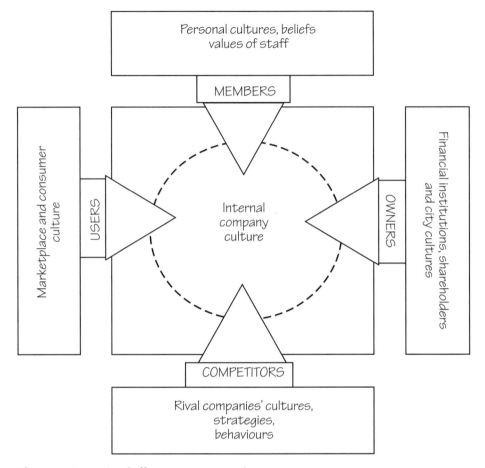

Fig. 5.1   Proportional effects on company culture.

Figure 5.1 illustrates the four main sources of influence on company culture.

The area within the broken line represents the balance of influence exerted by these four sources and in our experience *the influence of shareholders or financial institutions like the City and that of rival companies is far greater than either the influence of company staff or customers.* Senior managers in particular pay more attention to financial and competitor influence than to customers. It is only natural that such managers concern themselves with proper financial disciplines but it is easy to forget the customers who are the source of wealth. One of the aims of our innovation techniques is to attempt to remedy this imbalance even if only temporarily. This is another reason why we have built a large team who will engage on a substantial programme of customer contact and then take their experiences back into the organization in a powerful and concerted effort to break through.

The training has six stages:

1   Building a team.
2   Clearing the past.
3   Building a shared set of motivations for innovation.
4   Experiencing creative inquiry.
5   Unblocking the culture.
6   The role of the team in the Breakthrough Zone.

Stage 1   Building the Breakthrough Team

The purpose of stage 1 of the Breakthrough Training is to create a team, not just any team, but a Breakthrough Team. So, *what is a breakthrough*? Our definition of a breakthrough is 'something made possible that was not possible before'.

A Breakthrough Team is a team that creates breakthroughs, not just in terms of good ideas, but brand-relevant, new, customer-centred, economically sound propositions.

> Our definition of a breakthrough is 'something made possible that was not possible before'.

Cultural norms define what is 'possible' for a community; they operate both overtly and covertly. Even in organizations that claim to espouse innovation as a core cultural attribute, when they arrive at a crucial point of choice, all sorts of 'reasons' emerge for not implementing radical innovation and instead they default to changing something of relatively minor significance. Cultures have an inherent distaste for real innovative challenges. A large part of the 'job' of a culture is to preserve the norms and traditions.

Setting out to innovate means setting yourself up against your cultural norms. You are taking up a position that is inherently in conflict with the current status quo. To sustain yourself and your endeavours you must have a team that will stand with you in this conflicting position and remain faithful to your cause. Without this you will surely fail just as day follows night, unless you are sufficiently senior within an autocratically led organization to force things through. Even if this is the case and you are able to *drive* change through, there will still be a great deal of fallout in terms of resentment and procrastination exhibited by people who have been 'forced' to surrender their patterns and routines.

To be able to weather the strains of your chosen position, the most valuable commodity your team must create and maintain will be *trust*. Remember in Chapter 3 how we outlined the three types of relationship – professional, private, and personal? We need to build a team centred in personal relationships, founded on trust.

Trust is difficult to measure because it exists in the realm of feeling. It is one of those so-called 'touchy-feely' elements of human contact that professionals know is important, but often resist learning to master for fear of looking stupid. Without trust though, you have solid foundations on which to build. Inadequate foundations limit the size of what you can build. In the final analysis, whatever you think about trust and doing what is necessary to create it, nothing you build will be robust without it.

So within our Breakthrough Training, having set the ground rules for our time together, dealt with the issues of meals, fire regulations, health and safety issues and the location of the toilets, we then distinguish breakthrough. We answer the question 'what is a breakthrough?'

A breakthrough is something that is made possible that was not possible before.

But how do you make them happen? How are they sourced?

The source of breakthroughs is responding to unreasonable requests. Reason parallels the status quo. Things that are reasonable are already tested and practised until their results are as predictable as possible. It is 'reasonable' in a Post Office to expect that English people will form an orderly queue. It is unreasonable to go directly to the front when others are waiting. It is 'reasonable' to do whatever you do in your current business life because that is how the daily flow suggests you should proceed.

This reasonability is what leads to distaste for doing things differently. Doing things a different way feels unreasonable *unless* a reasonable justification for doing so is provided. In business this is usually in the form of a *'sound business case'*. To create and maintain an environment that encourages and supports the occurrence of breakthroughs, it is essential that we proceed 'unreasonably' from the word go, applying reason a good bit later than might normally be expected.

Business is there to make money, of course, as without it there would soon be no business at all. Discovering new insights that will provide successful products and services is rather like the princess trying to find the prince: she has to be willing to kiss a fair few frogs to find the ones that transform into the man of her dreams. That takes time, commitment and willingness to wait for the sought-after event to take place. Not only this, it requires investment and, as we know, responsible business practice requires a guarantee of a return on that investment. While it is true that what is innovated must contribute to profitability, to have profitability be one of the first tests for innovative and insightful activity is inherently destructive of it.

The question 'will it make money?' is a flawed starting point, although it is an important question to be answered further down the line. You cannot know the answer until you prototype and test it, and you cannot do that until you have an 'it' to test. You cannot know what it is until you have the learning necessary to give birth to it. You cannot give birth to it until it has been conceived. Prior to conception it does not exist to us. *How and where 'it' is conceived matters most right now.*

In order to create a breakthrough it is necessary to glean insights from a planned and focussed unreasonable activity. The word 'insight' is both over-used and misunderstood in business today. An insight is *not* the same as a good idea. The insights you seek rely on brand new learning about elements of our market, its customers, our cultural norms and the world at large. It occurs inside an individual *not* in the outside world. One of the first mistakes in the creation of insights is to believe that they are out in the world hiding behind a bush somewhere waiting to be found. They are the result of the world having an unexpected impact on us that changes what we know in some key way. They happen inside you.

Most if not all of us have constructed our lives to avoid the world and the people in it having an unpredictable impact on us for very good reasons. Many events in our early lives had a negative impact on us. Therefore we did the most sensible thing by avoiding such experiences ever occurring again. Making our own world as predictable as possible is a sensible way to avoid negative surprises. As most of these experiences sourced themselves in our dealings with other people, it is no wonder that we trained ourselves to make our interactions with others as predictable as possible. A whole set of rituals, customs and manners exist to make sure things stay this way. For businesses in particular, foresight creates stability and predictable forecasts are favoured. In the Breakthrough Zone we have to reverse that.

What you are about to set up is an unpredictable learning environment in which you all set out together to learn unpredictable things you are not yet aware of; then to put that learning into words in order to communicate it. From that which emerges you will be able to create anything you want.

When insightful impact happens to us it changes the way we see every-thing. It is as if we have woken up to something that we were formerly blind to and that, in all probability, we can't yet quite explain. Sometimes it can be exciting. Other times it can provoke feelings of anxiety. Likewise, it can also leave us feeling stupid for not having realized it sooner, and vulnerable – espe-cially when trying to explain it to someone else. It is an inner awakening that rocks our world leaving us temporarily off balance. This is an uncomfortable experience.

We believe that there are two types of insight. One happens almost instan-taneously and we call this 'Short Form Insight' (see Fig. 5.2).

Others occur over a comparatively lengthy period, and we call this 'Ex-tended Form Insight' (see Fig. 5.3).

You will see that whichever form it takes, the initial impact of insight takes us into disorganization and vulnerability, two things which professional people do their best to avoid. You must create an environment where they are welcome.

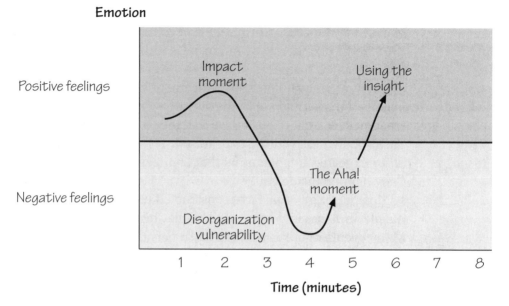

Fig. 5.2 The insight wave: short form.

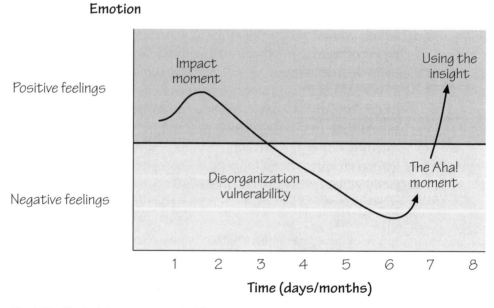

Fig. 5.3 The insight wave: extended form.

On the whole, it is only reluctantly that we learn genuinely new lessons as adults because of the widely accepted cultural notion that there is a point in our lives when most of our learning must be completed. Then we are 'grown up'. Additionally, getting ahead in the workplace seems to be accomplished more by knowing answers than admitting that we don't really know much at all. However, the first element of context required for true learning is the admission that there are some things we do not know.

How many times have you heard people in your working world say the words 'I don't know'? We have noticed that in business one of the most closely guarded secrets is that in reality everybody is making it up as they go along while pretending that they have got everything well under control. In today's market place the degree you have will have less and less to offer what you do every day. Whatever degree you do have, if you have one, will surely have served you well, but the half-life of the knowledge you acquired through it is getting shorter and shorter. What you make up, when, and how are more important.

To learn anything truly new you must first let go of any idea that you know the answer. 'I don't know' is the basis of all new learning. *It is the only fertile place for true insightful impact to occur.*

Early explorers certainly had absolutely no idea what they would find when they travelled beyond the horizon on the sea. The prevailing cultural belief in Europe was that they would fall off the edge of the earth. Imagine the kind of comments people must have made about those eager seafarers as they waved goodbye to them from the quayside. You might hear some similar types of things said about you before too long! Something in their spirit drove them beyond the horizon and away from their familiar and safe shores. They were true pioneers. This is what your team must become. Irresistibly curious pioneers are required, otherwise nothing truly innovative will occur except by accident – and such accidents are few and far between.

Essentially, too, this work is an expressive exercise. Although there has to be time for reflection and learning too, our main source for impactful discovery is in the expressed output from our creative processes. To uncover new learning it will have to be somewhere you can see it! A group of people keeping themselves to themselves will not get us very far at all. This is the sea we must sail.

So, you want to create an expressive team of people who can admit that they do not know the answer, that trust each other at a personal level, who are willing to embark on a journey with an unknown destination, powered by curiosity and who can co-create the future with the most important people to your business of all – your customers. Sounds like a tall order? This is how it goes!

Exercise one – creating relationship

Having set the agenda for the Breakthrough Training it is now time to create your team whilst giving them an experience of genuinely new insight-based learning at the earliest possible opportunity. This exercise is designed to facilitate an insightful experience in the arena of something that they experience every day. The arena is that of interpersonal relationships. Before embarking on this exercise it is ethical and advisable to have a confidentiality agreement with the group. We suggest that throughout the entire breakthrough process, in order that people feel they can express whatever they need to freely, that anything a person learns about anyone else during the time together never gets revealed outside of the group. Stress this as an important element, as you will have to challenge the 'sacred cows' of the business, as well as make mistakes, come up with bad ideas, be naïve etc. These may all be things that your current culture will have limited tolerance for in case they become career limiting in some way. To all intents and purposes they must be relatively secret sessions.

1   *Create space. Stand in front of the group with nothing to say, know or do.*
The first step in this exercise requires that someone stands in front of the group with nothing to say, to know, or to do. What they are asked to do is to stand and look at the other members of the team looking back at them. We ask that they do this for up to two minutes. While they are looking we request that they merely notice what they notice. We asked them to notice what is happening inside them, and what they notice happening outside them as they make eye contact with each person in the group for an 'uncomfortable length of time'. Why should we do this?

We are arguably more terrified of meeting other people than anything else in the world except death itself. Fear of other people is a more prevalent phobia than heights, spiders, snakes, or any other typically frightening aspect of life. For virtually all of us it is a phobia that we have had to learn to manage. We are forced to interact with others whether we like it or not. The bigger the results we want in life the more demands there are for us to form and maintain relationships with others.

We have developed all sorts of rituals and social habits that enable us to manage our anxiety as we approach other people. *Nevertheless, that is all we're doing: managing our anxiety.* We tend to enter new relationships self-consciously, which means we are predominantly concerned with ourselves. We are usually so conscious of ourselves that there is little room in our consciousness for the other person. We do not see them. We are very busy ensuring that nothing unpredictable can happen. We take control as soon as we can. The prospect of this exercise leaves people feeling anxious, and yet it is not life-threatening. Nevertheless everything about our anxiety tells us that it is. How did you feel the last time you had to present or make a speech? Come on now, be honest.

This, of course, is totally normal. Throughout our lives, and particularly in our early years, other people were a source of some pretty nasty experiences. We are absolutely certain that you will remember at least one experience at school of being treated by someone else in a manner that left you feeling wounded in some way. Perhaps you also feel in this moment of recalling that you experience many of the emotions you felt in that situation even though it happened so far back in your history.

In order to get into the kind of creative relationship that you will need with each other and the customers you recruit, you will all have to get better at meeting each other without your individual defensive behaviours being activated. If those behaviours start to run the show you will find it impossible to leave the quayside!

In this exercise the person in the front of the group just looks, makes eye contact and notices what they notice. Noticing what it is that you notice without interpretation is pure perception. Perception is the gateway to our treasure, insightful experiences.

2   *Create trust. Reveal something to the group that is important about you.*
Having created some *unfilled space* inside which a new kind of relationship can be built, we then request that the person *builds trust.* How can this be done? Trust is created by entrusting something *valuable* to someone else. We believe that this is always the case. If you give others something that is not valuable, then no trust is required at all. We know when we are being entrusted – it has an impact. We request that the person entrusts the group with something important about them. Note the words *'important about them'.* We do not ask for things that are important *to* them which may not always amount to the same thing. We recommend that whatever it is they choose to share it is not work related. Sometimes we request ahead of time that each person on the Breakthrough Training brings in an object to which they have a significant sentimental attachment. In this instance we ask them to introduce us to the object and what it says that is important about them.

Relationships can be defined by what is put into them – we want *personal*, not merely *professional*. The best personal relationships soon become private ones i.e. relationships in which just about anything can be said and heard. In a sense this is what we are seeking in developing the Breakthrough Team.

That this feels very risky for people to do is a mark of how impersonally we conduct most of our professional relationships. Yet it is the important aspects of our inner world that most guide our decision making, our choices, thus our brand loyalties, our buying habits, in fact just about everything. To reveal them to ourselves is hard enough, but to reveal those of which we are aware to others renders us 'hurtable' by them. This is key to the efficacy of this process. For this reason, *taking the micky is banned.* If people are to open up with us we must all learn to take care of them while they do so, otherwise they will only do it once. This is a rule in the Breakthrough Zone – *never take the micky.*

We have used variations of this exercise for many years and, without fail, as soon as one person opens up about what they hold as important about themselves, the group feels honoured, safe and willing to share themselves too. This is the group's first experience of the kind of revelatory insight that we seek.

What kinds of things do people reveal? The answer is anything and everything. What it means being a working dad or mum figures highly, and what they really hope for out of their parenting – fears, failures, triumphs and tragedies all surface in one form or another. Stories of illnesses survived, disappointments and losses emerge. Some people talk about their ethics, charity work, acts of heroism, depression. They speak about their love for people, places, activities and things. The human being inside each person arrives. At last it feels safe to admit to being human without fear of being condemned for it.

The relationships between members of the team grow palpably. Even people who thought they knew each other well at work sit open-eyed, open-mouthed and open-minded as they discover new and profound dimensions to their colleagues.

At the end of their period of speaking we request that each participant stands and listens to what people have to say in response. This is tightly controlled, and we will explain both how and why this is the case.

3   *Create acknowledgement. Listen to the group tell you what works about you.*
The group are now invited to feed back to the person standing in front of them. They are instructed that they must not criticize, nor are they allowed to give 'good advice'. They are, however, required to tell the person about the positive personal qualities that emerge when they speak as personally as this. When people show their passion to others, they reveal themselves. All sorts of useful qualities and personality facets pop up that the speaker can only ever be aware of if someone is willing to point them out. Whilst they are unaware of these talents they remain latent and unmanaged assets. It is like having £1000 in your pocket without knowing it, still feeling poor. By telling people that they have these qualities, they become real to them. Some research suggests that children only know they have talents when they hear about them three times.

Feedback at work is, on the whole, only ever given with any force or commitment when something has gone wrong and heads are being 'rolled'. Whilst criticism may have its place in the day-to-day running of a tight ship, expecting it to create a safe environment for breakthroughs is like expecting a boat made of ice cream to carry you safely down the Amazon. When we eventually work with our customer guests and invite them to open up and play with us at the depth we require, we need to acknowledge their contribution over and over again. Children thrive on genuine, specific praise from people Once they can see their talents they can get busy with them confidently. If we want people to use their talents, then the first thing they need to know is that they have got them and to know exactly what they are!

So, in summary, each person in turn gets to:

- create a space not filled with reflex social behaviour within which a relationship can be built,
- entrust the team with something important about themselves, thereby contributing to the building of trust,
- receive acknowledgement from everyone about talents and personal qualities that they might otherwise never become aware of, and
- be applauded.

4   *Write a one-minute letter. Create written evidence of those same things that work about the person you have just heard from.*

The final part of this exercise involves everyone writing a one-minute letter to the person, in which they simply write down all the qualities they saw. If it is true that children need to hear such feedback three times before they can believe it fully, then these are the second and third instances for each team member. This letter is delivered, and the next person gets a go in front of the group. When everyone has done the entire exercise and read their letters to themselves at least once we ask people to get into pairs and to read their letters to each other.

To create a Breakthrough Relationship you have to:

- create space for it,
- create trust,
- create acknowledgement on an ongoing and regular basis, and
- take care of people's vulnerability (no micky-taking allowed).

Stage 2   Clearing the past

Human beings find it very difficult to let go of the past. You might be someone or you might know someone who seems to do quite well at getting on with life anew after big changes. However, regimes are different. Put a number of people together and they will quickly form a regime. Moreover, many companies are more like military regimes than any other group of people.

Think for a moment about the language that dominates marketing cultures: strategy, launch, campaign, push, targets and more recently, 'guerrilla' and 'viral marketing'.

Once the regime is in place it likes things to stay pretty much as they are. Regimes are change-resistant entities. If reality eventually forces change to happen, the regime tends to behave as if it is a victim of the change. After change has occurred it is not long before the group reflex assesses the present as a poor alternative to the 'good old days'.

'Things never used to be like this', they say. Somehow what was 'bad' about the past gets filtered out of general conversation, and an increasingly rosy picture of what had to be left behind emerges.

Opening up to a new future requires releasing ourselves lock, stock and barrel from the past in order that some new 'good old days' can be created. That does not mean that everything that is past is bad, not at all. The past has provided us with opportunities galore. However, getting stuck there is all too easy, and all too natural a tendency. We must now do what is necessary in order to let go. Simply put, we need to see what we have created through our history, and then say goodbye to it knowing that anything of value can come into the future with us too.

Funerals, although not usually the happiest of occasions (in spite of the fact that many people seem to have hilarious stories about them alongside the tragic ones), are nevertheless a typical way for people to complete and clear aspects of their past. There is something about rituals that enables us to feel complete. People make speeches about their past with the deceased, wish them well and then say goodbye. Similarly, we may have farewell parties for friends going overseas, or stag and hen parties to say goodbye to being a singleton.

In organizations, we have seen good-hearted and talented people work miracles in teams, get extremely close to their team mates, achieve stunning results and then the team breaks up and the members move on without any form of thank-you or goodbye.

On top of that, we have seen any number of truly innovative ideas stunted and killed by cost-cutting or re-engineering. We have seen people take the risk to create fantastic market insights, then have their enthusiasm dented permanently by comments like 'We've seen people like you before, it won't last.' Sticking your head above the parapet twice in this kind of critical environment does not seem to be a smart thing to do. It could well be a career-limiting move!

Under the surface, the effects of such experiences rumble away unseen, their invisibility no antidote to the influence they exert over individual and group behaviour.

Let us refer back for a moment to our distinctions in relationship – professional, personal and private. The course of business impacts on people personally as well as professionally. They get hurt, jerked around, frustrated, enthusiastic, hopeful, dashed, desperate, angry, overjoyed; a whole spectrum of emotional experiences occur when they have their personal life invested in their work. When they get thwarted enough, they put it all away, become cynical and withdraw their emotional commitment because the prospect of further disappointment becomes too painful. To create breakthroughs you will need switched-on people not switched-off ones.

This next exercise is our best recipe for turning people back on again. We have turned around teams of insurance salesmen and women who had been sacked, and then when the breakthrough products we helped them create sold 400% of target in the first six months, were then re-employed at a lower rate of pay and in junior positions. This next process had a huge part to play in our success with them. It works because it is human first and foremost, as well as being honest.

It utilizes the most powerful tool in communication there is – listening without judgement.

Exercise two

People are asked to get into pairs and we direct them that, where possible, they should find someone they know less well than others.

In each pair there must be a number one and a number two. Number two starts by talking to number one for ten minutes about their history with the business. We instruct them to include the *facts* as they remember them and also the *feelings* that they had that were driven by those factual occurrences. We offer them an emotional vocabulary by telling them some examples of our own highs and lows in our own business.

There are a few simple rules to guide the participants:

- While one person is speaking for ten minutes, the other person is not allowed to say anything at all. They can make listening noises only.
- Any historical inaccuracies are to be tolerated without correction. One person's memory is, by definition, different from another's.
- The person listening must know that they will have to introduce the person who is speaking to a bigger group in the next stage of the exercise using this information.
- As ever, no micky-taking!

After they have finished, the roles in the pairing are reversed. The listener now speaks and the speaker listens.

When both people have related the facts and feelings of their histories with the company they then join together with another pair of people. This creates groups of four.

In this expanded group each member introduces the person to whom they listened to the new pair that they have joined. They have five minutes and are asked to emphasize their history in terms of the emotional impact that it contains. This has a remarkably therapeutic effect. Knowing that someone else has not only heard how you have felt, but that they have understood it well enough to report it to other people is in essence a cathartic experience. Being heard without condemnation by someone else is a most important experience as it allows us to put down our unfinished emotional business. It creates an emotional clearing. In this clearing it becomes possible to create a new future. Without the clearing we can only try to create a new future on top of an incomplete and unfinished past.

When all four people have spoken we ask them to join another group of four. This creates groups of eight. Again we ask them to introduce each other to the rest of the group. Once they have completed the introductions we then ask each group of eight to distil seven to ten themes that have emerged within the group. We ask them to list of these themes on a flip chart and then to present them to the large group.

This is always powerful. The large group gets to see its history in all its roller-coaster detail. Normally, there are enough recurrent themes for the group to realize that they have all been through a similar experience, and this is usually widely varied and often quite bruising. Because it has occurred within their business life people have usually suffered in secret. For many this will be the first time that they realize others have suffered the emotional highs and lows too. There is always visible relief. Rarely have we found bland accounts of working life. They are always filled with highs and lows. Already in the group they will be experiencing insightful impact.

The big group is now sitting in the presence of its history and we can ask questions relating to it. The first thing we check is how the group feels looking at it.

Stage 3   Building the shared set of motivations for innovation

Exercise three

After some feedback relative to the history that we have exposed, we then ask the bottom-line question 'What will happen if we just allow history to take its course and dictate the future?'

It is clear that history will create a future all by itself if it is allowed to. In every culture there are patterns, tendencies and cycles which, when put together, we call 'the drift'. There is always a drift. It is always there and it is always carrying its culture in a certain preordained direction. It is everywhere. Think about Christmas. How often have you decided that you would make next Christmas different? How often have you succeeded in having a different Christmas? Somehow, over time, we allow ourselves to drift in the direction of the Christmas we always have.

Families and businesses have an enormous amount in common in this respect. Look around you and you will see the drift operating everywhere. Somehow, with it sitting in front of us on the flip charts, doing nothing will seem like a slow drift towards decline and eventual disaster of one kind or another. Doing nothing is not an option any more. At this point the group can see and share the key drivers for change. We are at a point of choice and it is time to make up our minds.

We then ask the group 'What are the key motivators for our innovation project?' We ask them to express it where possible in a single sentence. Each group then presents their sentence to the large group. We collect them together and weave them into a single powerful expression of our reason for change.

Your project is now under way. The team has made a choice to act. Now you must practise some of the techniques that you will use when you meet customers in the Breakthrough Zone.

Stage 4   Experiencing creative inquiry

This section is in three parts and contains essential information on the nature of a creative inquiry, techniques to use, and how to shape and structure your creative processes.

Part I – creative inquiry

Creative inquiry begins with a question that requires an answer that we do not yet know. At the beginning of inquiry we often experience anxiety. Not knowing answers leaves us vulnerable. What do you do first? How should you begin?

A wise person once said to us regarding the writing of this book 'Don't get it right, get it written.' The same sentiments apply to our breakthrough inquiry. It doesn't matter where or how you start in an inquiry as long as you have a question. Once your curiosity is engaged, just get started.

Exercise four

Having played some simple and unsophisticated games to raise everybody's energy, we instruct them to break into groups of five to six people. Once in those groups we instruct them to invent a brand new game that has never existed before, that allows everybody in their group to play, and that is responsible in that it is unlikely to cause anybody physical injury. We ask them to name the game and be ready to play it through from beginning to end. We give them 30 minutes to complete this task and be ready to demonstrate the game for the rest of the group.

At first it sounds an impossible task to accomplish. Yet when we get into the Breakthrough Zone with customers, we will require everyone to embark on a series of creative journeys with no guaranteed results. This exercise exemplifies much about creative inquiry that is difficult. The instructions do not inform you how to do it; you have to make that up as you go along. In fact it is an unreasonable request. You are instructed to create something that does not yet exist; to the logical mind this sounds too tall an order. You are to be the joint authors of it; you are directly responsible and accountable for the result. When it is created it must be demonstrated; others will get to judge your creation. The process of its creation is entirely down to you. This, in a nutshell, is innovation.

A running order is created and the games are performed. Each group will have been through a pretty typical creative process – the unreasonable request and their resistance to responding to it, their decision to respond, their confusion and inability to make choices, their co-operation and building on ideas, and their ultimate formation of an innovative game that they can play.

At the end of the performances and our acknowledgements, we then ask:

'What did you have to do in order to achieve your goal?'

What they report is the stages of creativity:

- resistance;
- confusion;
- idea sampling;
- group formation and emergent leadership style;
- commitment;
- choice; and
- implementation.

It is true that groups can get stuck in any or all of these stages, but time and the 'theatre' of performance provide fantastic motivation to complete the task. We might then ask:

'What struck you about working together on such a project that surprised you?'

People will sometimes struggle to be coherent about what they specifically noticed that had an impact on them. Others will report quite clearly a level of impact that has dropped easily into language for them.

> The importance of this exercise is to point out that what we are seeking in everything we do together is any moment of impact that occurs and not necessarily a solution nor any explanation for it.

The creation of insight follows a tripartite series of events:

1 Impact – we are struck by something.
2 Inquiry – we question its nature.
3 Insight – we realize its significance and are able to express it in language.

We have found that groups in business default to explanation and problem solving when confronted by insightful impact. 'I felt so-and-so because …' In this sort of work, at this early stage, understanding is most certainly the booby prize. Impact is the chief resource for inquiry. Snap explanations stifle inquiry. Sitting with the fact that something different, inexplicable, puzzling and uncomfortable has occurred, is what we require. All the group has to do at this stage is drop the word 'because'. For once they can feel the relief of not having to justify themselves. The next stage is for the groups to conduct an inquiry and create insight. Consider these examples of simple impact that we have experienced working on specific corporate projects.

Whilst working recently with a large Australian financial services organization we noticed that when people mentioned the word 'project', without fail they chuckled. Everyone did it. This particular organization had experienced a shocking downturn in its fortunes. They had resisted admitting that they were vulnerable to the unmistakable market forces prevailing in the world economy throughout 2002. When those forces hit them, they hit hard. From the days of plenty had emerged famine.

Through inquiring into this simple and seemingly insignificant phenomenon of the chuckle, it became apparent to us that history had taught people in this organization that projects never finished. Hundreds were started and almost none could be traced to completion – after loud launches they gradually petered out and disappeared without trace. This anxious community of people had unconsciously developed this chuckle to express their scepticism about anything even vaguely resembling a project. Their engagement with anything 'project-like' was necessarily limited. In their culture to be seen committing to a project with any enthusiasm was interpreted by others as _naïveté_ of the most risible nature. In an organization that now needed everyone's entrepreneurial energy for its very survival this was an enormous barrier to survival. Realizing this made it possible for us to short-circuit the cultural expectations by dividing our work to provide visible results at every stage. Results became

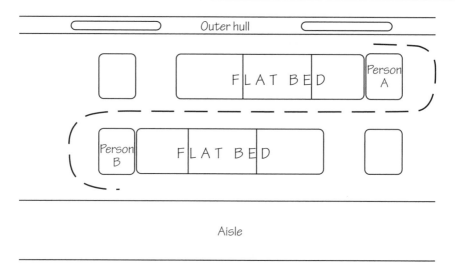

Fig. 5.3   Flat beds in Business Class – a rough sketch.

the first reassurance that 'projects' were now rationed only to those worthy of completion, and that actions could be taken with verve.

A European national-flag-carrying airline that has used our approach extensively for over ten years created flat beds in business class from another such insightful impact. At the time, in the early 1990s, cradle seats were the best that business had to offer. Working with customers in a creative process about the emotional story of travelling by air, every single group created a scene where people could lie down whether on a bed, a magic carpet or a massage table. The constant emergence of the same need was unmistakable. It was everywhere. Once the Breakthrough Team was persuaded and committed, a design company was found to deliver a solution. They solved another problem that had arisen in the customer process too: that of sleeping side by side with a stranger. Figure 5.4 shows their design solution with an ingenious rearrangement of the configuration of a pair of seats.

The games that your Breakthrough Teams have just created are models for the creative process, but are yet another resource for experiencing insightful learning. Ask the groups to go round and reveal moments of impact, to identify what struck them. Ask them to choose one of the things that struck them and to inquire into it until something dawns on them. After half an hour ask them to feed back their insights. It is common in this process for teams to joke about patenting their games although to our certain knowledge nobody yet has. Many of them, however, have been worthy of it!

The next stage of our Breakthrough Training is to experience some examples of methods that might be used in the Breakthrough Zone. It is a good idea to link the creative processes to topics for inquiry relevant to your business. Where to take your topics is an important issue. Where can you look for insightful impact? What kind of processes will expose what we are looking for?

Sources of impact

Now comes the time to relate the creative work to the research in hand. How do you set up creative exercises that will facilitate relevant impacts, inquiry and subsequent insight? There are innumerable sources for subject matter, but here we will discuss the ones which have proven richest for us:

- creative metaphors,
- disowned behaviours,
- withheld conversations, thwarted intentions and unfulfilled expectations,
- clichés, and
- direct questions.

We will generally discuss these exercises with examples in the next few pages and you will see that many feature customers as well as company staff. You can adapt them as easily for use in the Breakthrough Zone as in the team training. If you wish, you can ask staff to play customer roles in the training process as it gives them valuable practice at walking in their customers' shoes.

Creative metaphors
Looking at one part of the world through the lens of another is always revealing.

What might we see if we examined the world of air travel through the daily workings of a zoo? How does the experience equate? What could we learn about the nature of the experience of animals in a zoo and that of passengers on an aircraft? Is there anything about the treatment of animals in a zoo that might throw light onto the aircraft experience? What if we were to be put into a zoo for a period of incarceration? One of the first things that comes to mind is the lack of freedom and the dominance of routine. This seems to be something in common between the zoo and the aircraft. You get your food when the crew say, not when you want it. It's feeding time so eat up! We might also think of the zoo and wonder how such an experience could be imbued with delightful moments?

Creative metaphor can be used to replicate an experience and a context for inquiry into its impact on us. Working with a leading healthcare company that supplies both insurance-based products and delivery of the care, we noticed that many people felt they should have better access to healthcare for their loved ones. However, they were so anxious about the whole prospect of illness that they could not stay in a detailed conversation about it for long. Talking about the future of our health and well-being brings up that most difficult of topics – undignified illnesses leading to death not only for ourselves but also those nearest and dearest to us. This created a problem for sales as well as claims and underwriting staff. People who had bought the products had very little idea of the real scope of their policies seemingly due to their anxiety, and prospective customers became easily overwhelmed with detail and would pull out of the sales conversation and never call back. We saw this particular issue as being how to hold people inside a journey in which they were unable to see for themselves. Treating people with a sensitivity appropriate to their level of anxiety seemed to be important.

We invented a game. Customers were put into groups of four and asked to choose a member of the company and to blindfold him or her. They were not allowed to make physical contact with their 'victim'. They were told that their primary job was to keep the blindfolded person safe from harm and that they should do everything possible to inspire confidence in them. They were told to take them on a journey throughout the multi-storey hotel using words only. They could only touch them if an emergency dictated they should.

Our blindfolded brethren were nervous to say the least, but bravely went on their journeys. Some went up and down the emergency stairs, one group even went to the pub across the road!

When we asked the groups to inquire into the kinds of speaking they had to use to fulfil the brief for the exercise, what they had to say gave us the insight that enabled us all to produce a completely new approach to sales and customer service. The metaphor delivered radically new perspectives that also affected everything that was innovated. We will return to this exercise in the next chapter to further illustrate its place in the Breakthrough Zone process.

We often use building materials to help people express themselves within a creative metaphor. In a customer service inquiry with a leading British mobile phone retailer we took groups of a thousand staff at a time and divided them into two groups. One group of two hundred was trained to be customers and was issued a currency that we invented for the process. The remaining eight hundred were divided into groups of twenty. They were briefed to invent high street 'businesses'. The huge National Indoor Arena in Birmingham was divided into 40 retail areas, and 40 business groups were given materials (dowelling rods, silver paper, polystyrene cubes, cloth, torches, hacksaws, sticky tape etc.) with which to build a retail environment to deliver a service to customers that was *not* product based. The aim was to use the customer service values of the organization to deliver a customer experience that the 'customer' group of two hundred would be invited to buy. Customers would be canvassed as they left each 'business' to score their experience against these values.

The customer service scores were then multiplied by the amount of money taken during the one hour trading period. The highest overall scores for the top three were calculated and the groups rewarded with this same amount in cash sterling. Groups were invited to report back their insights.

The process was dynamic, creative, impactful and immense fun. The organization, its award cabinet crammed with customer service awards, is still the leader in its field in spite of extremely difficult market conditions. In this instance previously generated customer service values were experienced and learned creatively by the entire community within a day.

We ran a similar building process with general managers of a leading international hotel chain. Grouped into tens, we provided each group with a break out room and requested them to build an environment that they could all live in as strangers for an imaginary period of two weeks. Each environment had to contain significant elements of 'home' for each individual member of the group.

We then requested that they distinguish the ten key elements that made their environment a successful home for strangers. Once they accomplished this we asked each group to build a hotel brand based totally on these key elements, linking every aspect of the product and service to them. The results were ground breaking and led to a penetrating and innovative programme of training and development run by front-line staff called 'Welcome Home'.

Finding a creative parallel in which to explore aspects of your business and then to create a bold game to play within it will always generate new, insightful and relevant learning.

Disowned behaviours

Many products and services deliver a proposition to the customer that the customer then adapts to their own needs. These personal needs often occur within the secret aspects of customers' lives. Male students are not always the most hygienically focussed members of society. While working on detergents, for example, we have gathered the sense that people will often use deodorants or perfumes to cover up staleness in clothes rather than changing them. Particularly with young men, there is a tendency to use 'cover-up' products to hide dirt. How common is this practice, we wondered? Is there any product that might be used for more effective covering of odour from bodies or clothes? How would you market such a product? Are current deodorants being used in this way?

Give any product or service to people and they will adapt it in ways that manufacturers could never predict.

In 1924 a company called Kimberly-Clerk launched Celluwipes, a paper tissue-based product for the removal of make up. Research then revealed that people were mainly using them to wipe and blow their noses, which led to the relaunch of the product: thus was born the Kleenex.

Who can remember that Baby Gays were the first incarnation of the Q-Tip? Made originally to meet baby cleaning requirements, they are now used by model makers for fiddly paintjobs and gluing, machine-part cleaning, furniture restoration and all sorts of adult cleaning jobs.

Give any product or service to people and they will adapt it in ways that manufacturers could never predict.

Within the secret lives of us all are lurking many insightful realizations that are unavailable because they are closely guarded information that might feel too embarrassing or shameful to reveal. These areas of human behaviour are a veritable goldmine of useful commercial information. One manufacturer of instant coffee granules used an aspect of secret behaviour to promote his product during the 1980s. His TV commercials featured a hostess at a dinner party pretending to be a coffee percolator and making the sounds of percolation while actually preparing instant coffee out of sight of her guests in the kitchen. The guests never notice that they are drinking instant coffee, of course, and the point is made that Red Mountain blend is indistinguishable from real coffee.

To access these parts of human life in creative processes we have to be both clever and responsible. One means of access is through projective exercises, i.e. attributing others with the thoughts or behaviours that we wish to examine rather than owning up to them ourselves.

A leading manufacturer of soap powder recruited our help to discover how they might manage the prevalent and damaging connection between inexplicable skin conditions and detergents. Many people blame detergents for skin problems, yet scientists find it very difficult to replicate this causal link in the laboratory.

As part of our process with housewives we created 'The Gossip Game'. This supposed that we were all neighbours at a coffee morning discussing the new family that had moved in to a house in the street. The whole family had visible skin irritation and it was our job to focus on this distinguishing characteristic. The group embraced the game with relish, indulging in increasingly derogatory judgements about this unfortunate family, often prefacing their next comment with expressions of sympathetic pity, 'Oh I do feel sorry for them, it must be terrible but …'.

All of the judgements were damning, and all had a genuinely human ring about them. The skin rashes were evidence, it appeared, of incompetent hygiene, poor parenting, bad diet, lack of care and even that the children were 'at risk' in some way. In the mind of a mother a skin rash on their children or husband might become a route by which their care might be called into question. It could expose their incompetence. While there is little empirical evidence that washing powders are directly linked with rashes and skin eruptions, they clearly provide convenient scapegoats that cannot argue back. The damning attitudes which are then projected onto detergents as 'cause', became available readily within a game where we were pretending not to be ourselves, but role-playing as if we were others. It then becomes a point for discussion within the manufacturer whether to accept these attributions or to try to refute them.

The company concerned neatly side-stepped the issue by having a non-biological version of the powder to provide a more benign variant of the product. At the time of writing the non-biological variant accounts for nearly half of all sales.

Working in the airline industry we have discovered that passengers have a tendency to regress when they become anxious. They often behave like demanding children, sometimes exploding into fully fledged tantrums! There is a level of dependency on the pilot and the crew for our lives, let alone our comfort, that we have only previously experienced as children. We are truly in the hands of others, regardless of our status and power on the ground. Interestingly, we are reliably informed that business men favour kids' cartoons and computer games when travelling. Airlines that serve ice creams to business travellers have noticed that this is the preferred sweet. Being 'tucked in' at night by air crew is extremely popular. We have used this tendency to regress on several occasions to resource innovation in premium class travel by running a process called 'Throwing a Tantrum'. We play a series of simple and childlike games that require childlike behaviour and then ask people to imitate five-year-old kids making a stream of unreasonable demands – we create a group agreement that swearing is allowed, and that sex can be mentioned too. In fact this is so permissive that they can demand anything at all, legal or otherwise during their two-minute rant. We divide the participants into groups of four and have one person in the four stand and rant for two minutes. This means that the room gets extremely noisy, and the sound level enables each group to be unheard by the others. The job of the three others in each small group is to applaud and encourage the stream of demands from the fourth, and to remember the ideas that impress them. Having done the process with abandon, we then double up the groups and ask them to identify the themes that have emerged.

The demanding child in each of us has proven an extraordinarily rich source of customer insight over the years. If in doubt, create a game to expose this diamond mine no matter what industry you are in. You will be amazed at the results.

Withheld conversations, thwarted intentions and unfulfilled expectations

There are no-go topics and taboo subjects in every culture at every level. Countries have them as indeed do families. Working with a leading manufacturer of tampons and feminine hygiene products led us straight into the teeth of this issue. In fact within the two country markets that most concerned this manufacturer, Italy and Eire, the social and religious implications of the product usage were inevitably at the heart of the inquiry. How does a group of predominantly male facilitators open up an honest inquiry with women on such an intimate topic?

The simple answer is by asking. On the whole the people who are most impacted by social taboos are the ones most eager to talk about them when asked. However, the request to talk must come from a genuine and purposeful desire to know, not from profligate and voyeuristic indulgence. What we fail to realize from a 'professional' perspective is that many women talk about these issues together with no problem whatsoever. Giving permission for them to talk about such matters with you is merely accomplished by being interested, listening and contributing personal material from your own life too. The depth and breadth of what people will reveal is equal to the amount of non-judgemental listening you are prepared to do – as well as your willingness to reveal at the same level about yourself where relevant.

Death, sex, bodily functions, psychological and emotional trauma, ambition, fear – all are available conversations in an appropriate environment where no one is playing the 'expert' and everyone is a respectful human being. The more we see Oprah Winfrey type television, the more these taboo conversations become acceptable. Death, sex, bodily functions and the arena of psychological trauma etc. may have nothing to do with your business. If so, then do not go there. If they are, then you would be advised to go there without delay. These are meaningful issues to us all, they drive us in all sorts of ways and all of us are somebody's customers. We are not suggesting that you go there for the sake of it. We are suggesting that you be willing to consider that these human issues might have some bearing on your customers' choices – where and how is worth finding out. What people *do not* say to you should be of interest.

We have noticed that in some industries it is not so much that people are not saying things that are relevant, but that the industry has stopped listening to them. Some customers are so well trained that they will argue the impossibility of certain innovation on your behalf. We have heard customers tell organizations why they cannot do certain things even when the arguments have become obsolete due to technological or regulatory advancements.

A large British-based fast moving consumer goods company instructed us that they did not want to hear women tell them about how much they hate ironing and want the job done for them – even though this company's business concerns the process of washing and cleaning clothes. The fact is that people who wash clothes seem to hate ironing. However much you ignore or suppress this fact, it just will not go away. This is what the market wants, and in spite of this fact, no serious solution to this problem has emerged (except drip-dry or crease-resistant fabrics). The market is calling for a breakthrough, inconvenient as it might be, and the breakthrough required is in the ironing arena. We are waiting for a mechanical solution to the ironing problem just as those that have been found for washing, cleaning dust from the carpet, and drying wet clothes.

What you have stopped listening to because of difficulties that have been accepted across your culture constitutes an arena for a breakthrough product or service that is just waiting to happen. It is possible that your customers have stopped saying it to you. Everything that we tolerate is a breakthrough opportunity waiting to be exploited. Supplying to impossible aspirations is possible. Look at religions – they sell *eternal life*, and whether or not you believe one way or the other, they indisputably make an enormous income from it.

Organizations are often terrified to meet their customers for fear that they will do nothing but be angry, whinge and complain. We actively invite this for the first 40 minutes of every encounter, and even in the worst cases it rarely takes longer than this to complete. The thwarted expectations and disappointments of customers are a rich vein of insightful impact. It is arguable that from the moment we are born we must train ourselves to deal with disappointments. For this reason alone it is essential to get them out of the way in order that some new and creative thinking can occur. The benefit is that these things are usually top of mind and readily available. 'When the customer's pissed, don't resist, record a list or they'll persist.'

'When the customer's pissed, don't resist, record a list or they'll persist.'

With your team you must try this out. Choose an industry that is not in your market, but is familiar to you as customers. Collectively answer the question 'What's on your mind about …?' Insert the industry of your choice at the end of your question. Railways, roads, government, electricity, gas, water, builders, plumbers – the choice is yours. Listen to what people have to say. The rules are that people must speak one at a time, they must stand to speak, the facilitator does nothing but thank people for their comments and they get applause for speaking. As you listen, notice how much resource for deeper inquiry comes from peoples' mouths. We will be doing this exercise with your customers in the Breakthrough Zone about your business. Your team need to get used to listening without fixing, justifying or defensiveness.

Clichés

We were briefed by a famous telecommunications company to explore the nature of 'good communication'. The inquiry was to gain insights that would enable the organization to provide services and marketing that would increase people's usage of the telephone system.

We created groups of ten and challenged them to expose everything that they had ever learned about talking, and names for people that talk. What came up astonished us. The lists were extremely long – 'Empty vessels make most noise', 'Speak when you are spoken to', 'Children should be seen and not heard', 'gasbag', 'chatterbox'. The overriding impact that hit everyone was how damning and negative was our education regarding talking – nobody, it seemed, had ever been praised for being talkative. Even though others might be envious of an articulate person, praising people for their loquaciousness was very rare. Giving people permission to talk more and to feel alright about it might require some effort. Anyone that claims 'it's good to talk' might need to provide contexts in which people would be able to see how that could be the case.

Another arena that requires us to find creative ways to open up our talking is that of taboo topics. When asked to explore the active gender stereotypes still at work amongst a certain segment of customers we solved it creatively. We had women pretend to be men in the gents toilets in an imaginary night-club talking about women. The men had to listen with their backs turned to the action. Then the men got to role-play being the women in the ladies toilets talking about the blokes in the same imaginary nightclub. Besides being absolutely hilarious, it was an experience that revealed some extremely ancient attitudes, many of which were unspeakable in any other circumstances, but full of significance in the marketplace where they drove opinions and choices from the background.

Direct questions

Never underestimate the value of the direct question when asked by someone who genuinely wants to know the answer and who clearly will not use this answer to embarrass or belittle the respondent. What you are curious about is always worth pursuing. However, some questions are boundary busters that leave people in shock and shame should they answer. These questions need stepping stones towards them, i.e. short processes that establish permission to suspend normal rules. Sometimes direct questions can be answered using a mailbox. We might want to know about the usage of condoms. A discreetly placed mailbox where people could post answers to questions about their most innovative use of condoms would give an opportunity for them to respond honestly whilst maintaining anonymity.

We asked a group of 20–30-year-olds 'What do you think your clothes say about you?' and then 'What do you most hope they do not say about you?' Because we had established a trusting relationship with them and they knew that we were genuinely curious about how we use clothes to project an identity, they were really honest, often at their own expense.

Everyone, including the facilitators, must be willing to contribute their secrets as things emerge. Remember, praise and acknowledgement let people know they are doing well. As people search to find new learning, praise their every step. This will maintain their confidence to keep going. Get that right and they will go to the ends of the earth for you.

Part II – creative techniques

We have distinguished a number of areas that we have found fruitful for creative inquiries. Now it is time to categorize the different styles or techniques you can use to explore these areas or any other you might come upon. Creative techniques are the vehicles in our search for insightful impact. Put simply, they are the games we will play with our customers that will provide us with the information we are looking for. The best games are the simplest. The more complex the game is, then the more constraining it is likely to be. We want to create as few constraints as possible. Use simplicity as a rule of thumb. If the game needs more than two minutes of explanation, then it is probably too hard to be liberating.

You are limited in the techniques that you employ only by your imagination and boldness. We have already outlined some ideas that we have employed with companies in this chapter. Use and adapt them as you see fit.

There are some broad genres for creative techniques and we will expose them here before describing the next stage in the Breakthrough Training.

There are many ways to be creative. You can use *creative expression* (role-play, building tableaux, sculpting, the Tantrum Game described earlier, etc.), *creative contemplation* (visualization, day-dreaming, imaginative memory games, etc.), *creative production and invention* (building, as described above, and 'art-from-within' described in great detail in Chapter 6, write poems, songs, create new inventions, machines to accomplish hitherto impossible things, fantasy products, etc.) and even *creative discovery* (creative metaphors and projective games, 'what if?' inquiries, as described earlier).

Creative processes can be real-time or multi-stage where real-time is improvised and spur-of-the-moment, and multi-stage is more structured, each stage of output building on the completion of the previous step.

Creative expression

We find these particularly useful for energizing groups quickly. A simple series of tasks given in a limited period of time can inspire the group, get them into the group numbers that you want, and get them responding to your requests. A typical series of instructions we could start a process with might look like the following:

> 'You have five seconds to get into groups of five. Go!'
> 'You have five seconds to get into groups of seven. Go!'
> 'You have five seconds to get into groups of four. Go!'

These games are simple and can be accomplished by anyone. If you want them to be more inventive, and the group seems to be physically able then you might build on this exercise:

> 'You have 30 seconds to get into groups of six and the group must only have four points of contact with the floor.'

Repeat the instruction and say 'Go!'

Praise their efforts – set up acknowledgement as part of your creative culture immediately.

You might want to take the group into more expressive behaviours in which case you might issue the following tasks:

> 'You have five seconds to get into pairs. Go!'
> 'One of you is "A" and the other is 'B'. Decide now.'
> 'You are going to have an argument. Stand one metre apart and facing one another. "A" you can only say the word "Yes". "B" you are only allowed to say "No". As you argue using only those words, you have to get as loud as you can to win. The game will take one minute – how loud can you get? You are not allowed to touch each other. Go!'

These simple games move people into greater energy almost instantly. They find themselves breaking the normal rules with ease and having fun doing so. From here it is possible to take them into any expressive inquiry you choose, e.g. 'Things I hate about financial services', 'My worst experiences buying clothes', 'Things I wish someone would sort out.'

If you want to prepare people to role-play, then get them into brief games that involve behaving differently:

'Circulate in the room and greet everyone politely. Go!'
　　'Now as you greet people notice that they smell awful – stay polite.'
　　'Now greet them as if you are in love with them. Go!'
　　'Now greet them as if they are an old and treasured friend you haven't seen for ages.'

You can get people to be their favourite animal and then to become the human form of this animal. All you have to do is set up a playful atmosphere and instruct them simply.

Role-play is an extremely useful technique. It needs to be resourced with some preparation. If you want the group to invent an ideal customer service experience then some preparatory creative development needs to have been accomplished – how do we want it to feel, what are the key moments, what effect do we want the interaction to have on the customer?

Working with a telecommunications company we developed a role-play game in which two people had a conversation through a bed sheet being held up between them by two observers. One person was the speaker and they chose an attitude at random from a hat. This attitude was their 'speaking tone', (a few examples were panicky, level, distracted, passionate, bored, or angry). The other person chose a listening attitude at random from a hat (some typical examples were amused, happy, uninterested, distracted, bolshy, argumentative or cynical). They were to have a chat and notice what they noticed about the dynamics of the conversation. The surprising result was that in every group the listener was clearly the influencer of the conversation – more powerful against every measure that we identified. Very soon after that the company used the copy line 'It's good to listen' to complement its well-established line, 'It's good to talk'.

Working with family dynamics we have found role-playing simple domestic situations extremely revealing and often quite shocking, e.g. how the washing gets done from collection to completion.

One very revealing use of projective role-play that we use is a game we call 'The Best Psychic in the World'. We invented this game to surface insights into how people bonded with brands, and how those brands related to the formation of identity. People pair up. One person is the 'psychic' and the other is the 'client'. The psychic is the 'best and most highly paid psychic in the world'.

The psychic is briefed to look at the person in front of them and to notice any pictures that they have inside them relating to the other person, as well as any feelings or thoughts. Using this information they are to create a shameless account of the person's past, their present and their future and tell the other person with absolute confidence, disregarding any possibility that the story is anything but completely correct. When this is over and the client has had a chance to feed back, the roles are reversed and the game conducted the other way.

Next, each member of the pair has to construct a 'Brand Zodiac Chart' as the psychic for the other person, using logos, magazine ads, articles, etc. The questions they have to answer in their 'Brandological Chart' are 'Who have they been, who are they and who will they become?' expressed through brand loyalties and aversions. The results can be extraordinarily revealing. One person revealed that her deepest fear was that her generation '… is all about being yourself – but who is that? Brands help me be someone. They provide off-the-peg identities.'

Creating expressive games is an art that can be learned. Just make sure that you are willing to play too, keep the games relevant (even if sometimes necessarily oblique), respect what people reveal and give praise at every opportunity.

Become a collector and inventor of simple games and ice-breakers. There are many books available full of games. Listen to your children describe games they play in the playground and in class at school. They are a rich resource. The general principle to follow is use games like these to get the group to a level of expression that will form a platform rich in resources for wherever you want to go next.

Creative contemplation

If you want people to be more reflective and internally focussed, then do not do expressive games with them immediately beforehand. Get people to slow down and to notice things that require stillness and quiet to perceive.

> 'Notice the sounds outside the room.'
> 'Notice the sounds in the room.'
> 'Notice the sound of your breathing.'

Once people are in a more contemplative mood they are better resourced for internal image work in preparation for such processes as creative visualization or art-from-within (Chapter 6).

Creative visualization is an extremely useful tool. Everyone can imagine, although the ability may be underused and unpractised. It is merely an imaginary journey guided by the facilitator. In order to succeed with it in a group situation it is important that people have a chance to get into a comfortable sitting position; lying down will often cause someone to fall asleep and if they begin to snore you have an unavoidably disruptive situation from which there is no escape! Check that everyone is able to close their eyes for a protracted period of time as some people wear contact lenses that make this a problem.

Ensure that any visits to the toilet have been completed so that the group is not disturbed by people getting up and leaving the room.

Once they are in their seats adopt a soothing tone of voice as you follow a similar script as we have described above. Help them to relax by suggesting that parts of their body feel heavy and relaxed:

> 'You can feel your legs relaxing … your hands and arms … your neck … your head may be getting heavy … you are feeling extremely relaxed and at ease.'

When you sense that people are both still and inwardly focussed you can start your story. Here is an example of an effective first stage in a visualization that we use most regularly to inspire a group in their individual imaginary journeys. The journey begins by having people imagine that they are floating above their bodies, looking down on themselves sitting in their chairs. They then pass up through the ceiling, on through further floors and out beyond the roof of the building so that they have an aerial perspective of the building and the grounds that it is in.

We hover there for a moment, smelling the air and feeling the temperature, noticing the colours, in other words, we use our internal senses to increase the reality of the experience.

We then ascend up to the clouds, watching as the view expands – the town is visible and any local landmarks, then the outlying countryside, etc. We then arrive above the clouds into bright sunshine and a sense of freedom.

From here you can take people anywhere. You can float them slowly down to a town or city in the future, experiencing the world of their highest aspirations, to a holiday experience, to an idealized service experience, wherever you want them to create from. We would recommend that you do not introduce unpleasant surprises, or shocking ideas that might distress people deliberately. They will have made themselves vulnerable to your suggestions and it is important that you take care of them.

At the end of your exploratory journey always take time to bring their awareness back into their bodies as they sit in the chair. Some people will have become profoundly connected with their imagined world and to wrenched back into the room and expected to be awake and alert immediately will cause discomfort and in all probability low and tired energy. Coax them back gently.

> 'I am going to ask you to leave the world of your imagination in a moment and ask you to remember that you are sitting in your chair in a room in the ******** Hotel. Just gently wiggle your toes … then your fingers … arms … gently roll your shoulders … and when you feel ready, just open your eyes … open your eyes.'

They will have been in an internal world of their own construction and so to expect them to be buzzing with things to say will be misplaced. They will need to have some time to reflect on the internal experience they have just had before they report on it. You might give them time to remember as you remind them of some of the key parts of the story, and then allow them time in pairs to discuss what they experienced before they report back to the room. Often we provide each member with a pre-prepared worksheet that has reminders of the key questions and experiences of the visualization. Once they have re-visited and completed a record of their own inner journey it is a good idea to get into small groups to share journeys and look for themes.

You will find a detailed creative visualization from a real customer process described in Chapter 6. From this example you can get a sense of the product and brand-related tasks that you can explore with this technique.

You might equally take them into another creative process that we call art-from-within. Art-from-within is one of our most regularly used and powerful projective methods. You will find a full description of the set up for this in Chapter 6, but it is useful at this point to show you some of the marvellous and creative outputs that customers have achieved in this process.

Working with a tobacco company we asked people to draw on the topic of 'The truth about smoking', and 'How I see the tobacco industry'. The picture of the clown (Fig. 5.5) was produced in that very group. This is what they had to say about what they had drawn.

> 'It's a funny thing smoking. You do it with your mates and it's a bit of a laugh when you're clowning around and having a "party". But under-neath there's something niggling, like little devils laughing at you. I tried to show that in the picture, they're at the bottom creeping about. Wor-rying you all the time.
>
> 'As you can see the clown is all dressed up for a happy time but doesn't know whether to be happy or sad.'

Here are some further examples of the results that can be achieved as well as an idea of the range of subject matter that can be approached.

Remember when using this method that *the quality of the picture is of no importance.* What matters is the artist's learning from what he or she has depicted, revealed by their comments about their picture. We find that pictures from this process regularly and reliably provide an invaluable resource for hypotheses for further testing as well as confirmation of themes emerging from other creative inquiries.

In Fig. 5.6 we see a classroom. This expresses the feeling of an air passenger in an economy cabin on a long flight. The artist's notes say:

Fig. 5.5 The smoking clown.

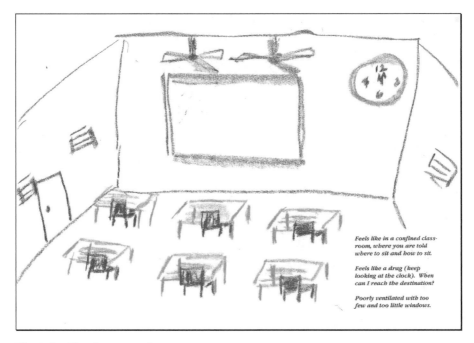

Fig. 5.6 The classroom plane.

'Feels like a confined classroom where you are told where to sit and how to sit. Feels like a drag (keep looking at the clock). When can I reach the destination? Poorly ventilated with too few and too little windows.'

Figure 5.7 represents the experiences of telephone conversations at work as opposed to those at home. In the lower half of the picture there is a crowd of smiling, relaxed and happy faces, whereas the professional faces above are serious, closed and even hostile. This is what the artist wrote:

'Work calls are exhausting and unpleasant. Not friendly. By the time I finish work I am so fed up with talking to people on the phone the last thing I want to do is answer the phone. When I do it's a pleasure but it isn't always very good to talk really.'

We think they reflect our points about personal and professional relationships quite clearly too.

Fig. 5.7   Calls at home and at work.

Creative production and invention

Children love to build things. Give them simple tools that require little mastery to utilize and they will astound you with the sophistication that they achieve if given enough permission and praise.

As we have already described, we often give groups, both large and small, basic resources for them to produce structure with. We have used this method in telecommunications, financial services, hotels, airlines, television rental and restaurant and catering companies. Without exception the results have provided an embarrassment of riches in terms of insightful learning. Be sure that you provide the right tools to work with. For example we find dowelling rods an essential part of the resource kit, but their worth is limited when there is nothing to cut them with; a junior hacksaw is useful whilst being relatively safe to have about in a busy environment. Be wary of box cutters or Stanley knives as they can be dangerous if left lying about.

There is very little that you cannot ask people to construct. We have requested everything from aircraft interiors, brand-monuments, uniforms for a new European Police Force, telecommunication devices of the future, environments for pleasure and well-being, new packaging for instant coffee – again, you are limited only by your willingness to imagine relevant applications. If you want some experiential insight into how your customers see you, then ask them to build something that reflects their attitudes. If want to know their aspirations, ask them to build something that embodies them. You will be amazed what you learn that no other research will teach you.

Creative discovery

This is a little harder to pin down. In many ways the whole of the Breakthrough Zone is a process of creative discovery as no preordained outcome has been established – what emerges is what strikes us and the learning that we derive from our inquiry into those impactful moments.

To a certain degree all of the creative techniques we have described have at their heart the opportunity to discover something unexpected. There is one technique, however, that has special significance for us in that the results it has produced have always created an excellent forum for a large group to talk about more visionary, even spiritual matters.

We sometimes ask people to take a quiet walk whilst thinking about a problem or issue and after five minutes of wandering to stop and look around them for something that attracts their attention. We ask them to stand looking at it for no other reason than it has attracted their attention at a certain point in their reflective time. We ask that if it is portable and legal to do so they bring it back, otherwise that they remember it and be prepared to describe it upon their return. We ask them to find the connection between the object and the issue that they were contemplating – what is in the spirit of the object that relates to the spirit of the focus for their contemplation? We do not claim that there is anything mystical about this process at all. The chosen item and subsequent associations call for a level of penetrative thought that forces unexpected connections to emerge. Try it and you will see what we mean. We call this process 'The Spirit Walk', a name suggested to us by a colleague in another creative business.

Any process embarked upon out of curiosity that has no particular expected outcome is a discovery process.

Now having explained all of that, it is time to return to the Breakthrough Training.

Part III – shaping the inquiry

It is time to revisit your STOP Statement. What is the essence of your inquiry? This is the time in the Breakthrough Training to give the group an experience of using creative processes in a way that relates to your STOP Statement.

If your problem is that customers are leaving your market, then how could you explore this phenomenon? What do you wonder about your market, your competition, what else your customers are up to that might conflict with using you or your products? What is happening in the world right now that is changing buying habits? What are the aspects of life that captivate or concern people today? Later, we can see whether or not what you produce and sell has any relevance to what matters most in the lives of customers. You might have a head full of theories about any or all of these things, but right now they are of no authoritative use at all. We are looking for something new.

Now is the time to choose how to pursue your inquiry with your team first, and then to expand it to your team and customers together. This is not to be run within the Breakthrough Training to get an implementable result, it is to get the team used to creative processes so that they can participate with the customer group as customers too. We all have a customer inside us. In the Breakthrough Zone we are all the same inasmuch as there is no 'us' and 'them'. There is room for individual expression too. There are no experts.

Your team have already produced a game and practised insight building from impact through inquiry. Now we are looking for impact only.

There are many starting places available. Loyalty to brands and products is of immense importance to any business. What are your team members' loyalties?

How might you grade them?

You could ask people to get into teams and to develop the 'Loyalty Top Ten' for each of three categories.

1   Relationships.
2   Activities.
3   Brands.

Notice that you are not dealing with either your product or service. However, you are exploring the elements and aspects of life that inspire loyalty as an attribute in the wider world of human existence. A list of what most inspires loyalty in your customers could be of crucial significance – especially if your product or service is not even in the Top 100 Loyalty list! What is the nature of the things in the top ten? What elements of importance are present the higher up the list one goes? If your product or service had some of those elements, how much further up the loyalty list of your customers could you go? How might that look in action? How might it affect service contact, sales, invoicing, marketing and communications, direct mail messaging, cross-selling, etc., etc.?

Let us imagine that your STOP Statement has identified that you have reached saturation in terms of penetration in your market, and that you either now increase your market share by winning business from the competition or you open up and expand the market by innovation in products or services. You do not have to choose one or other just yet. Now you have the task claimed by Star Trek: 'To boldly go where no one has gone before' complete with the split infinitive! What a prospect and how overwhelming. Where should you start?

Start with what we call 'wider inquiry', which is exactly what it says. Allow yourself to inquire into the wider world of you and your customers. Start somewhere other than your immediate business – think laterally not literally. Who is it you want to attract? What is meaningful to them in their lives? Where are their resources going? How have you been a part of their lives hitherto? Like the example of the Kleenex, how else have they been using your product or service other than the use you assert?

When working with baby boomers and financial services (pensions, investments, etc.) one of our starting points was to ask them what they knew about life that could only be learned by living beyond 40. The list was extremely enlightening – many things that were important in earlier stages of life were no longer powerful drivers in the second half. The people who had bought their pensions many years ago were motivated by different values and ideals from those same, now older, people about to reap the rewards of their savings. The company had completely lost touch with them as they had grown. Without understanding the real day-to-day meaning of life to this group of individuals there was no way of creating new relevant products and services to keep them in the market. That simple list exposed some profound and useful surprises.

Exercise five

Now create an inquiry for your team. What aspect of your customers' world do you want to step into? Remember that you are in the same world – you are a customer as indeed is every member of your team. Invite everyone to participate as a customer. You will need everyone's professional expertise later in the proceedings, but now we are looking for something new.

What creative techniques will you use?

To assist you in thinking more obliquely here is the Wonder Wheel (Fig. 5.8). In the centre circle you will see that we have written in a STOP Statement. 'Not enough mums want to buy our juice'. This is a simple and non-corporate expression of a simple problem that any producer of a drink might face. Inside the segments created by the spokes of the wheel we have written questions that might lead us into a greater understanding of how mums work in relationship with their lives and their kids' welfare,

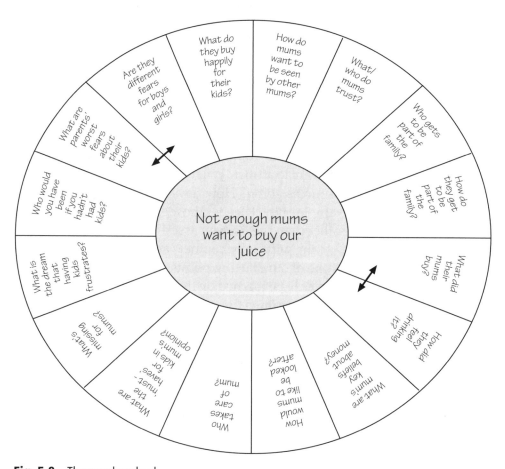

Fig. 5.8   The wonder wheel.

etc. It could be a useful exercise to split your Breakthrough Team into groups and give them an opportunity to wonder together. You could then collate the questions and inquire into the results.

Looking at our example of the Wonder Wheel the question 'Who would you have been if you hadn't had kids?' lends itself to a subject for art-from-within, quite simply set up without a visualization. The question about parents' fears for their kids would also do well in the process, but would need to be entered into sensitively and later in the Breakthrough Zone, when people are feeling familiar and safe with each other. It could be balanced out by broadening the topic to include hope as well as fear, for example, 'My hopes and fears for my children.'

Although focussing on fears might seem an appalling prospect, as parents ourselves we know that (a) we have many fears anyway, and (b) the chance to see that other parents have fears too is a relief not a burden. It might be an option in this instance to link diet with mum's hopes – e.g. 'What are you making possible for your children through their diet?' 'What could a poorly chosen diet do?'

'How would mums like to be looked after' calls for building something and role-playing in it. To charge a group with creating a machine, robot or person dedicated to the care of a mum, and then demonstrating it to the group could be extremely productive, fun and impactful.

'What did their mums buy?' calls for a conversation in small groups, recording of the responses on a flip chart in each group and then building into a short visualization in which they each get to imagine themselves drinking the drink and capturing how the experience feels. There might be a few people moved to tears in such an exercise. Tears are fine as long as you include them (i.e. do not ignore them), praise them for being so open and have it be a normal and acceptable thing. The feelings could then be recorded and fed back to the larger group.

'Who gets to be part of the family?' could be facilitated by the use of magazines and pictures of people. If someone else were to be included as a family member, what qualities would they have to have, how might they look, what would their purpose be? This could be done in groups or as individuals.

The process or technique you employ needs to be led by the topics for inquiry that you choose. Remember that right now we are training the Breakthrough Team, and although when you run your processes you will discover exciting possibilities, it is essential that you note the impact that caused the excitement and move on. The Breakthrough Zone is where we will derive our most seminal insights. This is a practice session only. It will lead to further questions, and will be crucial in helping you to design your inquiry with the customers in the Breakthrough Zone.

Having explored and experimented with some techniques with the group, it is time to collect the recorded data for future reference and move into a session on how each member of the team needs to be at the Breakthrough Zone event with customers.

Stage 5   Unblocking the culture

'The way we do things around here' is quite a useful operational description of culture. There is, however, a key component missing. Culture also includes 'the way we *don't* do things around here.' In other words, what is *not* allowed is as important as what *is* and because you won't see what is not allowed it plays a more secret and invidious role in shaping the company's behaviour. We know of one great organization which has developed a culture of great civility and reasonableness. This is fine and these are great people to be with, decent, intelligent, considerate and thoughtful. Unfortunately, there is an invisible and harmful downside to reasonableness. If you are to maintain cultural norms in this organization you cannot be unreasonable. As we have pointed out, the source of breakthrough is unreasonable requests and so this culture, once known for its innovations, now has to buy rather than develop its own. Every few years it acquires a new 'hot' brand or product and after a few years turns it from an exceptional into a reasonable one.

There are also long-term effects in a culture where you can't be unreasonable. In such a community it is very difficult to say 'no' to anyone, especially if that 'no' follows an earlier 'yes'. So it is very hard to stop projects or initiatives once they are started. There are *hundreds* of extinct projects going on in this culture because no-one can easily stop them.

Exercise six – the T-shirts game

We got this idea from the phrase, 'Been there, got the T-shirt.' It is a piece of vernacular, meaning 'I've done that already. I don't need to do it again.' It occurred to us that T-shirts had all manner of things written on them that revealed (or could reveal) things about the wearer, his or her attitudes, beliefs, orientations, etc. At the time we were looking for a way to play a game demonstrating the blocks inherent in a company's culture. We wanted something that would be fun and informative at the same time. T-shirts provided the ideal vehicle. Here is how it works.

A few weeks before the team training ask yourself, your team and maybe even your client/internal investor about the way things get stopped in their company. Ask them particularly to think of any phrases that are going the rounds in their office, particularly those that can be used as put-downs. Include things like suspect statements of intent. Here are two common examples:

- 'We must do lunch sometime.'
- 'I'm behind you 100% on this.'

When they get stuck, invite them to ask assistants and colleagues until you have six or seven different phrases. Then have these phrases printed onto T-shirts.

At the Breakthrough Training divide your groups up into sixes or sevens. Ask two people to be supporters, two to be neutral and two to wear T-shirts. It doesn't matter if there are one or two more neutrals in the group. Then set the group the task of discussing how the breakthrough project is going and what it will take to move it on.

In this discussion the supporters must promote the project, the neutrals are undecided and the T-shirts must come from the attitude that the T-shirt suggests to them. So, from the two examples above you might develop an attitude of insincerity. The T-shirts don't actually have to use the actual phrase printed on the shirt, although it usually produces a great laugh if they do manage to fit it in!

Here are a couple more examples. These two are things which are commonly said about breakthrough ideas as they come up for discussion:

- 'We tried that before.'
- 'We've never done it that way before.'

While these two appear to be opposites, very often the attitude behind them is exactly the same. Both are past-based comments about something new and untried. Although they may be perfectly accurate observations, this does not make them valid. The attitude behind them is often that of throwing doubt and caution into the mix and can be used to distance the speaker from commitment to the project or to fire an 'I told you so' warning shot. These kind of statements always aim to sap the enthusiasm and energy accompanying the ideas. Often they are motivated by unconscious envy.

Two more examples will serve to complete a set:

- 'My diary is chock-a-block for the next six weeks.'
- 'I'll get back to you with a date for a meeting.'

These two are often used to stop the initiative by employing delaying tactics. They are extremely common in organizations because they have the secondary advantage of proving to the group how busy (and therefore important) the speaker is.

It is very hard to circumvent these 'stoppers' without practice. They have probably become accepted tools in the culture for saying 'no'. But they are indirect and you cannot be sure what they mean. They may also be used together in groups or aggregations of resistance. To work through or around them takes practice because it is counter-cultural.

No self-respecting actor would ever do a great play without rehearsals. This is when they practise different tones, interpretations and nuances through the lines they have been given by the writer. We in business tend to hope that we can respond differently without any rehearsal whatsoever. This requires a level of interpersonal flexibility that many people will never develop without some chance to experiment.

Responding differently to cultural resistance requires rehearsal, and for this the T-shirt game is extremely valuable. Confronted by the phrases and statements that are commonly used to resist change in your organization, your team can practise different gambits and conversational strategies.

Some of these strategies are as follows:

- To *include* the resistance (i.e. incorporate it – rather like using the cynicism of employees to predict the kind of problems that past attempts at change have thrown up and thus be able to avoid or eliminate them in future). 'I think you have a great point here. Thank goodness you threw that one up. Bearing that in mind, what would you do to ensure that it does not happen again?'

- To *defeat* the resistance (i.e. develop a rational argument that exposes the flaws in the current point of view being used to resist – very difficult and rarely successful). 'You see, your point of view does not hold water, although I can see how it could appear to be valid at first sight.'

- To *enrol* in it and champion it to such a degree that the original perpetrator begins to sell your benefits back to you! 'Oh my God, you're so right. In fact I hadn't seen it that way at all until now, and we should pull the whole thing and go back to the way we've been doing it all along. My God, I can't believe I did not see this. What would you do in my place? Cancel the whole thing? My God you could be absolutely spot on here!' This is a pretty manipulative method and can backfire if you are not good at it.

- To *ignore* the resistance – a hazardous strategy unless you are absolutely certain that their resistance is thin and uncommitted. Some people just need to test the certainty of the leader by throwing some 'cardboard spanners' into the spokes to see whether or not the bicycle has enough momentum to keep moving regardless.

- To *confront* it, i.e. to state categorically that it is clearly a spoiling point of view being represented and that the motive is to stay inside the cultural comfort zone. This too can become positional and lead to polarized views.

- To *empathize* with the anxiety that has led to the adoption of a resistant strategy, and thus short circuit its power over the perpetrator. 'I think it's absolutely right to be cautious about this, in fact I feel much the same way. Tell me more about how you feel as I think we have got a lot in common in that respect.'

- To *satisfy* it. 'What would you need to have in place for you to be happy about this?' To fully satisfy resistant strategies you need to be able to uncover the personal agenda that is hidden behind the resistance. See Chapter 8, 'Dealing with Cultural Resistance' to understand this better. Selling ideas relies on them being accepted into a culture that is based on another set of ideas. This is by far the most reliable strategy for successfully subverting cultural resistance.

Running the game as a role-play, you can ask the people developing the counter-strategies to develop and demonstrate their favourites after the game has been played. The neutrals can provide invaluable commentary by speaking about how their allegiance or disaffection with the project was affected by the 'meeting'. The T-shirts can have the most impact of all if they are willing to expose the real feelings driving their remarks.

Stage 6 The role of the team in the Breakthrough Zone

The next time that you meet as a group will be on the morning of day one of the Breakthrough Zone event. Before you leave, it is important to let people know who and how to be during the process. Here are some guidelines.

1   Each one of you, including the facilitator, is to be *in* the inquiry. In other words, everyone needs to be in the experiment as a customer. Nobody knows the answers or outcomes at this point, and unnerving as this might seem to some, this is exactly the right way to be.

2   Having experienced the kind of creative process that will be included in the Breakthrough Zone, people on the team will be well placed to encourage and guide their customer team-mates on the day. They are co-facilitators in the respect that they will be the role models for your customer guests through their level of participation.

3   Having experienced creating personal and trusting relationships with each other, as soon as they arrive at the venue on the day it is essential that they do not clump together into a company group and exclude the customer guests. You want everyone to feel included from the very beginning to the very end. How they are welcomed is important.

4   The insights of the Breakthrough Team in their role as customers are just as valid as those from the actual customer community.

5   Let the team know that if they are stuck or in doubt at any time throughout the session they can ask for help, either from colleagues, customers or facilitators. No one knows the answers but the facilitators will have experience in working through some of the recurring types of problems (inability to reach agreement, avoiding the topic, being overly cautious, deferential and polite, struggles for ascendancy in the group).

6   No one on the team is there to justify the business in any way. The first hour of the Breakthrough Zone event can be very difficult if there are a lot of unrealistic observations and 'unreasonable' complaints about your organization. This will pass. While it happens it is important to keep listening.

Now they are ready for the Breakthrough Zone.

6 | The Breakthrough Zone

Arrival and the first morning

Sooner than you expect, the dates for the Breakthrough Zone event will arrive. In this section we will take you through a set of ideas about what to do, and when and how to do it. The suggestions here are based upon a wealth of experience with large groups working on commercial problems. It would be exciting for us were you to use these as a springboard for developing your own approach and let us know how you get on!

Some exercises will resemble those of the Breakthrough Training but be subtly different in emphasis and purpose. We will describe in full anything that we haven't covered before and refer you back to an earlier description if appropriate. Given the strength of corporate cultures and their resistance to change, it is no bad thing that the team will work through some things more than once. It helps to provide confirmation and confidence in their discoveries. We always say if something happens once it is an occurrence, if it happens twice it could be a coincidence. If it happens three times it is time to take notice!

Another characteristic of experiential work is that it is different every time you do it. It is affected by context, community dynamics, process and purpose. This is the true nature of 'real time' data. Every time you ask you get a slightly different answer. Which is the truth? All the answers are true at the experiential level: what happened did happen. The best way to test the validity of your answers is to ask the important questions several times and from different perspectives in different settings. If the data is robust the same central theme in the responses will recur, although the way it is expressed will vary. If you have a problem which has impact on the world rather than just a local stage, how many times and in how many locations should you repeat the investigation? Our answer is probably three times at most. We have just completed an inquiry on three continents. By the time we reached the third we were dealing mostly with variations in shade rather than fundamental differences. This style of work illuminates needs that are common across cultures and which are deeper than those satisfied by impulsive or casual choices.

We usually run the days in the Breakthrough Zone between 09.30 and 17.30. Outside the main room have a registration desk. On the desk should be laid out all of the name-lists for the attendees, together with their nametags. Ask all participants to wear their nametag in a place where it can be seen. This desk should be staffed by two people including your programme manager, the person with overall responsibility for logistics in the Zone.

Involve your whole Breakthrough Team in accompanying participants to their seats when you ask them to take their places. Your team should already be briefed to spread themselves among the participants from the customer community. You will almost certainly find that the chairs fill up at the back of the room first. It is not uncommon, if there are a number of latecomers, for the front rows to be nearly empty. Do not worry about this at this point. Let them just sit wherever they feel comfortable.

At last you are standing in front of the room ready to go. It will probably look a bit like Fig. 6.1.

The details of this set-up are explained in the resource section.

We usually start the proceedings with one facilitator at the front of the room. If you are he or she, you will probably be feeling pretty nervous right now.

We suggest you say, 'Hello everyone and welcome to our session. It's really good to see you here and I'd like to thank you for giving up your time to spend it with us. We know how important your time is and we promise not to waste it.'

Then you can select or construct your own version from all or any of the things below that we might say in an opening. We are aiming to create safety and structure so that people feel secure, to demonstrate that it is safe to speak to the group and that whatever anyone says will be respected and not used as ammunition by the facilitators or the group, nor as fodder for jokes.

When you begin to speak, remember that informality is the order of the day. Just as you all spoke to each other personally in the Breakthrough Training,

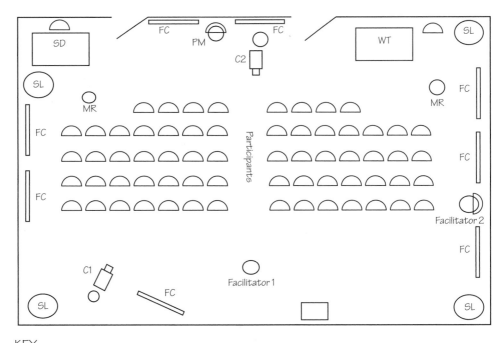

KEY
SD   Sound desk
SL   Spot light
FC   Flip chart
MR   Mike runner
PM   Programme manager
C1   Camera one
C2   Camera two
WT   Water table

Fig. 6.1   Recommended room layout for Breakthrough Zone opening.

be personal now. Look at people as you speak; actively watch them listening to you.

Be honest about how nervous you feel. Then introduce yourself in the following stages.

Introduce yourself

'My name is _____ and over the next few minutes it's my job to outline our purpose for being here and some of the ground rules and guidelines that will help you make the most of your time with us. As you know we are here as a community to discuss _____(topic) and we'll get to that in a moment. But first, a little bit about us and the nature of this event so that you have some ideas about how it's going to work.'

Introduce the style of working

'During the next two days we will work in a whole variety of ways. We'll be creative, play games, analyse what we notice and have feedback sessions. We will work as a large group like this, as individuals, in pairs and in small groups. You can be sure we'll have fun.'

Introduce the people from the company

'There are a few people for you to meet from the company. Here they are. Would you stand up please? There are quite a few aren't there? They are from different parts of the company and they're here to participate too. We need help to find some new ideas, so nobody is an expert.'

Introduce the facilitation team and the logistics

'The facilitation and support team is made up of myself and (co-facilitators), the programme manager who will handle logistics and things like breaks and refreshments. You may also have noticed the cameramen and the sound desk. These are so that we can create a record of this event, which can be edited and shown to other members of the company so that they can experience this too.

'On cameras are _____ and _____. On sound is _____. Very occasionally we may ask you to repeat something if the cameras missed it while changing tape or location.

'We will work from 09.30 to 17.30 each day with normal breaks in the morning and afternoon and a lunch break of an hour. There'll be food and refreshments available during the breaks.'

Take people through the fire drill and point out the exits. Let them know where the loos are and be honest with them about the security of their valuables.

Create safety

'You don't have to know anything to do this workshop. You've been invited because you're exactly the people we want to conduct this inquiry. Let's get started with a bit of practice at speaking in the large group. I'm going to ask a question and if you want to say something then just raise your hand. Let's have a practice run. Raise your hand if you're nervous about talking in front of this group.'

Encourage someone with raised hand to stand and speak. Show them how to hold the microphone so that their voice can be heard around the room.

In this opening session it is tempting to have the cameras pointed at the facilitator. It is much better to have them pointed at the audience where they may start to pick up movement, posture and expressions in the room. We hardly ever use any footage of facilitators in the finished film and we are always short of good shots of people listening and reacting to illustrate the atmosphere in the room.

Now for the first key moment in the Breakthrough Zone the time has come for the participants to start speaking rather than the facilitator. Usually we say something like this:

> 'Now it's time for us to start hearing your views and ideas. Has anyone got any questions or concerns about the set-up or the venue?'

If there is anything, ask the person to stand and speak using the microphone. Always follow the discipline of this procedure. People will soon learn that only this process for speaking will be closely attended to in the large group sessions. There may be one or two questions about things like parking or lunch. This is a good time to ask people to turn off their mobile phones.

When the group is ready ask 'What's on your mind about ...?' In the gap insert the product or service that your inquiry is about.

The facilitator's next job is to wait. Sometimes someone will respond immediately, on other occasions it can take what seems like an eternity before a half-hearted hand is raised somewhere. But it will happen. These people have come here to make themselves and their ideas known. It is important not to force them at this point. Show that your invitations are meant seriously and that you are willing to wait.

When someone volunteers, they may try to speak from their seat without standing or waiting for the hand-held microphone. Be patient and ask them to stand and wait for a second while the mike arrives. Listen and do not interrupt, even if they ask a question – let them get to the end before you reply. The whole room will be watching how you handle this first interaction – whether you are a safe pair of hands around nervous people and whether you listen or interrupt. Most people are used to being interrupted at all times, by colleagues, bosses, family or friends and it will seem a little unfamiliar to speak into such a large 'listening'. This is, of course, one of the special attractions of the Zone that will soon begin to work its magic of encouraging people to come forward and make themselves known. Usually this first contribution will be short and before you know it the speaker will have sat down again!

Now comes an important bit – however short, whatever was said, it is time to practise acknowledging people for their contribution. We usually say something like:

> 'Thank you. You are really brave; it takes real guts to go first. We have a custom in the Breakthrough Zone of applauding people's contribution, just because we all know how much it takes to be willing to speak out in front of a large group like this. So we'd like to give you a hand.' (Lead clapping.)

Although it may sound a bit contrived, this acknowledgement is an absolutely vital ingredient of the Breakthrough Zone. Remember in the Breakthrough Training that we featured acknowledgement. This is where it starts in the Breakthrough Zone. When they meet an environment where praise rather than blame is the norm, people are surprised and a little embarrassed at first. They rapidly come to enjoy it and you will hear spontaneous applause and verbal acknowledgement breaking out in the various work-groups as the event progresses.

When they meet an environment where praise rather than blame is the norm, people are surprised and a little embarrassed at first.

As a facilitator you must take responsibility for maintaining the culture of acknowledgement. Do not allow it to be put aside, for although they may not say anything, everyone will notice. It will prove to be one of the greatest assets in the Breakthrough Zone.

After this sharing from the first speaker invite contributions from others. There will usually be a flow of five or six people waiting to speak in this opening session. After this initial burst things may appear to dry up for a while. Nowadays we offer a second topic in this opening session because our analyst/report writer has told us that she finds these opening remarks very helpful in forming an early appreciation of the kinds of things that are top-of-mind for customers. These comments are as likely to be complementary as critical. So, after the initial five or six we might say:

'What sticks in your mind from a recent experience of _____?' (the relevant product or service). Once again be ready to wait, relatively still and silent at the front of the room. Some of our best openings have been an hour or so in duration, but there may not be that much material readily available in the room. There are some important considerations for the facilitator in this session:

1   Resist the temptation to comment on, cap, or otherwise complete people's contribution. You are not required to do anything with what they say. Allow it to be sufficient on its own. Just say 'thank you'.

2   Notice if your attention is repeatedly drawn to anyone, either in the form of positive or negative regard. If there are such impulses

and they are strong, tell your co-facilitator about it at the first opportunity and ask him to keep an eye on your interactions with these individuals.

3   It is quite normal for some people to try to speak several times during an opening session, almost as if they are hungry for attention. As a rule of thumb do not ask the same speaker to speak more than twice unless there is absolutely no-one else coming forward.

4   Resist the desire to correct or provide extra information on top of what people say, even if you know it would be helpful or appreciated. We are building people's sense of the value of their own speaking; it needs to be done a step at a time. Do not get drawn into refereeing a dispute. Allow opposing views to co-exist in the room. If a conflict persists simply say something like: 'I've noticed that there are various shades of opinions here. We'll have plenty of time to work through these over the course of our time together. Perhaps we could hear from someone else now.'

5   If someone gives critical personal feedback to someone else, commenting critically on either the content or manner of their contribution, ask them to wait a moment and firmly and gently explain that we will not get far if we cut each other down. Reassure the critic that we will welcome his or her contribution, provided it is not directed at correcting others. Everyone's experiences and points of view will vary to one degree or another and they are all equally valuable to us.

6   You will have dealt with the contribution from the client team in your preparation session but if you suddenly get a stream of clients wishing to speak, take one or two and then re-invite participation from the non-clients.

You will reach a point when you will know the opening session is done and it is time to move on.

Getting to know you

At the start of this session the facilitator makes something personal of himself available to the room, which may not have been called for in the first session. The reason for this is that we are about to ask people to make themselves more personally available and we never ask our participants to do things that we are not willing to do or able to demonstrate ourselves. It is important though not to use these first personal revelations to 'rock the room' as in, for example, 'I spent the last five years in prison and have just got out on parole', or, 'My mother died yesterday and I didn't know whether to come today or not'. Keep it within the bounds of acceptability, sharing feelings about pastimes, friends or family. But it is important to move the tone towards what we call, 'speaking from I'.

Next it is important to acknowledge that we are about to do something different and to get permission from the room to change tack and activity. At this point, our facilitator usually says something along the lines of: 'I'd like us to play a few games just to get the energy moving in the room. They are pretty meaningless games, just a bit of fun. Will you play with me?' We have never had a group refuse to play in 12 years of running these sessions. However, there are one or two important tips about this change in activity. Make the session sound really easy and inviting, and raise your energy a bit higher than that already in the group. So, in effect, the invitation rings out around the room as a call to come and have fun.

Second, make the invitation quickly and as soon as you have finished speaking say, 'Now, let's get out of our chairs and move them back to give us some space.' In other words the group are doing the session before there is much chance for debate. It is once they are up and moving about that you can give them further information about taking care of themselves physically as they move around. Often we can feel a sluggishness in the room for the first few seconds as people are getting up, but then once the chairs are gone the atmosphere is different. People start to notice each other, approach each other, form pairs and trios and the energy begins to rise.

As in the last chapter, we play some simple warm-up games. They need to be quick, simple and easy to execute.

There are a few extra guidelines:

1   These are warm-ups, don't make them too long. Our opening game sessions usually last no more than ten minutes.

2   Use this session to leave people in appropriate groupings or numbers to start whatever it is you want to do next. This saves time and reassures people about the continuity and logic of the process.

3   It is often a good idea to let participants get a look at each other arranged by height, birthday month, or colour of eyes. This fosters the sense of variety in the community and allows for different styles and types of groupings to occur.

4   Keep your energy as a facilitator just that bit higher than the groups. At this early stage it is important to make the games easy and doable by everyone. Don't set 'tests' that only a few can pass.

Clearing the past

'Clearing the past' is an unusual phrase. We use it to describe a process that allows all of the participants to get as 'up-to-date' in their experiences, preferences and opinions based on the topic, product or brand as they are willing to do. In this session we ask *the client Breakthrough Team to act as customers* and describe their customer experiences with the company or brand. If you recall, back in the Breakthrough Training, they have already cleared the past with respect to their working experiences in the company. Mostly we will run this session fairly early in the first day. There are a number of reasons why this is a good idea.

1   It is something everyone can do. Since it relies upon past experience, everyone in the room is qualified in some respect and can make a contribution. It is a very good exercise for developing the sense that everyone has something to say which is of value and that there is time and space enough to allow this to happen.

2   We know, too, that group dynamics and the lack of familiarity between group members will influence much of what is said in these early encounters. Nonetheless, the effect of working independently in small groups and then summarizing and comparing results across groups provides a natural way of letting the factors that are of most importance come to the surface. An additional benefit here is that the groups gain experience in working through different, even contradictory stories without one invalidating another.

3   Because it is set up using a structure that gives an equal amount of time for every person, it helps to iron out the unevenness in participants' experience of the topic. It helps especially to allow the client group to contribute from their more extensive relationship with the subject, but does not give them any more time than anyone else. It has a remarkable effect in demonstrating the validity of everyone's contribution and the fact that knowing a lot about something can be a disadvantage as well as an advantage.

4   It is essential preparation for starting to notice what we have already described as the 'drift', or otherwise the 'future created by the past'. This time it is focused on the brand or product but it is amazing how often the company and brand drifts are identical. It is vital that people have some sense of what will happen if this group do nothing, that there is a future already waiting to happen, so to speak.

5   It is also essential preparation for the innovation, brainstorming or ideas sessions. It is very difficult for people to build a new future on top of feelings about the past. In our experience things which have left residual unexpressed feelings keep re-emerging in the form of complaints or recommendations throughout the programme. This is OK in one sense, but there is very little freedom for invention when this old baggage keeps appearing in the room. Better to get these things out into the open first and give the room space to make choices about whether to include them, resolve them or let them go.

Before starting the process, the facilitator must have counted the total number of participants and have worked out the arithmetic for groupings. People need to start the exercise in pairs or threes and build up the size by taking their first partners to meet other partners. Try to make sure that the final groups at step three are no bigger than 12 people at most.

Here are three examples:

Total number of participants	Step one	Step two	Step three
21	9 × 2 1 × 3	4 × 4 1 × 5	1 × 10 1 × 11
33	15 × 2 1 × 3	7 × 4 1 × 5	3 × 8 1 × 9
46	23 × 2	7 × 4 3 × 6	3 × 8 1 × 10 1 × 12

This is how we set it up:

'We're now going to build the information that we have at our disposal about the subject or our meeting. To do that we'd like you to get into pairs (or pairs and trios – see chart). Work with someone you don't know in this exercise. When you've found a partner find yourselves a space and sit down facing each other.

'Choose someone to be A, the other to be B. Each of you will now take five minutes to talk about your experience of brand or product X (the topic) bringing anything you like to that conversation. It is important that you include feelings as well as facts. How do you feel when you buy or use X? Notice that five minutes is quite a long time and you will probably get to the end of your first burst of speaking fairly quickly. Be patient and something else will come up, be willing to follow your train of thoughts and share some of them.

'While one of you is speaking, the job of the other is to listen. Try to keep your part of the exchange to a minimum. In fact, notice you want to speak and don't. Just listen.

'We will call out when the first five minutes is done and it is time to change. The speaker will become the listener and vice versa. It doesn't matter if you repeat what the other person said in part if it is true for you. Just say whatever it is that you have to say.

'Please don't take any notes during this ten minutes, we will tell you the next stage of the exercise when you are done.'

The facilitator must time this. We usually let the group know when they have one minute left. Trios will get just over three minutes each, rather than five.

'The next step is to join up with another pair or group (see chart). You will now find yourself in a foursome. The job now is for each one of you to take two minutes to share *your partner's* story with your new group. The time starts now and it will take eight minutes to complete this.

'If you are uncertain about an important detail, tell it as you recall it and your partner can correct any errors when you have finished, but not before! Don't forget to include feelings as well as facts.

The facilitators support these new groupings and encourage the participants. When it is complete we say:

'The third step is to find another foursome and make a group of eight (there may be some slightly larger or smaller groups – see chart). In this group we have a slightly different job; it is to start to distil the themes from our personal stories into a group record. Do not be afraid to include different, even contradictory elements. We would not expect everyone to feel or think the same about anything. Try to notice the top seven to ten things that came up and again, don't forget the emotions and climate of your experiences as well as the facts. Record them on a flip chart.

'We'll take 20 minutes to do this.'

The final step is for each of the groups to feedback to the large group on their experiences in this process and the themes they have come up with. In most sessions we find a degree of repetition in these themes and they provide a useful set of data about the way in which the brand, product or service is performing. They are particularly helpful in uncovering:

1   What the company does well from the customer's perspective (which is frequently not the same as the thing that the company prides itself on).
2   The context of the product in people's lives, what and how much they have to say about it from their own experience
3   The effect, or lack of effect, of new advertising, positioning, product variants, launches and re-launches. The company's awareness of the details of the product's history is usually much greater than the customers. But the customer's history of *using* the product demonstrates a much more intimate relationship with the thing itself than the company's.
4   Patterns of problems or recurring issues.
5   Issues of morale or motivation in service brands.
6   Sudden changes in strategy, direction or policy and their effects.
7   Moments of triumph or great breakthroughs.
8   The background conversation, climate or atmosphere that pervades attitudes to the brand from both the points of view of customers and staff.
9   What is stuck or missing in the brand, product or service.

It is important during this session to encourage customers rather than staff to present the feedback. Sometimes, if customers are particularly nervous they do it in a pair with a staff member for support.

Usually this whole process takes around an hour and it is not unusual for the group to experience a well-deserved sense of satisfaction as it views what it has managed to accomplish in this relatively short time, considering that it started out as a group of strangers. What is especially surprising to us as facilitators is how quickly the boundary between staff and customers starts to dissolve, and we find ourselves among groups of people developing shared perspectives with room for everyone's input.

The future created by the past

This is often the 'crunch' or 'killer' exercise in the first session. The process reveals something that is very likely to happen in the future in a very powerful way. For the company staff, it is only the second time they have seen this revealed in a logical and practical way. Almost invariably this past-based future will confirm both the nature and extent of the issues that generated the inquiry in the first place. It will almost certainly match the predicted future created by the staff team in the breakthrough session and will provide confirmation of their own discoveries. In process terms it serves to move the group from a mode of operation which is descriptive/factual to a realization that there is something at stake for everyone in the room. If we don't do something, there is a future waiting to happen based on events that are already underway.

This is how the process goes. We have just finished clearing the past and it may be time for a break. If so, take one, if not press on – either way stay in the same groups. Here is a typical set-up for this exercise:

> 'We'd like now to explore something new with you. Think for a moment about what you're going to do about your fitness. If it isn't fitness for you, think of something else where you keep making promises you don't keep and talk about that instead. Take a moment with a neighbour to assess honestly what is going to happen. How many of you are going to end up doing pretty much what you always do? How many times have you made a resolution to do something about it and if you did, how long did you keep it up for? Gyms know that they will get a lot of new members just after the New Year (resolution time) and that after a month or two they'll never see them again.'
>
> (Pause to allow neighbour conversations for several minutes.)
>
> 'You can begin to get a sense of how strong the grip of the past in the form of habits is. We may justify or rationalize it by saying "that's just me", but we tend to let habits run the show. Try discussing doing something different at home and see what happens. If it's not a standard conversation in your household people will wonder what you're up to. They may even ask you if there's something the matter.
>
> 'There is, we say, a *drift* in human events which is powerful and invisible, like a tide in the river or sea. Things are already going a certain way. Just imagine how powerful such a drift can be at the community level where many thousands of customers and companies are involved. We'd like to explore the drift for this company, created by this past that we've all participated in describing. Here's what we'd like you to do.
>
> 'Look at the themes and patterns you've observed. Imagine, if we do nothing, if we just allow things to continue on their present path, what will have happened five years from now? What is the future that is already happening to us? Let's take 15 minutes to develop our ideas about that in our groups.'

Follow a similar process of allowing the groups to develop their ideas and then feedback to the large group. Use a different order for the feedback this time and ask different people to present wherever possible. Maintain your enthusiasm as facilitator for everyone to have a go and speak to the whole group.

The main effect of this process is to start the shift from the kind of 'involved observer' stance that may be used to clear the past towards the acceptance of responsibility that is required to develop and implement the innovations which will create a new future. We might say something like:

> 'Now we've had a look at the future that's waiting to happen, is that what we want?'

Usually there is a substantial amount of head shaking or avoidance of one type or another going on in the room. If the avoidance and discomfort is the predominant sentience, we might say:

> 'How many other groups of people of this size and depth of experience do you imagine there are working on this problem right now? The fact of the matter is there is only us: we are it. We are the people in the driving seat. We are the people who can make a difference to this pattern of events. Are you willing to do that? Please will you help us develop a future that you choose rather than this one that's waiting in the wings?'

A genuine request for help is rarely ignored. At this point you will have a willing group of customers who will have been given ownership of the future for a company. When else will they have been entrusted with such a project? Reassure them that they will have all the help and resource that they need to get this done. Let them know that the results will not necessarily be the actual items they invent, but the learning that we do together which will form the basis of the future. You can guarantee that they will surprise themselves; they always do!

Standing in a clearing

Having cleared the past and put away the baggage – at least for a while – the group will now be left with a 'clearing'. People will look around, fairly pleased with what they've accomplished as if to say, 'OK, that was easy – what's next?' It is tempting to get straight into fixing the problems but in our experience that usually produces some fairly narrow solutions which have the disadvantage of being reactive, or born out of issues that are already imperfections in the company's greater aims or purpose. We need to get in touch with something deeper and more enduring if we are to create breakthrough solutions.

Think about where we are for a moment. We have now a group who have met in a couple of different ways – as a large group and as smaller task-oriented groups – and which has accomplished a great many things for a group of strangers within a couple of hours. Confidence will be fairly high and people will be ready to move to another level of inquiry or exploration. The question we really want to ask the room is: 'what is the deepest and most enduring customer need that could be fulfilled by this brand or organization?' But most times people are out of touch with their need states, at least to some degree and we must find creative ways of letting the group reach its deeper needs and desires.

Here are a few examples of the kind of thing we might be trying to reach for:

> 'What needs could air travel in the 21st century really satisfy? What needs do we perhaps have when we travel today, yet have put away because we fear they could never get met?'
>
> 'What needs is a mother trying to satisfy when she chooses a soft drink for her child?'
>
> 'If you look a bit more deeply into the reasons why you shampoo your hair, what do you find?'
>
> 'What needs do we have for healthcare? What would the relationship with a perfect healthcare provider be like?'
>
> 'What needs are unfulfilled in the domain of domestic chores? What is it that we long for that is inhibited by current domestic routines/ products?'
>
> 'When we travel, do we need to be held or supported in some way? What could the brands or reputations of destinations, travel companies, hotels or resorts provide us in this respect?'
>
> 'What desires do we have for diversion, fulfilment, satisfaction that we haven't found an experience or product or service to meet?'
>
> 'When we do one of many small daily acts, like buy a newspaper, drink a coffee, eat a biscuit, is there any deeper, more enduring need that we are touching with this small act? If there is, how may we contact that to deliver better satisfaction without feeling inappropriate or ridiculous?'

As you can feel from asking these questions of yourself, each one can quickly take you off into a place where not only do you not really know the answer, you may not know if there is an answer. It is easy to get quickly into ridicule once we find ourselves in a place where we don't know the answer – especially if we are in a public forum. 'What on earth are they talking about – the satisfaction of small things – I never heard of anything so ridiculous. I drink coffee because I'm thirsty!' From a process point of view it is our job to provide a setting and some stepping stones that allow people to stay in an inquiry in which they may not know what to do or what questions to ask.

There are a whole number of tactics and processes which we might do to facilitate this.

1   Give people an exercise that requires a non-verbal output. *Examples*: construction exercises – art-from-within, role-play, sculpting, building an environment. It is somehow much easier to create an output when released from the conventions of sensible, rational speaking.

2   Give people an exercise which allows them to explore the associations or imagery of the field of inquiry without judgement or assessment. *Examples*: visualization, spontaneous writing, a fairy story, Brand on the Couch.

3   Give people an experience which unleashes emotions and then direct them to explore the topic inside of a feeling or emotional experience. *Examples*: tantrum, the Brand Gang, a Brand World.

4   Create an exercise that forces people to reflect on something in an unusual manner. *Examples*: Spirit Walk, a non-smoking planet, life without aeroplanes, life without cars.

Each of these techniques serves the purpose of giving permission to the group in the Breakthrough Zone to bring resources and activities that they have never used before to focus on a brand, product or service. What does a Nescafé song sound like? What does a Ribena machine look like? What would happen in a role-play of a perfect visit to the bank? We have already given descriptions of Tantrum and visualization, and will cover art-from-within later in this chapter. Another interesting game is Brand on the Couch or Brand Therapy. Here is how it is played:

Set up either twos or threes. If you use twos, one is the brand the other is the therapist. If you prefer threes, one is brand, one therapist and the other is an observer. Here are the instructions:

'I'm talking now to the brands among you. You know you have problems. You know you have a past. You know what you want for the future. Perhaps you're optimistic, perhaps not. Anyway, its time for your weekly visit to your therapist. Go and lie or sit in front of him and just talk. Try to say whatever comes into your mind and take ten minutes to just talk about yourself (as the brand) to him.

'Now for the therapists, your job is to listen. Keep questions to a minimum but don't ignore requests for help or information. As you listen pay attention to the themes, links and chains of thought set off inside you. Also pay attention to the brand's and your own emotions throughout the period.

'At the end we will add an extra two minutes for you to give the brand your interpretation and counsel.

'If you are an observer, here's what you do. You observe. You observe them and you observe you. What are your feelings as the session progresses? You will have a couple of minutes to give your input at the very end.'

Expect some hilarity. That is good as when we play we are spontaneous. Taking things too seriously can be evidence of anxiety. This is a game and the results will be enhanced if people are having fun. Moments of serious realization will stand out all the more prominently.

You can then build these outputs in groups as a kind of group therapy session and feed them back to the large group.

In essence what we are encouraging here is a form of *freethinking* that captures chains of associations and connections that would otherwise be invisible. We believe this to be an invaluable route to insights or breakthrough thinking. What we are trying to do is to bring elements of the inner monologue of normal everyday thinking out into the open where it can be shared as a dialogue between a group of people working to express an experience or solve a problem. This is very similar to psychotherapy where a client might be free-associating in front of the therapist without knowing at the time the meaning or value of their words. Because of the open nature of the dialogue new insights and directions become available or trigger off other memories or responses in the group. When the group is asked to comment on or review these experiences very often new learning becomes available.

'Standing in a clearing' is usually done in pairs or small groups. Since it is often the first example of a creative exercise for the whole group it is important to take time over it and ensure that everyone has enough resources and permission to have a go. Sometimes we will demonstrate it ourselves in front of the room. We might demonstrate a tantrum we had during a traffic hold-up – something that is very familiar to most people. Or we might prepare an example of art-from-within to share with the group. In another set-up one facilitator might ask the other to adopt the posture he or she 'felt' when it was his turn to come to the front of the room. Or to strike the pose that illustrated their feeling when someone said something that they missed or that was difficult to understand. This is what we call a 'sculpt'.

Here is an example of a set-up for a sculpt related to the activity of doing the washing or laundry at home. People are divided up into groups of eight or so:

'We would like to understand the dynamics that operate in your household around the activity of doing the washing or laundry. Choose someone in your group to be the one whose family will be represented and then ask her to think about who the key characters in her family are.

These key characters are family members that influence the washing process in some way. She may decide to involve all of the family members, or just some of them. Next ask her to pick other group members to represent her family members.

'When she picks her characters to role-play family members, she should pick them from among you. Then she must give each one a short brief about that member's attitude to the washing. Are they helpful or unhelpful? Demanding or indifferent? Involved or uninvolved? If she is able she might also give each one a typical comment that the family member would say or think about the washing.'

Then when the characters are selected, for each character ask:

'While the washing is happening, where are you and what is your orientation in a physical sense? For example if, like a small child, you were trying to help but getting under your mum's feet, you might lie down and grip one of her legs as if holding her back. If you were off at work and thinking that what you are doing is much more important than doing the washing, you might put yourself a long way off and stand with your back turned to the activity at home, while talking about a "very important meeting". Ask your protagonist to arrange each role player so that they adopt an appropriate distance and attitude. You may have had a grandmother who always fussed about cleanliness; what did she typically say? What does her voice in your head sound like? Have someone play that voice and repeat her words in the appropriate tone of voice. To indicate the fact that they were an inner voice they might stand close behind you, or would they be in front of you, encouraging, challenging or admonishing?'

As facilitator, patiently encourage the protagonist to brief each participant on location, attitude, posture, and dialogue (if any) and tone of voice. Then help the protagonist move around placing each of the participants in their relevant place and pose. They do not have to stand holding their postures until the facilitator calls out 'adopt the posture' when everyone is in place. As a general rule keep dialogue to minimum, just potent words or phrases will do. Take your time to build the tableaux, character by character. Allow each one to relax once they have perfected their performance. What we are building here is a psychodynamic representation of the group influences affecting a person who is engaged in doing the washing. This is the real life dynamic that drives attitudes to detergents, washing machines, ironing and relationships with other family members. This is the vital stuff. Once we have built it, we ask everyone involved to give feedback to the group on their experience. This technique is based upon work done in a field called psychodrama and we are grateful for the instructors at Spectrum in London for teaching it to us.

When everyone is ready, ask the protagonist to locate herself within the group and to strike a particular posture that seems commonplace when doing the washing for her. Then, when everyone is in place call out 'adopt the posture' and the group all adopt their characteristic posture and location. Then ask the group to hold it there for a few seconds and pull the protagonist out of her posture and invite her to look at her 'picture'. What feelings does she have? What does she notice?

Next, ask everyone to relax and then go round one at a time and ask each participant to momentarily recreate their posture and as they do so to describe their thoughts and feelings.

All manner of insights can arise from such an exercise. Here are a few examples.

1   In a sculpt about doing the washing a protagonist noticed that while she was holding other family members in mind as she sorted clothes, no-one was holding her in mind. They were all going about their day without a thought for her. Consequently she started to feel resentful and unnoticed by her family as she went about her domestic routine. Her fantasies turned both to escape and criticism of her family as she did the washing. Eventually her mind became so angry that she projected onto the clothes as 'representatives' of her ungrateful family. She found herself handling the clothes and the machine quite violently.

2   In another washing sculpt a man doing the washing noticed that he had to pretend to be uninvolved in this task as he had doubts about the 'manliness' of it. This had the consequence of increasing quite dramatically the number of errors that he made and led to inefficiency, the task taking up more time than it really needed to. This in turn led him to dissociate from the activity and do it absent-mindedly. He often made mistakes and had to do it again. Have you ever wondered where all of those socks went?

3   In a sculpt about drinking coffee at home a protagonist noticed that she always hid the jar of instant coffee because she felt ashamed of it. She wanted a form of packaging that was more fun and expressive of coffee values – but not one that simply pretended to be real coffee – she wanted something attractive in its own right.

4   In a sculpt about being a passenger onboard an aircraft, a passenger noticed how frustrated and angry she felt as she listened to cabin crew chatting behind a curtain. When she dug down for

a reason for her anger she noticed that she was feeling scared and alone on her journey and wanted a reassuring presence nearby who was interested in her.

Analysis of any one of these can be used to generate insights about some of the hidden aspects of people's experience that could make a difference to a manufacturer or service provider. It was just such a role-play that planted the seed of the idea of 'Taking Care of the Lives in Our Hands' for a healthcare company. It was from another such role-play that a passenger noticed how he felt when dumped in airport 'Arrivals' at 5.30 am on a cold English morning. From that insight the arrivals lounge at Heathrow was born.

There are some other things to bear in mind too.

1   It may be necessary to demonstrate a whole sculpt from beginning to end with a few people and then release the room to have a go themselves.

2   If your creative exercise involves an individual journey like a visualization it makes sense to get people to build their personal stories into a group experience before reporting it back. This keeps the feedback to a manageable size. It also encourages people to build the meanings of their experiences in a visualization when they have to explain them in a group.

3   Do not worry if you hear things you have discovered in research before. You will have to trawl through a lot of familiar territory in order to get somewhere new. Treat this as reassuring confirmation.

4   Make sure the film crew capture the feedback sessions – oh, and continue to get the customers to present; they will get a sense of accomplishment from it and you will get useful footage for your video.

The lunch break

If you are going to provide hot food – and we always do – you will need to co-ordinate the timing of the break with the readiness of the food. We have found that we get a lot of complaints if we only provide snack-type food. This kind of work uses up a lot of energy. Remember an army marches on its stomach.

With the best planning in the world somebody's dietary needs will have escaped notice. There are often more vegetarians than expected, someone who must have gluten- or wheat-free food, someone who cannot eat dairy products. Handle such 'emergencies' with grace and good humour. Don't reprimand people; minor food crises often show up in a large group and everyone will notice how they are handled. Most hotels and conference centres will be accommodating.

Insist that your Breakthrough Team and your facilitation team eat with the main group. Even if the facilitators and team have things to discuss, ask them to reserve that discussion for a short section of the lunch break so that you can spend time with participants. It does not help to get into worry sessions during the breaks: everyone, facilitators and team alike, needs some down time during this kind of event and you may hear all sorts of interesting things at the lunch table.

The first afternoon
Starting off

We usually begin this session in the large group in the formal setting of theatre-style seating. We ask people to speak to the group about what they noticed in the morning/lunch sessions. Again, we do not comment on people's contributions, we just continue to applaud them, thank them and ask for more speakers to add to the session. We are building confidence as much as noting what people say at this point. We aim to get at least four or five people who haven't spoken in the large group so far to speak up at this time. We often prompt for this to encourage people to come forward:

> 'People tell us that they're very nervous about speaking in front of such a large group. Well, here's a chance to have a go. We'd like to know what you thought of lunch!'

In the afternoon you will have to energize the group with short games more frequently. All over the world we have noticed that afternoons get sleepy after 2.45 pm. For this reason we tend to reserve more physically creative processes for the afternoon.

What you do on this first afternoon will be determined by your brief, objectives and the questions you want to inquire into. Our suggestion is that you expand your inquiry further using either questions from the Wonder Wheel or those that have emerged from the work in the morning. If things have struck you, then follow them where they lead. We find we are constantly updating our thinking, and sometimes our whole approach as the Breakthrough Zone unfolds.

Here is a series of examples from a session to explore customers' experiences in hotels:

1   In groups, talk about a time when you went to stay at someone's home as their guest and felt really welcome. What happened that felt good? What were the elements of each story that made it a good experience?

2   In the same groups, role-play arriving at the hotel. What happens? What is desirable/undesirable in this experience? How many of the elements from the stay in someone's home were present or absent?

3   Visualize going to your room for the first time. Take 30 seconds with your eyes closed to 'look around' in your mind's eye. What do you see? What are your reactions to the various elements of the room? Size? Décor? Facilities? Accessories?

4   Using the elements of home from the first part of this exercise create a story to act out for us. Create a truly 'homely' hotel, one that was trying to be a home away from home, what would it be like? What must it have? How must staff be? What about room design? Stick relentlessly to the elements you distinguished in part one.

5   Score other brands against your key elements out of 20: Intercontinental, Marriott, Holiday Inn, Renaissance, Post House, and Crowne Plaza. How are these brands similar? What are the differentiators?

6   In your group, have a look through various brochures, menus, promotions and publicity for this range of hotels. What do you notice about them? What impressions do they give you? How do you feel when you think about the invitations they are making? Create an irresistible invitation to stay in your hotel – you could make a TV commercial, a newspaper advert or a direct mail brochure.

7   What are the awkward and embarrassing feelings that people feel in hotels when they are away on different kinds of trip? What do people pretend that they are not feeling? What do they cover up and how do they do it? Think about eating alone, going to the bar, returning early/late to the hotel, arriving, leaving.

Such an exercise might take 45 minutes to generate findings. Then each group can feedback to the room on its discoveries and the whole room can comment on patterns or insights that seem to be emerging as the process unfolds. For people used to conventional focus groups this can prove a remarkable experience. In conventional groups it is common practice to follow a similar or identical protocol in each session. Then you start again and do exactly the same with a different group. In this large group you can get a perspective on a whole range of inputs at the same time and in real time start to notice the things which affect you, how various elements are related and how one thing influences another, a bit like in the sculpt. These are dynamic results.

These patterns or early insights will often lead to your next exercise and it is a good idea in process terms to keep some time free at the end of the first day. Stay in close contact with your Breakthrough Team and once the group have presented the small group work described above, create a tea break or loo break and ask yourselves if there is a question waiting to be asked/answered in the room? If there is, is it a question that people can answer creatively straight away, or do they need a process to help them get into it more deeply? If they do, it is up to you to come up with something relevant and get ready to set it up after the break. It is very important that you stay open to this live and improvisational structure. Nobody knows what twists and turns a large group will take in its development process. If you have all the exercises lined up and ready to go you will end up with a McDonald's style workshop where all the food has been cooked already and there is no room to create to order. This McDonald's menu is, unfortunately, the status of many of today's focus group discussions where functional details and specific questions have taken over the agenda from promoting a properly formed group discussion where new and spontaneous conversations may occur.

Remember in the previous chapter the blindfold exercise that led to massive changes across the commissioning company? On the first day of a process for a healthcare company, customers were asking for something which they called 'cradle to grave healthcare'. This was emerging as a consistent factor from the small groups with their various topics as described above. We had noticed many blank, uncomprehending faces among our client community. What on earth were the customers going on about? This company provided care through the instrument of financial insurance, which was how care got delivered.

It was apparent to the facilitators that the client team needed an experience of what it felt like to be cared for by an invisible carer when you were in a vulnerable situation. When folk are ill they cannot know for certain which direction their illness might take, they are temporarily rudderless, cast adrift in new territory with only their expert carers to advise them. Who would lead them through this uncertain terrain? How would they like to be led? What did it feel like to have to surrender control of one's fate to an outside agency?

Quickly we improvised a set of blindfolds and formed our group into threes and fours. We conducted the experiment as described in Chapter 5. Forty minutes later they were all back in the room. Many were visibly moved and shaken by the experience. There was a completely different level of regard for each other between the participants, both among the blind and the sighted.

Next we had everyone distil the learning from his or her experience. What did it take to care for or 'hold' someone through an uncertain experience with all the potential hazards and stumbling points along the way? Over the next half an hour the meaning of caring and holding people in their need became clear to everyone in the room.

This is a classic example of experiential learning. The client community had to give up their expertise and *put something at stake* to get through to a new perspective. In this exercise they had to suspend their normal level of autonomy and put themselves (mildly) physically at risk. For people who are used to calling the shots in their business environment to put themselves in customers' hands in this way calls for courage and daring, but the gains are immense. The executives get an experience of the emotional and physical journey that their customers go through and this leads to insights about the need for relationships and process components that can have a profound effect on the business. It is unfortunately a truism that many of the processes currently in place to connect businesses to their customers are nothing much more than elaborate corporate defence systems through which the company exhausts its customer as they climb hurdle after hurdle while they listen to recorded messages and push the buttons on their telephones, waiting to speak to someone who cares. Even if they get through the entire preamble the customers might eventually end up speaking to a newcomer in a call centre who knows less about the issues than they do.

> If businesses had to go through the things they put their customers through they would soon go elsewhere for their product or service.

If businesses had to go through the things they put their customers through they would soon go elsewhere for their product or service. It is extraordinary that though everyone hates automated voice recognition systems they are proliferating across the world so that you can hardly pick up your telephone without reaching a recorded message of some kind or another.

Closing the first day is usually done as we started it, as a large group in the theatre-style format. This is always an interesting session because the atmosphere in the group is now completely different and everyone can feel it. People often get up to say how amazed they have been by the experience of working together, how kind and understanding the company group (Breakthrough Team) have been in their willingness to listen and help out. Others will notice how tired they are and we will suggest that people get an early night because there is another whole day to do.

We usually finish with a review of what we learned during the day, again taking the main points from our participants and Breakthrough Team adding one or two observations of our own. Often we will ask participants to notice any passing thoughts or realizations they have overnight about what they have done, so that we can start in the morning with some considered reflections on our first day's experiences. We will often make recommendations to take it easy in the evening and get some rest. After long experience we know how this level of creative endeavour tires people and that they might not recognize their tiredness in their excitement about the day.

Day two
Morning session

It is important to take a moment to recognize where we are in the process at this point. As people gather in the room and say 'Hello' there will be a completely different atmosphere from the first day. There will be more talk and comfort between people than at first. This is now a large group that has:

1 Experienced the issues of membership and belonging in this community and has seen what it takes to stand out and differentiate oneself from the group and that it is safe to do so.

2 Shared experience of both generative and analytical work (creative exercises and distilling results) and has accomplished both without disaster.

3 Accomplished the task of bringing some of its inner world out into the public domain where it has not been held up for ridicule. Instead it has been valued and used productively.

4 Experienced being valued and applauded for the willingness to speak or to take a risk in creating something.

5 A confidence and maturity in its deliberations that is hardly ever seen in survey work. It has also experienced a 'valuing' of its creative output that is rare in group work and so it is ready and prepared to make more creative leaps on related or new topics.

6 An acceptance of experiential, creative and rational debate as contributors of equal merit to an understanding of issues, products and services.

7 A growing and trusting relationship with peers and clients that is based on taking journeys of inquiry together with unknown outcomes, where the client is as much a participant in uncertainty as the customer – where everyone has been in the same boat!

From the facilitators' and Breakthrough Team's points of view this group has formed a community around its own agenda in terms of the important themes of the main topic – it was invited to do so at the outset in the very first session. Hopefully this has been reinforced by the facilitators' sensitivity to the issues in the room. It has not been hustled into opinions on a set of functional or tactical issues as is usual in consumer contact session. Thus present in the room are the customers' own priorities, their major concerns, their own vocabulary, together with their own sense of what is stuck or missing from the company's products or services. We have also experienced valuable contributions from the 'customer side' of the client team. Also present is a sense of its own power and value as commentators or users of things that empowers it to set out on another day's creative journey without withholding or avoiding tackling new or unusual tasks.

If you think about it, these first-day events are quite extraordinary experiences compared with most of daily life. The group now has a sense of its worth and capabilities that few of us encounter ordinarily. Much of the time we don't really listen to each other, we are so intent on our own agenda that we pass quickly through our contact with others only noticing whether it will inhibit or facilitate achieving our own ends. We join teams and leave just as quickly when the work is done. We commute, pass by each other in streets, cafés and shops. We are very often 'alone together'. The community we have built on day one is different from this. It is genuinely able to take some risks without fear of ridicule in creating new ideas.

Quite often in this opening session there will be a readiness to share and comment on the proceedings of the first day with the benefit of an overnight break to reflect on them. People have somehow integrated their earlier experiences and can often see them from a different perspective. Here is an example from a group of seventy women talking about sanitary protection. One woman stood and spoke very emotionally in a way that grabbed the attention of everyone in the room:

> 'What I thought was that I hadn't had an easy time of it yesterday. Suddenly I thought of Chad Varah. I don't know if people know him, he's the man who started the Samaritans. And the reason he started the Samaritan's Helpline was because he went to his parish church one day and a man was digging a grave for a young girl, and he asked, "What did she die of?" The gravedigger said, "She committed suicide", and he said, "Well, why?" because she was only fourteen.
>
> 'The man said "Well, she started her periods and was so ignorant and uninformed and terrified that she killed herself."
>
> 'And I thought yesterday about our vision for the future of Tambrands ten years on and I was quite disappointed how timid we all were. My son will be a grown man by then and really I would like a world where the whole thing has stopped being a problem, where women can actually be women and enjoy it, where people are in tune with their body and celebrate it.'
>
> Female participant, 35 years

In addition to a willingness to work at this kind of level of significance when speaking, the group has also flexed its creative muscles and found that it is able to collaborate successfully in the area of idea production, performance and improvisation. It is ready to create almost anything we ask of it – in almost any domain, whether rational or emotional, sensible and straightforward or wacky and way out. Perhaps even more importantly, those engaged on the sensible projects will encourage and value the efforts of those tackling the more way out topics and vice versa. This is because, as we can notice from the speaking above, there arises a sense in conscious communities that we could all be doing more to tackle important issues, make our voice heard or bring our realizations to those who can make a difference. The group has begun to sense its power to transform things!

An important consideration

It is vital on this second day to consider what the client team will be left with in terms of physical as well as experiential outputs. What will we have to reflect on and review as evidence of the customer's contributions once the workshop is done? Many companies are overflowing with information about customers' opinions but have little in-depth appreciation of the contexts in people's lives where their products live. Additionally, they may have a poor understanding of the needs and compensatory mechanisms that make up so much a part of a modern life where their products might have a role. Much of what we consume is as a reward, treat or compensation for enduring something else or for waiting for something or someone. Many of the things we pay for help us to put aside more deadly fears or feel that we are making significant progress along some path that exists only in our minds. Even though such a path is purely in our heads, it is an important determinant of our behaviour and choices.

This compensatory element of consumption arises partly because we must all deny or ignore so many of our emotional needs and impulses just to get by in our busy daily lives. The frustration of waiting for a bus may be relieved by the consumption of a chocolate bar or cigarette. The feeling of not having lived up to one's potential may be overcome by driving an SUV which has a cabin not unlike that in a modern jet plane and a seat which puts the driver far above the person in a 'normal' car.

If you find yourself chuckling at these stereotypes it is worth remembering that it is not just one or two of us who are engaged in this kind of behaviour; we are all involved. From the high-flyers with their palm tops and frequent flyer programmes to the person who lives way down that country lane in a house powered by wind and sun, and drives a clapped out 2CV. We are all using our consumption patterns to indicate preferences and send messages about our beliefs and values to the rest of the world.

Thus some substantial outputs, which inform the company about the emotional landscape in which its products dwell, will often provide a vital 'gallery' of evidence to support the insights and outputs from the rational and experiential discoveries from the workshop.

Construction exercises

With these things in mind, we often start the second day's creative endeavour with a projective construction exercise. In this work the participants' ideas and feelings will be projected out into the creation of something that represents them. When a large group works in this way the outputs form a very exciting review of the underlying drivers in the relevant market place. We can literally see in the room what constitutes the customers' perception of the brand and how it might meet their needs.

Here are a couple of examples of construction exercises that we often use.

The brand world

Here the participants are given a set of physical resources and asked to build a 'world' that represents their experience of a brand. It might be a place that we can walk into or sit in, a model we can look at, an artefact or icon that symbolizes everything about the brand or something entirely different. In the resources section you will find a list of things we would normally provide for such an activity.

Brand worlds that we have built in recent projects include:

- British Airways – the world of 'Club',
- Nescafé – a 21st Century Nescafé,
- Ribena,
- Horlicks,
- Lucozade,
- the service function in a financial institution,
- the interior of a new aircraft,
- the high street of the future for Carphone Warehouse, and
- the gas station forecourt of the future for Shell.

We have always found this kind of construction very illuminating in surprising ways. All sorts of things can be seen in these physical representations that cannot be described easily in words. How will Nescafé look in ten years? What will a gas station forecourt be like in 2020?

Art-from-within

This is the construction process that we use most often. It was brought to us eight years ago by Nicky Forsythe and we will describe its set-up and outputs in some detail so that you can use or adapt it for yourself. In the resources section we give details of the things you will need to do it.

One of the great advantages of this process is that everyone can do it and everyone produces their own original output. These individual efforts can then be discussed and evaluated for themes and insights by their creators. We usually do this exercise in 'tables' of eights or tens where each table is working on a theme. So in a recent BA project the tables worked on a set of subjects like:

- Concorde
- First Class
- Club World
- Club Europe
- Economy.

Through their illustrations of feelings and sensations in the different cabins a great many innovations were put in place from Beds In Business to World Traveller Plus.

Here is the script for a typical set-up for art-from-within. Imagine the scene where all the participants are seated around tables of eight to ten people, there are pieces of high quality A3 paper in front of them and boxes of pastels in the centre of the table.

Art-from-within

Automatic drawing can be used as a powerful way of tapping creative resources we literally 'never knew we had'.

The process is simple: you start off by assuming that a part of yourself that you do not know and are not in control of is going to do the drawing. Then draw! Start by picking up any colour or colours that feel right to you; make marks or divide the page in the first way that occurs to you. Then relax in the knowledge that the process is already under way: what you have done is *already* meaningful: it is the beginning of something that 'wants' to be drawn or expressed. You don't yet know what this 'something' looks like: you just watch the process of creating it unfold; you are a passive observer of your own process.

You might want to focus on a specific issue on which you'd like some insights. However, do not *try* to draw anything relating to this issue: simply note that you want some insights in this area and leave an unknown part of you to do the work.

Check any tendency to try to recognize or name what you are drawing, or to rush in with rational interpretations of your work while you are doing it. Equally, do not *try* to make your work meaningful or beautiful: in fact, if you find yourself getting stuck on the notion that you need to do something 'good', the best thing to do is to give yourself full permission – or even to set out purposefully – to do something *bad* and *meaningless*! (This can yield some astonishing results.)

Your 'rational brain' may well be busy making judgements like:

> 'I don't believe this works.'
> 'This is meaningless.'
> 'Maybe this works for artistic people, but not for me.'
> 'I can see something is taking shape here, but I don't believe that it has any deep inner meaning: it's just scribbles!'

This is a sign that everything is going as it should: the rational mind likes to believe that *it* is in control and knows what's *really* going on. In fact, this side of you will often deny or flatly refuse to believe that there is any other part of you at work here.

Just accept these thoughts, if they come up; carry on with the process and see what happens.

Eventually, you may well find you reach a point where your 'mindtalk' subsides or stops completely: you become unaware of the passage of time, totally absorbed in what you are doing and oblivious to what is going on around you.

Then, when you feel complete with your work, sit with it for a while and allow it to communicate to you: what comes to mind when you look at it? What thought processes does it set off? Do you see any shapes or forms that have meaning to you? (Don't be afraid to acknowledge and to see things that you never overtly intended to draw.) Also, notice what you were paying attention to when doing your drawing: was it a particular feeling? Were you drawn to certain colours or combinations of colours? Were you preoccupied with outlines and boundaries or with forms; with harmony or with contrast? What do these things mean to you?

Finally, after giving yourself enough time to really explore your work receptively, acknowledge three insights that have come to you as a result of doing this, and write them down.

When everyone on your table has finished we will start a 'Go Round'. In this we will take it in turns to talk about our work and what we can see in it – or what it means to us when we look at it. Look at your work again as you listen to others talk about theirs: you may find you see things there that you didn't notice at first sight. You may also decide to do a series of such drawings: if you do this, you will find that following the pattern of development of your drawings is a fascinating and rewarding process.

Then, once questions are done, the process can get underway. It can sometimes be necessary to encourage silence in this session, but not always. If you do feel it wise to ask people to stop talking and return to their creation try to do so in a light and pleasant manner and avoid reminding everyone of the tyranny of the classroom!

After 30 minutes everyone will probably be done. Some may finish in five minutes and we often ask them to do more drawings. Sometimes they wish to get up and walk around and look at others' work and we discourage this. If they must get up we usually invite them to leave the workroom for a few minutes once they have fully written what their drawing signifies to them on the back of it. Others will become so engrossed in their process that they would go on for hours. Give them as much time as is feasible without the rest of the group getting too bored.

This last is an important discipline. Ask the group to review their work and write the main things that come to mind on the back of their illustration. This will help by providing a series of verbatims that can be used to 'title' the work at the feedback stage and by providing an aide mémoire for you when you are reviewing the outputs at the analysis stage.

Once everyone has finished drawing it is time to begin the Go Round, in which each will take a turn to talk about their drawing and show it to their table. We usually film this process for use in the video later. Seeing the passion with which people express themselves in this simple exercise is very convincing for members of the company or organization who were unable to be at the customer workshop.

When the Go Round is complete we ask each table to extract the themes from their work and to create a gallery on the wall to exhibit their work in a thematic fashion. Then the whole audience takes a tour round the gallery and looks at the work. It is usually very clear what important themes are emerging for the customers in this exercise.

By the time art-from-within is complete it is usually time for coffee.

The specifics session

It is common for our clients to have a whole series of specific issues that they would like feedback on. For example, in a study of hot milky drinks our client wanted to know in detail about people's sleep patterns. In a study of a children's treat the client wished to observe the interaction and dynamic between mothers and their children. In an airline project they were particularly concerned to get feedback on all elements of the ground experience as well as the airborne one. In a healthcare project they wanted feedback on how people felt about their experiences with the call centre and the claims process. In a computer project they wanted to know how people allocated responsibility for problems with their computers, e.g. was it a hardware or software issue and who was to 'blame' for the difficulty?

It is at this point, after coffee on the second day, that we will often tackle these specific issues. The large group is now well resourced having explored in some detail both its opinions and emotions surrounding the product area and related experiences. In this state of heightened awareness we have found that the group can get quickly into appreciation of detailed issues. They are also able to give specific feedback that does not have to include all of their issues that might relate to other aspects of the subject because they have had plenty of time to air these and work through them.

Thus in the computer example above, while beginners were very frustrated by their early experience with their computers, they were able in the specifics session to admit to the extent of their ignorance and confess that often they did not understand even the simplest of terms like 'program' or 'desktop'. Often their early telephone sessions with the helpline would devolve into someone explaining to them in a very basic way how to do something step by step. This, inevitably, left them feeling like a small child at school – even if they were grateful for the help they had received they felt humiliated by their ignorance too. They were not children, they were adults and it felt dis-empowering to own up to their ignorance at this level. This was the very opposite of the feeling of power and competence they had been hoping for when they bought the computer.

This led to the insight that computer companies, both hardware and software producers do a lot to create expectations and very little to manage them in their advertising and promotions. The advertisements are all about size, speed and power, nothing about the wise and appropriate application of all that potential. There is an obvious opportunity for someone to connect with new owners of computers with a sensible and basic course. The nearest we have seen to that is the publication from Reader's Digest, 'How to do just about anything on a computer' which tackles a whole series of simple processes in a text full of photos of normal people doing normal tasks. It is interesting that this publication comes from a source which is adept at providing DIY (Do-It-Yourself) manuals for a whole variety of common needs. In other words it took someone not from the computer industry to create a book for customers who were not from the computer industry either! Reader's Digest DIY manual for home improvements is currently priced at £14.00 and ranked number 124 in Amazon's best sellers list. Can you imagine what a profitable product that is? This book sells year after year after year.

Now this is more than an interesting digression in our opinion. There has been a notable slowing in the uptake of computers, particularly in the area so important to manufacturers – that of upgrading and modernizing. We believe that a good part of that slowdown is driven by the disappointment of customers with their initial purchase. That failure to manage expectations and to put in place support and 'Help' programmes that didn't keep customers waiting for hours on the line is now coming home to roost. When computers were 'Hot' everyone wanted one whether they could work them or not. Now that the fad has cooled, the lack of investment in their customers by the manufacturers is showing up in stagnant sales. Bill Gates might well give a billion dollars to worthy causes but have you – one of his customers – tried ringing Microsoft for help?

Of course, this is nothing new. The motor industry learned that follow-up service was just as important to their purchasers as the gleam of new vehicles in the showroom. Some manufacturers who have resisted this insight are dropping inexorably down the sales leagues as customers revert to companies who are courteous, service-oriented and interested in their on-going business.

So, in the specifics session all sorts of things may come to light that lead to breakthroughs in their own right. This is where customers get a chance to get their hands on the kinds of issues that bug them, whether the company thinks they are problems or not.

In this session we would typically have groups of six to eight working on an each area of concern to customers. We would encourage the customers, not the client, to specify the problem areas. Usually the customers work on things that interest the client and if they don't, you must ask why not? The client team would join in these groups too, spread evenly around the topics. It is important that the client team get a sense of the language, feelings and issues that figure in their customers' worlds.

We would often ask each team to produce a list of the most irksome issues in their area of concern and to produce prototype solutions for each. We might structure these solutions to range from low-cost quick wins, through to longer-term high-investment options.

We have to say that for most of our clients this is a new and astounding session. Having a well-formed group who have become sensitized to your product/service working at pace to identify problems and create solutions is not only of immense practical value, but gives a real sense of the passion with which customers will work for you on things which are of benefit to both communities, customer and company. It is truly a win–win situation.

Lunch break

The final afternoon

We now have a large group that is as well resourced as it can be to contribute to the development of your business. For this reason, as we have said in other places, it is a good idea to bring to the Breakthrough Zone an issue which is worthy of this level of input. Decisions about packaging details or promotions do not really lend themselves to this level of inquiry. You are, hopefully, searching for the answer to, or a way through your STOP Statement.

Consequently this last session is often used to build or prototype the best solutions that the group can achieve given their heightened sensitivity and their desire to help the client. This desire has been mightily enhanced by the client's interest in them and willingness to work with their ideas. These people will really want to help you. There is no rocket science here; this is merely a matter of reciprocity. It is similar to the situation where you go to someone's home for dinner and you have such a wonderful time that you end up staying late, talking of all manner of things as you help them do the dishes and clear up.

Here are some examples of the things we have created in this final session:

1 The perfect healthcare experience
2 A call centre that works for customers
3 An ironing revolution
4 The ultimate in-flight experience
5 A perfect frequent-flyer programme
6 New products in the soft drinks area
7 My healthcare company
8 The interior for an intercontinental submarine vessel
9 A bank that is on my side
10 Insurance company interactions that treasure customers in every way.

Usually our group is again divided into working groups of 8–10 per group, although at this stage you might find groups as large as 15–20. The community has learned how to work on a task together and to divide up areas of responsibility. Occasionally we have witnessed the fascinating process of all 70 or so of the participants engaged in one project.

Often we ask the group to create an experience of the solution that will let us sample the benefit they are trying to achieve. We may not be able to try the 'actual' product, but perhaps they can create a sense of it, an environment or experience that conveys the feeling they are hoping to get across with the actual thing. We can recall very well the expression of sun, sex and vitality that a group brought to their image for a new Marks and Spencer. The group were concerned to counter the elements of dowdiness, lack of sex appeal and slowness that they felt about M& S in 2001.

This experience may include props, places or environments, role-plays, advertising, customer propositions, promotions or all of these. What customers create gives the client a very good feel for what is stuck and what is missing in his current offer. And as the clients co-create with the customers they can feel their own sense of the appropriateness of the solutions too. Inevitably, not every idea is as good or as relevant to a particular client as every other but can you imagine the quality of this experience compared with asking people for their opinions at 8.30 pm in an anonymous room in a small town somewhere in the UK? In the conventional focus group what is the level of commitment of the respondents to reaching inside themselves to help us solve our problem? What you get out is always related to what you put in. Commitment shifts reality.

> 'Until one is committed, there is hesitancy, the chance to draw back, always ineffectiveness. Concerning all acts of initiative (and creation), there is one elementary truth, the ignorance of which kills countless ideas and splendid plans: that the moment one definitely commits oneself, then Providence moves too.
>
> 'All sorts of things occur to help one that would never otherwise have occurred. A whole stream of events issues from the decision, raising in one's favour all manner of unforeseen incidents and meetings and material assistance, which no man could have dreamed would have come his way.
>
> Scottish Himalayan Expedition

If you can't find the energy, commitment or resources to work intensively with your customers you may well find other roads to your solution. However, we doubt that they will be as customer-centred as a session like this.

The last creative session will turn the event into a kind of 'show' or exhibition of the best solutions or new ideas that can be reached by the community. There is often a huge amount of laughter and applause in the room, but if it is lacking we do our best to remind and encourage our community to acknowledge themselves and others. The film of this show will act as a record of the themes and creations that can be shown to others. A word of caution here though: we have found that the finished film must not be too explicit in revealing the vulnerability or showmanship of the participants. Things that happened in a well-formed group where trust was high and people were taking risks can look very crazy in the boardroom on a Tuesday morning! We will be selling the insights, not the way we got to them.

Leaving the Breakthrough Zone

We leave between 45 minutes and an hour for the final feedback and closing session. We usually set the room as it was for the very first session so that the group can notice the difference in atmosphere even when we are all seated in a formal arrangement. What you will notice too is how easily the group now falls into compliance with a simple request from the leadership team, how they acknowledge and accommodate each other and how well they have learned to work in this large community. As we have said elsewhere there are several key components to building this atmosphere: safety (particularly freedom from criticism and ridicule), security, permission, acknowledgement and equality combined with clarity, warmth and structure from the facilitation team.

At this time the group will be ready to give their final feedback or to do any last-minute exercises to cover components that remain unexplored. We usually remind the group of the primary task or central objective of the session and ask for their feedback on that: so if it were, say, 'the future of flying', what do they think about that now? What message would they want to send their sponsor, the client? There are usually some lively and important messages in these last few minutes.

Next it is time to round off the group and to facilitate an appropriate ending to this unusual experience. We will often ask the group members to take a good minute to look around them and notice the people they have worked with over the past two days, as well as any they haven't. We then invite the group to comment on their experiences and, using the microphone and the discipline of speaking one at a time, we all listen. You will sometimes hear remarkable things about friendship, delightful moments, tiredness, and above all, a desire to stay informed of progress on the project. People want to know that the hard work they have put in will have an impact.

In our view it is important that we make some response to this interest without over-promising levels of involvement that we cannot deliver whether for lack of time or reasons of commercial secrecy. Here are some practical solutions we have found:

- The most senior person from the company thanks all the customers and promises to send a letter or email in a few weeks' time to thank them formally and to update them on the project.
- We create an email 'newsletter/chatroom' community, usually hosted by someone in the client community where customers and staff can continue to contribute things that they notice, new ideas and thoughts. Usually several members of the customer community become enthusiastic contributors to this.
- People who are interested leave their email address so that we can update them at some future date – someone from the client community needs to take responsibility for this.
- People who are interested in providing feedback on ideas as they develop, perhaps in focus groups or smaller workshops, let us know and we create a database of 'interested' customers who might play a role at a later date. It can be valuable to compare the views of educated with naïve customers as concepts, prototypes or new ideas go forward.

It is important not to over-commit at these sessions. The customers have helped us greatly but they have been properly rewarded for their contribution both in financial and social ways. It is not essential to form an ongoing community unless you really want to, or it has some value for the project going forward. Look honestly at your motives for holding on to some sense of engagement and be ready to let go if it does not really serve the programme. We have a great deal of difficulty saying goodbye and this is the time to do it!

Remember to thank everyone, including:

1   the venue staff;
2   the film crew;
3   the Breakthrough Team;
4   the facilitators, programme managers and support team; and
5   above all, the customer guests who will have given their all!

As the event finishes it will be important to facilitate the speedy and accurate distribution of any rewards agreed. Try not to leave the calculation of variable amounts like travel expenses to the last moment or you will create a queue a bit like those familiar to people who visit their banks. We usually arrange two payment desks, one from A to M, the other from N to Z.

The facilitation team will still have quite a number of things to attend to:

- a concluding session with the Breakthrough Team;
- collecting and labelling all of the outputs from the session; and
- packing up and getting away from the venue without leaving any commercially sensitive or important information lying about.

The 'wash up' session

Once the customers have left it is important to have a few moments with the client team. There are two key objectives for this session:

1   to give people a chance to get anything that is worrying them off their chests; and
2   to direct them towards the next set of activities and to prepare them for the Insight Zone.

Set a time limit for this session. Sometimes the group fly into conclusions and solutions at this point. You can pre-empt this by stating that we now need to maintain an open mind about what we have experienced. Ask the team what had impact on them.

It is very interesting at this session to notice how, even after an extraordinary and wonderful session some people can immediately start to devalue and dissect their experience. Since this will be the last moment in the Zone for everyone it can be important to promote a balance in the feedback that does not discount the experience.

At this point in the process the experience is still raw and there has been no opportunity for assimilation and integration. These will take place over the next few days and nights. At the end of their time in the Zone people may feel anxious that they have missed their opportunity to say something, or concerned that the 'result' cannot be seen in front of them like a shining star. If there is any complaining much of it will be as an attempt to avoid blame or responsibility for not having a concrete result. Correspondingly small niggles about the process may form the centre of much of the wash up:

> 'I thought we were going to spend more time on the actual products.'
> 'There were bad dynamics in our group and we didn't really get past them.'
> 'It was all very engaging but what did we really learn?'

We are in the presence of our old friend anxiety. Suddenly the team charged with the ultimate responsibility for a breakthrough is sitting in a circle of uncertainty with their minds overflowing with massive amounts of feedback, insightful ideas, and no framework inside which to understand them. This is because the things that made an impact are lost at this time among the tiredness, the relief at having finished, the mourning for the lost group combined with the unprocessed nature of the 'result'. Everything feels a bit like an anticlimax. Did we make it or not?

Sometimes we will offer a facilitation structure for this session and the final go round:

> 'We'd like everyone to share their best and worst moment from the event. Spend a few minutes sharing your experience with your neighbour replaying your highs and lows and then we'll take feedback from everyone in turn.'

Usually we do not attempt to encapsulate, summarize or reinterpret this feedback. We just let it be. Now is not the time to get defensive or to try to be clever, just reassuring.

Next we remind people that in a few days' time we will meet for the Insight Workshop. Our job there will be to develop a new awareness leading to a set of realizations based on the events in the Breakthrough Zone. We point out that realizations may come as much from what did not get said as what did. Did customers seem the way we expected them to be? Were the issues the ones we were expecting? Were the strategies we had in mind before we started likely to resolve their issues? What were we expecting that didn't happen?

Of the things that did happen we ask the team to notice what had real impact on them and talk a little about the nature of impact. We also ask them to notice their insights – things they have become newly aware of as a result of the Breakthrough Zone – and to bring these with them to the Insight Zone.

Then we say goodbye and go.

Resources list for the Breakthrough Zone

Refer to the resources list for Chapter 3 where the information regarding necessary accommodation and basic resources has been listed. In addition to this we have prepared a further list that includes some of the more tricky resource issues you might consider.

1   Ensure that you have a name badge for everyone with their first name in a large enough font size to be readable at 5 metres distance from them. At the registration desk have a computer and printer in order to be able to create badges on the spot.

2   Two or three hand-held microphones that are linked not only to the sound desk for recording, but also to a public address or speaker system so that speakers can hear their voices amplified as they speak. If people can not hear evidence of their voices through the microphone they will not hold them up. This will make the sound recording very poor.

3   Lapel mikes for the facilitators. It is important that they have both hands free as they speak. Make especially sure that when the participants are working that the microphones are switched off, or the volume is cancelled. It is all too easy to have private or side conversations booming out of the sound system while the facilitators are chatting in the loo or outside the room!

4   If you are going to use construction exercises, then ensure that you have appropriate and safe tools and materials for their use. People will prove incredibly resourceful in seeking all sorts of items from the surroundings. Here is a list of some of the resources you might use:

- dowel rods;
- polystyrene cubes (all sizes);
- Foamcore boards (expensive);
- corrugated cardboard on the roll;
- tissue paper;
- crêpe paper;
- small torches and theatrical lighting gels;
- string, masking tape, raffia, gaffer tape;
- junior hack saws, scissors (never use Stanley knives or box cutters unless used under close supervision);
- calico or cheap curtain lining material;
- big felt pens;
- baking foil (essential);
- enough bins to dispose of the sundry messes people make;
- a strategy for dismantling structures, disposing of them and cleaning up between sessons;
- a digital stills camera to record the constructions.

5. If you are going to use art-from-within, you will need the following:

- A3 art paper – err on the side of generosity with 4 sheets per person;
- chalk or oil-based pastels;
- wet wipes (pastels can be messy!);
- spray fixative in order to avoid the art work smudging when you collect it in;
- Blu Tack or other mounting adhesive that is acceptable to the hotel or conference facility; and
- a digital stills camera.

7 | The Insight Zone

Simplifying some difficult concepts

 The Insight Zone is one of the most difficult events to describe. This comes about because it is essentially a place where one sets out to create or raise awareness and then to forge new connections based upon that awareness. As such it is a place of new thoughts, memory and contemplation combined. It is also to be hoped that as well as mental processes participants will experience the shadings of emotion and valency. They may feel excited or saddened by an experience or drawn to some element while repelled by another. We are using the idea of valency as it is used in chemistry to describe the feeling of a bond of attraction or repulsion between a person and an idea or activity or another individual or group. It is our aim in the Insight Zone to access all of these experiences and to distil the learning from them. There are all sorts of methodological intricacies here and we shall do our best to steer clear of excessive complication and keep the Insight Zone simple.

However, there is one requirement for participation in the workshop that cannot be ignored or short-changed. That is the willingness to look inward, to gaze at data from the inner world with the same degree of candour as we bring to our observation of what is on the outside. This presents us with our first methodological issue, for just as we have surely been trained in our ability to discern the outside world through our education and development, we may not have been equivalently trained to examine the inner world.

Indeed the most inspired and gifted practitioners of 'inner seeing' suggest to us that there are all sorts of immediate problems for people undertaking this activity. The first and most important problem was noticed by Freud who observed that even when people were encouraged to speak of *anything* they encountered in their thoughts, no matter how seemingly irrelevant or unwholesome, they could not do so for more than a moment or two.

The kind of freethinking required for an uninhibited creative inquiry might not be as easy as it ought to be. We will describe in a little more detail some of the more common problems encountered in this work and some ideas about how to help people around them.

We shall also spend some time in this section drawing on examples of insight from other projects and experiences so that we can guide you in process terms. Not that these insights are necessarily brilliant or earth-shattering, but we include them so that you can see how the method of freethinking is applied and worked with using the tools of reflection, analysis and interpretation. Additionally, we offer some ideas for doing this creative work in a group setting.

Let us begin with a fresh sequence of free thoughts as our starting place. They are produced just as one of us sits here writing this. Here they are.

> 'As I write this I am looking at my desk and I notice the grain in the wood. Next I see the picture of the wild and bare branches of a tree on a book that is lying there. I think momentarily of my father and his death many years ago. I sense tears not far behind my eyes. I notice a tension in my mouth, my lips are pressed together as if I would say something. "Oh Dad!" comes to mind.
>
> 'A sense of relief fills me and I can see the nearby objects in the outside world more clearly. There is an interesting blue light on a hard disk standing half a metre in front of me. I think blue light, then red light, then Red Light Zone. I am for a second afraid to follow my thoughts. My next thought is: "Amsterdam" and suddenly I find myself humming. Then I think of a woman I know who once lived in Amsterdam. I met her briefly here in London the other day.
>
> 'I find myself singing, barely audibly. The sound of the notes is 'Dum-di-dum', but I can discern no tune. I am embarrassed. I have produced some ill-formed and primitive sounds for no apparent reason. Why could I not detect a song behind the notes?'

THE INSIGHT ZONE   145

Making connections

Next it is time to review these associations and to generate ideas about them. Here is the chain of thoughts that occurred when the author reviewed the associations:

'If you knew me you would know that I often think of my father when I see wooden surfaces, especially those that have been crafted in some way. He was a carpenter you see, and I very much wanted to follow in his footsteps. He preferred me to follow my talents in the classroom however and discouraged my woodworking ambitions. The sigh, "Oh Dad!" I think reflects my regret and exasperation that we didn't manage to see each other's point of view while he lived and were often at loggerheads over values and behaviour. But why a sigh? I feel it is a sigh of reconciliation for as I sit here I am practising my craft – that of writing; and this is my woodwork. Just as I watched him in his workshop many years ago, so I am in mine and it is the early morning, a time I associate very much with him. I remember that when I was fifteen I had a newspaper delivery round and he would get up to make me a cup of tea at 5.45 am before I went off to do my round. Right now I am trying to deliver again, this time it is a manuscript – in other words a lot of new[s] papers – for this book! I could do with that cup of tea now!

'My feelings rise to the surface as I follow this chain of associations and this surfacing of emotion leads to another association, that with the Red Light Zone and I am momentarily puzzled. Then I notice the word Zone and recognize that it is one I have thought about several times already this morning as I write and review elements of our manuscript. Is there something attractive about the idea of a Zone? I am reminded of the book *Flow* by a man with an unpronounceable name and how athletes describe the sense of being in the Zone when they hit peak performance. Am I trying to gear up my energy to help me reach some kind of Zone in my writing this morning, aided and abetted by the ghost of my father with the cup of tea?

'And the woman from Amsterdam? That is a private matter. But some time later in the day I catch myself singing those few notes again. And this time I am able to extend them to the point where I recognize them. I am singing a hymn, "O God, our help in ages past" is the first line of the song. What is the significance of that, I wonder? Is it another appeal for help?'

So, of what use is all this? One thing that we would wish to make really clear is that this activity of speculating on the free wanderings of the mind is in itself an immensely valuable creative tool. Like a detective story, the incidents or perceptions that touch our minds can be regarded as clues to the backdrop of wishes and desires that move moment by moment though each one of us. It is, you remember, the deepest customer wishes and desires that we are trying to elicit in our efforts to make brands, products or services more desirable, relevant or exciting. They too move in this way.

> One thing that we would wish to make really clear is that this activity of speculating on the free wanderings of the mind is in itself an immensely valuable creative tool.

However, we are only too aware that, as Freud observed, this is not a straightforward matter. The best support we can offer is to break this process down into simple, replicable components so that anyone can follow the creative journey to insight if he or she follows these steps.

Looking again at the example above, the first thing we have done is to *reproduce* as accurately as possible an actual sequence of experiences, in this case a train of thoughts. The next step was to *generate from* this primary data a set of associations or hypotheses which derive from it. The third step is to *generate an insight* or *preferred explanation* for the sequence, which might or might not be the ultimate truth but which was invisible during the original experience. The defining quality for this generated idea is that *it must help us see more fully into the heart of the matter*.

Here is another way to divide the creative process into steps:

1   reproduce;
2   generate from; and
3   generate.

The central insight generated from those above is that insights are generated, not found. They are elements of awareness translated into language.

In pure abstract painting and freeform jazz improvisation we find examples of 'generated' expression, although even here origins, themes and influences can be detected or imagined.

An amusing and elegant commercial example of this may be found in Greg Rowland's excellent analysis of an instant food product, Pot Noodles. This is an instant noodle snack that is made by adding hot water and waiting for a few minutes. Greg's analysis led to an advertising campaign based on the line: 'The Slag of All Snacks.'[1] Here is a short quote from his paper.

> 'The answer, while not exactly staring us in the face, is never far away in popular consciousness. The answer was pornography.

'It was time to whip up another paradigm to investigate the relationship between porn and real love:

Real love	Porn
Mutual care	Individual gratification
Authentic	Fake
Eternal	Transient
Deep	Shallow
Real emotions	False emotions
Priceless	Cheap
Effort	Easy
Beauty	Crassness
Beyond money	Commercial
Wholesome	Degraded
Natural	Technological
Long term	Quick

'It was immediately apparent that the relationship of Good Food to Pot Noodle had some startling similarities to that of real love and the semiotic universe of pornography. Indeed, when we mapped Pot onto Porn, the idea of pornography seemed to express the brand's values more precisely than in a relationship with Real Food.

'Moreover, porn is also about victimisation. Certainly, many participants in the porn industry are themselves victims (though some are highly paid victims.) But more importantly, porn makes men victims of their basest desires and impulses. In particular, the greater accessibility of pornography compared to ten years ago means that smut is a far greater part of young people's lived experience than ever before. Electronic media – and in particular the internet – has made porn instantly accessible ...

'So we suggested to the client that Pot Noodle could be seen as a form of Food Porn.'

Greg Rowland[1]

Interestingly, although it led to a rise in sales almost overnight, the campaign also generated a lot of controversy. As a reader of this book, we can invite you to view this rather special piece of commercial insight by downloading it from:

http://www.semiotic.co.uk/case-study/pot-noodle/

You can see how his overlaying of one paradigm, that of real love as contrasted with pornography (base desires gratified), onto another, real food versus snacks has given access to an insight about Pot Noodles as a snack (base desires gratified) – that it is a 'pornographic' element in the world of food.

The job then is to help our team get into this kind of freethinking frame of mind after their experiences in the Breakthrough Zone. However, we use the Pot Noodle example as a technical demonstration of technique and process only. So far pornography has played no role in our programmes!

First we must consider the 'When' as much as the 'How' of this task. What is the appropriate time to call the Breakthrough Team back into the Insight Zone? If you remember from our diagram, we have noted that there are both short and long forms of the Insight Wave, so it might prove a good idea to visit the insight process on more than one occasion. Yet there are certain expectations and structural considerations with regard to the innovation process overall that need to be considered when deciding on timing. For one thing, business is almost always in a hurry. People are used to getting into action almost as soon as an event occurs or an issue arises. We discuss this phenomenon later too. Nonetheless, your Breakthrough Team will almost certainly want to get on with it pretty soon after the Breakthrough Zone event. People will be worried about forgetting what happened, and anxious that they are required to somehow keep all this data on their radar screen when they have a day job to do.

Usually we run the Insight Zone two or three days after the Breakthrough Zone. We have found that any time during the first seven days after the Breakthrough Zone is acceptable for most projects. Any longer and you will start to experience drop-outs and non-attendance. The Insight Zone is a full day's event facilitated by the same facilitators who conducted the inquiry in the Breakthrough Zone.

The Insight Zone – primary task

The primary task in the Insight Zone is to drill down into the primary data and to notice which aspects or elements had impact on participants. What do we mean by primary data?

1 Primary data includes all of the experiences in the project since the first briefing. What do you remember and what affect did it have on you?

2 Any memories, associations or other data that have come to mind, which seem in some way, no matter how remote, to be connected with the project.

3 Your own thoughts and reflections upon these memories or experiences.

4 Actual verbatim comments from the workshops or bits of behaviour that you remember.

5 Any elements of character, posture or tone that struck you and made an impact.

6 Experiences from your participation and any affect they have had on you.

7 Residues or inexplicable elements that have stuck in your mind, including faces, expressions and characters as well as things that were said.

8 Unexpected or memorable things that have come to mind since participating in the project.

9 Hopes and fears about the project and their relationship to your participation.

10 Your (secret?) predictions about where the project will end up.

Our task is to access all of this without sifting, sorting or prioritizing. Our assistants in this endeavour will be our Breakthrough Team-mates who will notice their responses as well as our own to the primary data so that we can use these to create insights a bit further down the line.

Here is a key piece of information about the Insight Zone:

We expect that you would take four hours to complete this review of primary data. This is not to be hurried. We aim to savour this data as we would a good meal, the objective is to taste it again, and allow ourselves to be swept away by the associations and realizations it provokes. As we have tried to show in our brief discussion of freethinking, there is no alley or pathway that might not yield something useful or a connection hitherto unseen.

Now it is time to start our walk through the Insight Zone.

Step one – getting back together

You should aim for as many of the client team from the Breakthrough Zone as you can muster. If everyone can attend then that is so much the better. Ask anyone who cannot come to send you their insights and the things that struck them, by e-mail before the Insight Zone event.

Once you are reunited in the room, spend a little time on sharing about any and everything that has happened since the Breakthrough Zone. People may need to talk about the effects of their experience, the volume of work in their in-trays or other matters. Take some time until people are ready to re-connect with the project.

Step two – resourcing the Insight Zone

A common tool in our approach is to use examples based upon participants' experiences in everyday life. In this way we can ask people to work in a way that we need for the workshop, by re-examining something they have already done. In this session we are aiming to create insight and therefore we need examples of personal insights in the room.

We want these for several reasons:

- They will form an incontrovertible demonstration that everyone in the room is capable and qualified to have insights.
- They will illuminate some of the qualities of insights.
- They will show how, once acted upon, insights change everything.
- They will demonstrate that a period of struggle, feeling lost, of being about to give up often if not always precedes the attainment of insight.
- They will show how the exact moment at which insight strikes or occurs is never predictable. You might have one at any time.

Here is an exercise that will help you get to personal experiences of insight.

In pairs please attempt the following.

'Recall a time when you noticed or admitted something that changed everything. It could have been something like a relationship that wasn't working or that you had met someone who was the most important person in your life! It could have been something you noticed about yourself, about others or the world. The more profound the impact of this realization on your life, the more it will help us in our work today.

Look back over it thoroughly and try to describe fully:

- How you were in the time leading up to this realization.
- When, where and how the realization struck you.
- Whether you had any precognition of the realization or not.
- What happened after the realization.
- Whether you struggled to resist the realization or not.
- If and how you implemented the realization.
- If you kept it secret, what effect did it have?'

Allow each person a good 20 minutes to complete this, ask their partners to take notes as they speak if that will help. The importance of this exercise cannot be overstated, it will demonstrate:

- How insight/realization is at the heart of transformation.
- How difficult it is to accept an insight that changes everything.
- How resistance keeps swinging us back to the way we were.
- That people are already well-qualified as Insight Engineers.

When the work is done, invite each pair to share back to the larger group anything that they noticed or that they think is of value to the larger group. Once a safe atmosphere is established also ask: 'Is there anything of importance from this exercise that you suppressed from the group? We do not want to know what it was but it might be important to reflect for a moment on what impact it could have on our perceptions if it was publicly available. When we move on to recalling the Breakthrough Zone it is important that we do not suppress things because they make us uncomfortable or are difficult to explain.'

Break

Step three – revisiting the Breakthrough Zone

Now it is time to work through our experiences in the Breakthrough Zone. We must say that this is the step that is almost always shirked in discovery projects. Because the model of reality that dominates our culture is based so firmly on the idea that observations of the outside world will yield whatever information we need, many inquiries miss the point that it is the effect of these observations on our inner reality that really matters. Instead they push for longer and longer lists of 'facts' many of which have no use or value whatsoever. We have sat through many presentations of 70 charts or more where everything of value was contained in the first three slides. Quality not quantity is the key to this process. Quantity is important, but the ways in which quantity forms an important element of work in the Breakthrough and Insight Zones are the following:

- The size of the team and the customer group means that we are likely to get several perspectives on anything we encounter.

- The length and depth of the work in the Zone mean that we have the opportunity for thoroughness in our reflections on the experience.
- The expressive processes, emotional climate and volatility of the large group enhances the likelihood of our being affected by our activities (i.e. we are more likely to notice what is going on).
- Our extended period of contact creates enough safety for more secret or hidden desires to surface.
- The large extent of the working group's control of its own agenda removes much of the facilitator bias of many so-called 'research' studies.
- The amount of time and the flexibility this gives us allow for more working through of difficult issues. We are not confined to the linear 'ask the question then move on' structure of standard interviewing or discussion formats If something is interesting we can approach it from another perspective or have another go at it.

Here is a typical set-up for the session in which the group revisits the Breakthrough Zone customer experience:

In groups of four please attempt the following.
    'Please now take the time to recall and describe your own journey in the Breakthrough Zone. What we are looking for here is not your ability to remember all the exercises we did and what the outputs were: we already have that information. We want you to start from the day before the Breakthrough Zone, or even earlier, and recall anything that you remember about your inner dialogue as you approached this event.

    '"What did you think about it the day before?"
        '"What were your thoughts/feelings as you approached the venue on the first day?"

    'Taking this as your starting place, try to adopt the style of freethinking and allow your associations to wander over the two days. It doesn't matter if you change the order of events or find one thing mixing with another. We are interested in how the thing occurs for you internally. Ask another member of your team to take notes for you.'
    You should allot a time of 20 minutes for each person to complete their review. In our experience, people will probably get to the end of their first run-through quite

quickly – in five minutes or so. Soon after that other things will begin to come through and so they need to be ready to receive and report them. They may come in and interrupt ongoing thought processes. Ask participants to try to bring them out into the open quickly without worrying if you are making sense to your colleagues.

Another thing to do is suggest they go back over their first run-throughs and ask 'why did that have an impact on me?' for each of the key events there.

'When you dry up, invite your colleagues to ask you to talk more about anything that interested them. Do your best to accept and reply to their invitations. Ask them for help if you're stuck: what interested them? What aspect would they like to hear more about?

'It is also important to give your colleagues permission to redirect you if necessary. So, for example, if you get stuck at the level of describing behaviour they might want to know more about feelings. If you are bogged down in an emotional landscape they might want to know what actually happened next.'

After each foursome has completed their revue take a short break. Get people on their feet, move around, shift the energy but all stay in the room if possible. There is a kind of brainstorming effect which is desirable here as we push against the barriers of our defences and resistance to allow the deeper aspects of our experience into the room. Too many breaks in concentration may not help. The whole session should take about 90 minutes. But do not despair or worry if people need two hours. The facilitators can think of ways to co-ordinate activities between different groups moving at different speeds.

Once everyone has taken part it is time for a first attempt at generating from our reproduced material. Try this as a word game. Each member has to start a sentence with:

'I never realized that …' And then complete the sentence based on something they have realized from listening to the reviews of the Breakthrough Zone. Go as quickly as you can and then record your realizations until you have ten or more. Have another go after a break and see if you can get up to 20.

We have now reviewed the workshop and generated a set of realizations as outputs.

Step four – building the realizations

The next activity requires us to build with the raw materials we have at our disposal in order to generate more ideas from it. Go back into the same fours. Now each member chooses one of the realizations and starts speaking using the following phrase:

'If I had realized that, it would …'

and then completes the sentence and continues to talk as if the realization was his own. He must talk for at least two minutes. It might be a good idea to take notes of this process too. The aim here is to promote ownership of the realizations and to build them by taking them on board and starting to examine their consequences and the possibilities they create. You can try out some other leads in this exercise too:

> 'The main thing that would change if that is true is …'
> 'The belief I would have to give up in the light of this realization is …'
> 'The kind of people who might know about this are …'
> 'The thing that most surprises me in the light of this is …'
> 'One product that this realization calls for is …'

It is not unusual for a process of working through like this to yield lots of 'eureka' moments. Do not inhibit these, follow the Muse, but do return to the discipline once an idea has been born or something seems resolved. As a culture we are far too limited in our ability to work things through. This is why the same mistakes and misfortunes occur over and over again. We could learn from our errors but are too busy running from them to let the learning take root. We seek distraction or diversion almost immediately and in this insight process we are attempting to harness this impulsivity in service of the review of the Breakthrough Zone.

Step five – feedback to the group

We are now in possession of a great deal of original and reworked material and it is time to share this among the whole group. This process of sharing ownership acknowledges the right of the whole team to 'own' anything that is produced by the group and to develop it if it calls them. Allow the groups to choose what they wish to bring back to the main group. Give them a simple guideline:

> 'We would like to hear about anything that had impact in your work this morning, for whatever reason and anything else that you think we should know about.'

Building the listening

It is extremely important at this stage to build the listening of the whole group in the knowledge that we have a lot of new 'babies' in the room and there will be a great deal of vulnerability about, even if it cannot be seen. Take ten minutes to coach the group in 'listening for possibility'. By this we mean to show them how to adopt what is often referred to as open listening but to go one step further and ask for each thing that has impact on them – for whatever reason:

'And what does that make possible …'

A simple way to reinforce this is to set an exercise for the large group. After each group's feedback the other groups have five minutes to develop possibilities from the feedback. They must get at least three – one or more of which must be a new product or service.

By now you will have established enough faith and trust in you as a facilitator to carry the group in this exercise without further elaboration or explanation.

Lunch

Step six – a different perspective: visiting the gallery

It is always good practice both to ground your developments in customer needs and to look for existing realities that, when seen through your emerging insights and new distinctions, confirm their value. One of the techniques that we commonly use to support this activity is to take the team back to one of the key customer outputs. Often we use the art-from-within, both because it is so expressive and because it lends itself to opening up interpretations and new avenues of inquiry.

Immediately after the Breakthrough Zone we start to sort the pictures from the art-from-within looking for themes. We arrange them into groups based on these and type up some of the descriptions created by the customers to explain their work. Then, early in the morning before the Insight Zone starts, we put the pictures up in the room where people will be working. We try to arrange them in the most helpful and intelligent way possible.

Then after the steps where they have reviewed their own experiences, we invite the team to visit the gallery of pictures and notice what has an impact on them. After this we allow more time for their groups of four to discuss the pictures and any things arising from them.

Figure 7.1 shows an example of a picture generated by a participant in the Breakthrough Zone. It shows hands reaching out from an aircraft seat. It depicts the relationships and communities from which the passenger feels cut off and with whom he might need to be in contact.

Fig. 7.1   A passenger's desire to stay in touch while in flight.

Step seven – paradigm swapping

Earlier we referred to an analysis in the snack market which overlaid one paradigm onto another. If you recall it was the paradigm 'Real Food' overlaid with the paradigm 'Real Love'. So that you can use this type of analysis in your insight process we have broken it down into simple steps which you can adapt to suit your material. Here they are:

By this time your project will have generated quite a lot of ideas about things that are stuck or missing from your brand or product. You will also have a good deal of information about peoples' desires and ideals. These sources will include input from both your team and customers.

Examine these outputs and try to draw them into a set of distinctions. A distinction is a very useful tool for organizing perception: it is created by giving a name to a phenomenon or occurrence. Thus distinctions, like insights, are created not found.

Making distinctions is the perceptual tool that allows us to describe the world we experience. The world we perceive is exactly in line with what we are able to distinguish. Let's take colour as an example. Babies don't see colour. Colour has to be learned. In fact there is no such thing as colour, colour is electromagnetic waves of different lengths. Objects absorb energy according to their make-up, some materials absorb different wavelengths from others.

The light waves that are not absorbed are reflected and we can 'see' them. It is the absence of the absorbed wavelengths that have us perceive something as being of a particular colour.

But whatever the physics of it, once you have learned to see colour, once you have distinguished it, you cannot *not* see it. People have very different facilities with the distinction colour. Artists have a rich resource in this distinction, colour-blind people much less so. Although there is some agreement about the names of colours, its likely that we all see something slightly different when we look at things.

There are other distinctions than colour though. Emotion is a distinction. Love. Hygiene. Gravity.

Eskimos have 28 different words for snow. In their homeland being able to distinguish the type of snow they're in is a survival issue. Over here we only have one word for snow. Or do we? There's slush. And sleet. The point we're making is that the kind of snow you experience is determined by the distinctions for snow that you have available. Another example is the distinction 'anatomy'. While you and I may have a sense of our own bodies, it would be hard for us to perform surgery. We simply don't have the distinctions, nor do we have the practice at applying them.

Let's return to the idea of distinctions based on things that are missing for customers and the team. Here is an example:

For air travellers *space* is missing.

Now we expand the idea of space until we determine some ends of a continuum. Here is an example:

Confinement	**Freedom**
Cramped	Expanded
Trapped	Free
Withheld	Expressed
Barriers	Openings
Imprisoned	Released
Constrained	Unabashed

Next, brainstorm other continua that are related closely or distantly to your original, e.g.:

Confined	**Free**
Coralled	Open
Miniature	Giant
Packed	Strewn

Now we pick one that interests us, one that is not completely synonymous with the original.

Miniature	Giant
shrunk	stretched
chip	chunk
compact	enlarged
micro	macro
tiny	huge
tight	loose
visible	invisible
bud	bloom
cubby-hole	arena
detail	whole

Next we have shaded a couple of words that had impact on us: giant, enlarged and arena. We had never heard these words in this project before. Then we focused on one that interested us – arena – and started to *generate* with it.

'Your very own arena'
'a public or private arena'
'an arena for work, rest or play'
'a comfortable arena'
'your own fully configurable arena'

Something struck us about an arena being conceptually much bigger than a seat. What if we designed each cabin's available space from the concept of a 'fully configurable arena'? What if the seats that weren't occupied could fold away and serve some other purpose? What if the tray had edges to it that you could turn up so that they formed sides and things couldn't fall off? Soon a veritable stream of ideas about the cabin can be generated. This is a simple example of working with distinctions based on something that is missing and by stretching it, mining for insight.

As you will have noticed, this process also follows the basic steps for creative thinking:

- *Reproduce* – write down the things that were stuck or missing.
- *Generate from* – develop distinctions and continua from these.
- *Generate* – invent new product concepts for your product.

Step eight – building insight platforms

You will soon realize that when the Breakthrough Team generates a 'killer insight' or two, they can start to build these into whole new positionings, products or services. Here is an example of a customer speaking in the Break-through Zone during a session run for an airline:

> 'I was just thinking about a flight I had in the other morning. It was a great experience, I was fortunate enough to be in one of those beautiful sleeper seats and I slept all night. But unfortunately when I arrived in Gatwick I had about two hours to get into London for a meeting and I wanted to change my shirt in the worst way because I slept in it all night. There was no room on the plane, the loo was too small and so I ended up in the Arrivals hall in this little concrete commode trying to put a shirt on. When I got to the meeting an hour and a half later, the first thing I did was apologize for the way I looked. Actually it was the way I felt, simply because the last thing I remembered from the whole flight – which was a very enjoyable experience – was the changing of my shirt in a loo in Gatwick airport and it brought everything down to that as opposed to everything else.'
>
> Male international traveller

Putting this quote in context, it helps to know that we had spent much time in this particular Breakthrough Zone looking at check-in and on-board experiences. How could we make it all more hassle-free and enjoyable? Suddenly, in the room someone was speaking about an element of the journey which the airline had never considered itself responsible for – arriving. Arriving was missing. The truth of the matter, if this passenger was to be believed, was that the airline dumped its passengers the minute they left the plane. While they were welcomed into the flight with considerable courtesy and ceremony, they were left to fend for themselves the minute it landed.

This was a killer insight. It was from the review of this in the Insight Zone that the Arrivals Lounge was born. The first one was at Heathrow in London. Here are a few things that passengers have said about it:

> 'We're here on our honeymoon. We have to keep to our budget and so this is a real blessing. We can't check into our hotel until noon and so we shower and freshen up before going into town for a look around.'
>
> 'I got in at 5.30 this morning. I'm here to meet some chaps at 10.00. This is an ideal place to change my travel clothes for business and put the final touches to my documents for the meeting.'
>
> 'First rate, brilliant. At last someone is thinking about the passenger's journey from door to door. Well done!'

Remembering what happened on that programme, we recall how vulnerable and defensive the team felt about the criticism made by this passenger (a

New Yorker as it happens). What they had to go through to start the process of building their insight was to put away their own defences and denial:

> 'It's not our fault, every airline does the same thing.'
>> 'It's passengers' own responsibility to make arrangements for their arrival.'
>> 'Passengers don't want to be bothered, they just want to get away from the airport as soon as possible.'
>> 'You can't expect us to spend a lot of money on arriving when no-one else does.'

Then, suddenly someone in the team said:

> 'By the way, what time do our flights from the US start arriving in the morning?'
>> 'Six-thirty', someone replied.
>> 'Yes and there are flights arriving from about 5.00 am from other destinations', said someone else.
>> 'Where are people supposed to go at that time of the morning?', someone added.
>> 'What on earth do you do if you can't check in to your hotel until 15.00?'
>> 'What if you've come for a meeting and it doesn't start until 11 or 12 o'clock?'

All around the team it was beginning to dawn on people that these early morning arrivals left their passengers with quite a problem; one which the airline was apparently unconcerned about. Nine months later the Arrivals Lounge was opened.

In another Breakthrough Zone, conducted on behalf of a telephone company, one of the objectives was to help drive call volumes. How could you encourage people to use the phone more? During the Breakthrough Zone a very interesting role-play got started where we observed two people having an imaginary phone call. One thing became crystal clear; the listener had more influence in the communication than the speaker. If someone was willing to listen, the speaker would end up offering all sorts of interesting comments and opinions in order to keep up their end of the conversation. This was quite a revelation, particularly for the men in the audience. Many of them had viewed telephone talk as simply a means to an end. You said what you had to say as quickly and efficiently as possible and then put the phone down.

Building on this realization, the Breakthrough Team were able to conjure a scenario where a man rang home simply to listen to his three-year-old. The child makes charming but unintelligible noises into the phone, while dad who is on another continent, presumably on business, simply listens with a beam of delight on his face.

In another scenario a teenage daughter rings home from college. Her father picks up and straight away says, 'I'll get your mother.' The daughter says, 'Hold on, I want to talk to you dad!' Father's face shows puzzlement followed by delight as his daughter starts to tell him about her adventures. The campaign was supported by the copyline: 'It's good to listen.'

In process terms we often arrange the team into new groups for the work of Building Insight Platforms. We sometimes ask that these are groups who could meet again after the Insight Zone to develop and further their ideas if necessary. So it might be important to consider a mix with a varied skill base, competencies or experience. It is also important to consider how overseas members might continue to make a contribution too.

Once in groups, we set the primary task:

> 'Reviewing all the realizations and information you now have at your disposal, put yourself firmly into your customer side and ask, "What is the single thing this company could do that would make the biggest difference for customers, either in terms of overcoming a current problem, or providing something new that would meet customers' desires?" Then please devote the next hour to developing that opportunity. As you do so you will also expand the realizations generated by your initial insights.'

Thus begins the first stage of crafting insights into linked and related 'platforms' and building opportunities based upon these realizations. There are a number of aids or support structures that you can put in place to support this work.

- Sometimes we have an artist present who is very experienced and quick at realizing ideas on paper. He will draw up some of the group's ideas as they emerge.
- It is not uncommon for us to keep a set of construction materials close by so that people can build things if they need to.
- We have invited actors to participate in the Insight Zone to help role-play and characterize particular emotions, processes or communications.
- We have invited senior sponsors into the Insight Zone so that they may participate in the work as it progresses.
- We have made available a whole set of music CDs and magazines so that people can create Mood Boards, or atmospheric realizations of their ideas.

Step nine – review and new directions

After the afternoon break it is a good idea to take feedback in the form of a short presentation of their work from each of the groups. Once again use the 'listening for possibility' structure outlined earlier, where the listeners have five minutes to create contributions in the form of 'builds' on the groups' work. You will remember from one of the earliest processes in the Breakthrough Team event that developing what works rather than criticizing it is one of the core components of this innovation style.

We want to remind you that it is not easy to keep to this. We are so programmed to criticize that it is automatic. Our defences are invariably aroused by anything that shifts the status quo even if we did not like the way it was. The furore and sense of hostility to the London Congestion Charge is a classic example. Yet who has not complained bitterly: 'they need to do something about all this traffic!'

It is vital for the facilitators to stay vigilant and supportive – particularly of raw or emergent notions – at this time. Babies can look ugly when they are first born. The parents within the Breakthrough Team may be genuinely exhausted by the struggle of overcoming their own resistance. To walk straight into a wall of fire will surely extinguish any passion they have left. Be prepared to defend the emerging ideas and their protagonists and invite the critics to examine the intention and effects of their attacks. It is not as if our world isn't packed with funny or silly ideas. Who ever thought a fictional person called 007 would have turned into a worldwide industry? Or that hobbits would become all the rage, or Barbie, or Fruit Shoots, or Computer Pets? Come on. It might be a qualifying feature of anything that is to take the world by storm that it seems silly or even horrible at first. Who can now recall the vicious attacks on 'Yuppies with their mobile phones', that formed nightly articles on TV and in the newspapers? Do you have a mobile phone today?

You must learn to welcome all contributions. You really do not know if they are the ONE or not!

Once the insight work is done, there is one more extremely important job for you and your team to accomplish before you all go home. As strange as this might seem, you are all going to listen your way to success. How to set this up is fully explained in the following chapter.

Note

1   Rowland, G. (2003) 'The Slag of All Semioticians', MRS.

8 | Dealing with Cultural Resistance (The Listening Programme)

Setting up the Listening Programme

Insights are born of learning that is derived from the impact of something happening. Impact occurs unexpectedly. Unexpected impacts are noticeable to us only when we are open to them and willing to remain aware of them. Inquiry is one of the ways to make ourselves open to impact. This is what we have been doing in the Breakthrough Zone and onwards into the Insight Workshop. Only the people who were at the event will have experienced unexpected impacts there. But what of the people who were not there? How will you engage the people in the organization that you need to implement anything new and convince *them*?

There is a view in the world of naturalism that apes create culture by adopting ideas demonstrated by other apes. The ideas that work get adopted, and the ones that do not fall by the wayside. If this is valid, and cultures are an amalgam of ideas that work, we must ask, 'work how?' Working means that they suit the agendas of the people within the group. Ideas that stick will be those that support the most powerful agendas, and those that do not will be seen to be unsupportive and thus will be sidelined. You might think that a certain practice makes absolutely no sense whatsoever; yet when you try to change it to a more sensible one you will always meet resistance. The fact is that it meets someone's requirements otherwise it would not be that way. It may not be business-focused but, without doubt, someone's undeclared agenda will be serviced by it.

Changing a culture requires that you either sell it new ideas that support existing agendas, or you sell it new agendas. The latter is extremely difficult except where the organization is facing some kind of inevitable catastrophic failure. Then the need for a new agenda becomes the price of survival. In such circumstances the group must adopt a new agenda, often with great difficulty. But, ordinarily, organizations rarely change their overriding agenda without compulsion.

Let us imagine for a moment that you are travelling on an aircraft towards a new and exciting life in your dream location. It has taken years of planning and strategy. At last you are on your way towards your dreams. Without warning the aircraft inexplicably develops engine failure. The immediate problem has asserted itself whether or not you like it. How important is the colour of your new bathroom suite now? Any life at all looks better than hitting the ground at high speed. Survival is a powerful motivator.

The level of change you wish to create inside your organization will dictate the choices that you need to make. As a rule of thumb, the bigger the change, the more power you need. Like it or lump it, this is the way of the world.

The process you are now about to enter ensures that everyone in the team is involved in a programme of engagement and enrolment of the key movers and shakers in the organization. Before we go into the actual nuts and bolts of the Listening Programme there are some things that might help.

The nature of resistance

In Chapters 4 and 5 we established the existence of three broad kinds of relationship:

1   professional,
2   personal, and
3   private.

Let us recap on what these are and how they operate.

A *professional* relationship is based on transactions, for example if I do something for you, you will either pay me or do something equal in return. There is a mutual and hopefully beneficial exchange. This is the nature of the professional relationship. It is exclusively transactional, and normally excludes significant emotional expression of any kind. The contract is simple.

A *personal* relationship is based in communication about aspects of human life that are important to the individuals involved. Participants might share information about their children, about successes and failures, disappointments and aspirations. The contract is complex and usually undeclared, remaining latent in unexpressed hopes, expectations and fears. Certain forms of personal relationships are labelled in a way that suggests an agenda – a 'date' for example suggests a romantic or sexual agenda – but most are not.

A *private* relationship is one in which information that brings up strong emotional responses can be shared, for example bereavements, traumatic events and private problems. This is a relationship in which virtually anything can be said and anything can be heard without fear of rejection or humiliation. The contract in this case is dependent on ongoing experience of the necessary safety. You would stop sharing things in a private relationship where your confidant revealed all your secrets to all and sundry.

Generally speaking in the working environment the professional relationship is the one that prevails. On the surface it appears to be the least messy. Very often should anything personal or private arise within a professional relationship it will soon be stamped out; 'Let's keep this professional shall we?'

To be successful in the implementation of insightful innovation from the Breakthrough Zone, it is vital that you continue to form and maintain personal relationships within the working environment. So called 'highly political' cultures in organizations are those in which people's personal and private agendas are kept secret while everyone appears to be maintaining the professional agenda. If the only overt agenda is the professional one, it follows that everything else is covert.

> We *all* have personal and private agendas.

We *all* have personal and private agendas. These agendas contain our most important objectives for success in whatever it is that we do. Absolutely no one on earth goes to work for professional results alone. Success in the professional arena supports everything that is personally and privately important to us by paying our mortgages, feeding, clothing and educating our children, supporting our hobbies, meeting our status needs, etc. However, in the day-to-day working environment, what is personally important to us must be kept out of sight most of the time.

In Chapter 3 we described how power is invested by those with it, to those without it in order to get a profitable return. In fact everyone in every culture is an investor and on the whole the expected return on any investment is undeclared. Cultures are hierarchies of investors, and you are one of them which is one of the primary reasons you are reading this book!

Learning how to spot what is most important to both your senior and junior colleagues is vital in understanding how best to enrol them. What is most important to people is what runs their so-called 'hidden agenda'. It is hidden because it has no place in a professional environment; there is no room for it because it is 'unprofessional'. It may also be hidden because it is unpleasant, manipulative, driven by ambition, greed, envy or any of the other perfectly normal but less acceptable elements of our personal make-up. What return do they expect on their investment of effort at work? Unless what you are proposing to them includes the satisfaction of their hidden agenda, you are likely to have difficulties in persuading them to go along with your point of view. Lip service may be the best that you get.

The bottom-line question you need to be able to answer is 'What is it that you really want?' If you do not have the kind of relationship with them in which you can ask this directly and expect a straight answer, then you will have to find out by other methods. You will have to become a detective. What does their behaviour suggest to you that they want that might be difficult to own up to? Have they got a PA? PAs can be the most informative people of all if you can gain their confidence. On the whole, once they realize that you are genuinely on the side of their boss they are likely to be happy to help you understand what makes him or her tick.

What is their reputation? What about the gossip? Although it is rarely if ever worth much when taken at face value, there are sometimes trends and themes in gossip that can be informative. Gossip is based on projection: that is, we use it to attribute unpleasant parts of ourselves to others so that we can be 'rid' of them. So it is a distortion of reality but if many people buy into the same gossip about a person you might at least try out the idea that it has some validity. If the gossip were true, what would their hidden agenda be?

Find people that have a good relationship with them and see what they know about their preferences regarding new ideas, their history with innovation and what kind of things they have championed in the past. By developing as wide a profile as possible you will get to know something about their preferences and motives. The most powerful way to do this is to 'walk in their shoes'. See the world as they do as far as possible. Make sense of their ways by imagining that they are your own. What might lead you to behave like that? As you understand who they are and what fires them, you will learn to pitch new ideas in such a way that the benefit to them is taken care of as a by-product of your communication with them.

You might think this manipulative. It is to an extent. All influencing could be interpreted as manipulation. The hidden agenda is manipulative; if it were not it would be openly visible. It is one of the great open secrets of the power game that is modern business – that often what is going on is not what it seems. What is happening here is that you are growing and using your perceptive abilities to relate what you are doing to the needs, both overt and covert, of anyone who can lend authority to your project. The cancerous form of manipulation is that which seeks its own advancement at the *expense* of others. We do not advocate this as it is short-lived in its results, and leads inexorably to a breakdown of trust which is fatal to a breakthrough project.

All customers deserve us to seek out what they cannot admit they want and then create ways to satisfy them that are decent, legal and honest. These senior people are also your customers – they pay you for your services. They deserve satisfaction too.

Selling something risky to a senior executive who is just about to retire is likely to give you problems unless you give him or her some sort of relevant assurance. Handing the credit for success to an ambitious senior, having protected them from the consequences of failure, is likely to buy you loyalty and trust that you could not create any other way. It is just the way it is and relationships, as we always say, are the source of results.

Mastering this will also help you in your work with customers. Customers are driven by personal *and* private motives to purchase most things. Never forget that you too are a customer. The professional psyche cannot fully grasp the customer experience as it is always trying to work out the logic of the human being objectively. It can only watch customer habits and behaviours from a transactional perspective. You will need to do better than that; you will need to walk in the customers' shoes. At this stage what we mean by 'customers' is predominantly those to whom you must sell your new ideas.

Whether or not your company is in a period of stability, you can be certain that whenever you encounter cultural resistance to new ideas it is the result of someone's anxiety. They will be anxious because they will be unable to grasp how what you are proposing will affect their agenda. They may also be anxious and uncertain about your personal agenda. As we have suggested, the most powerful agenda is the personal one, and it will almost certainly be secret. However, once activated, it will spread its interpretation like wildfire. It will use the gossip grapevine to do this. If you do not enrol people, the anxious influencers certainly will. You need to move fast. Unless you are able to reassure their anxiety you will fail fully to enrol them.

There are many euphemisms in the corporate world for anxiety. Admitting fear to colleagues often feels like an admission of weakness or incompetence. On the whole, people will admit feeling uncomfortable or that they have misgivings, but they'll never admit that they are terrified; and terrified they will be, especially if you're proposing a real breakthrough solution.

The first lesson in dealing with resistance is not to take it personally. We do realize that it is personally hurtful and is often subconsciously designed to be so. Nevertheless, it will serve you to remind yourself that it is not personal to you, however personally targeted the tactics might be. Although it might appear that someone in a senior position is blocking you for the sake of it, or junior staff are undermining your recommendations, their resistance is their nervousness in action. It is not, unless you have an enemy on your hands with an old score to settle, driven by their desire to do you down for the sake of it. If you experience blocking or undermining you are sure to be in conflict with someone's personal agenda. Working out what this hidden agenda is and satisfying it will set you up to succeed.

The next thing is to understand something more about the nature of resistance. Figure 8.1 is a simple diagram that will help.

Each of the four boxes contains a method of resistance that all of us use to manage our anxiety to one degree or another. When confronted by something that makes us anxious we might revert to behaviours driven by any one of the reflex reactions named in the boxes:

- pleasing;
- avoiding;
- blaming; or
- plotting.

This 'Four-Box Resistance Model' suggests that there are four typical types of resistance to anxiety which show up as behaviours. Each of them is, in its own

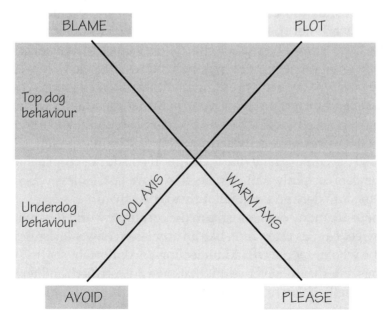

Fig. 8.1 Resistance to change: four common forms and their interaction.

way, a response to the anxiety that a call to change provokes. If you look at the diagram above, you will see how they are related, as well as some further ideas about their character.

Blame is a 'top dog' tactic and pleasing is an 'underdog' version of the same thing. In other words, blame comes from a high level of confidence and pleasing from a low level. Research shows that many parents redirect their anger and fear about their own problems at their children to whom they feel superior by dint of their seniority. However, the same people might never express anger towards their elderly mum, but disguise it by pleasing behaviours – dutiful visits, flowers, pleasantries, etc. Neither of these behaviours changes anything about the situation. What is interesting about them is that they are both visible to an observer and both have a warm or heated emotional tone.

If people start blaming others or trying desperately hard to please, you can be sure they're worried. They are indirect behaviours inasmuch as blaming rarely occurs to the person's face, whilst pleasing simply obscures and denies the issue driving the anxiety.

Blame never moves anything forward, nor does pleasing. Both maintain the status quo and are based on a belief held by the blamer or pleaser that they are powerless to do anything about the situation. They might actually be resisting acknowledging that they have power.

We have seen people blaming their boss in loud and certain tones, who suddenly realize that that same boss has entered earshot. In a microsecond a heated tirade becomes a smiling welcome, 'Oh, hi Dave, we were just having a cup of tea. Would you like one?' Moving from blame to please along the warm axis can be accomplished in an instant!

These two types of resistance are both overt. Once you know blame is in the air, or that you have the feeling that people are nodding and saying 'yes' to you without really meaning it, then it is time to bring out the biggest gun of all – listening.

We have already talked about our work with the large healthcare company. Their field sales force were extremely resistant to change. A new customer proposition was being implemented and the way sales were conducted had to change. We worked with them in a large group. We had been warned that they were the most cynical and 'difficult' bunch of people in the entire organization. In itself this warning was an example of corporate blaming based upon the senior management's fears of a rebellion in the sales force. The participation and commitment of the sales force were critical to the success of a new product, sales culture and strategy.

Our first action was to tell them what the customers had told us and what we had made of it. We then invited them to give us their most blaming and cynical views. They told us everything, enjoying themselves greatly as they did so. Next, we asked them how they would go about enrolling a cynical bunch like themselves. They then taught us what would be needed to overcome these problems and difficulties. One of the key insights was the need to inform their administrative support teams about the sales force's real needs. We listened to them as they did all the work and then thanked us for it! Not only that, they then taught each other how they could change their sales style to reflect the new customer proposition by sharing best practice and experience. They engaged and enrolled each other. We listened. The blaming became our greatest resource.

Listen to the people doing the blaming or pleasing to discover the nature of their worry.

Plotting is a top-dog strategy for influencing and manipulating. Avoiding is an underdog strategy where the plotter believes that his only power lies in going missing. Both of these strategies are covert. At the receiving end of these you are left with an uneasy feeling that something is going on but you can't quite put your finger on it. Confronting someone about it will usually lead to them telling you that you have a problem and that they are doing nothing at all. They are likely to portray a picture of innocence.

Plotting usually involves playing one person off against another. 'Well it isn't my point of view at all, but John is saying that you …', or 'Everyone else thinks that …' Self-appointed representatives giving you well intentioned information about what others are up to is a sure sign that you have a plotter at work. If their cover might be blown or their confidence wanes, then it is time for the plotter to hide. Symptomatic behaviours are: no answer to telephone calls or e-mails, and missing crucial meetings; they become difficult to find and pin down to any specific agreements.

The solution is to point this out without blaming them and, where possible, to discover with them what their main objections are. Remember that these behaviours are driven by anxiety. To reassure them you will need to access what they are anxious about. Until this is exposed, they will continue to plot or avoid. While this is happening, all their creative commitment will be diverted into obstructive games to block any innovation at all. Deal with it through listening. If you are listening and communicating with enough people with enough influence, you will find that some plotters will convert, whilst others will disappear completely.

We both remember going to a large organization for a board-level briefing preceding a large breakthrough initiative. We were told in no uncertain terms that the company needed 'a radical transformation'. We spent some hours listening to their commitment to change and all that was necessary to keep them at the head of their market. They were refreshingly convincing. When we broke to go to the toilet, one of the most vociferous advocates for radical change suddenly delivered a personal warning to one of us in an unmistakably antagonistic tone:

'We give people with new ideas two years around here. Don't expect this to go anywhere.'

Astounded by the directness and vehemence of this comment, we returned to the same meeting. This particular person continued to say one thing in the boardroom and be as covertly obstructive as possible outside … we could never get him to meet with us separately and he cancelled any attempts we created to listen to him. The mission grew and his influence diminished. He left the company shortly afterwards.

Do not forget to spot your own resistance when it occurs. It is as easy as falling off a log to sit with the team blaming, plotting, avoiding and pleasing all the people that resist you and your ideas. Watch it carefully. You must get to know your own patterns of resistance to anxiety, otherwise you will be a victim of them and convince yourself and the team of your powerlessness. Build power by doing the things that make a difference, not indulging in things that maintain the status quo.

While all of these resistances are perfectly natural – and we all do them from time to time – they will lead to persistence of the problems and delays in completing your mission if not dealt with where they exist. You need your Breakthrough Team to be aware of these and how they operate. One of the best ways of helping the team to work around them is to share this information with them, own up to your own favourite resistance strategy and invite other people to discuss theirs. Then expose the cultural favourites. It is important that these things are out in the open where they can be seen for what they are – indications of anxiety.

When encountering resistance in someone who is key to your project moving forward there is one turbocharged tool in your kit – *listening without resistance yourself.* This means that you do not try to convince them of the need not to worry, nor sell them your ideas. You just listen and include their worries. What do you do when you see one of the so-called 'mad' people in the street, the type who shuffles along muttering the same thing over and over again? Perhaps the reason he's doing this is because no one ever heard him? Once you let something land by listening without judging, the speaker is often freed from the anxiety. Trouble shared is trouble halved.

Conducting the Listening Programme

Having spent two to three days in an Insight Workshop, you will have privileged information. No one in the organization has access to the same primary data as you and your Breakthrough Team. It has affected you all enough to create new learning. You have shared a creative journey with your customers. Yet somehow you will have to communicate these findings to others. How can you do this effectively? The corporate reflex is to put together a PowerPoint presentation and try to inform everyone that way. But ask yourself for a moment, what happens to you when you are in a presentation of that type? Especially if it is all about something you weren't invited to. It's like looking at a pile of someone else's holiday snaps. It is tiring just thinking about it. You cannot get the power of the Breakthrough Zone process into a presentation.

Relationships are the source of results. Look at what you created with your customers in a weekend just by being in relationship with them in a different way, up to different things. This is what we are now going to set up for the team. Everyone on the team is going to get into relationship with the people who are most important to the success of your project in a different way, up to different things.

Relationships are the source of results.

Using a flip chart, ask the group to identify all the people in the organization who are absolutely essential to have on side in order to move forward, and list them: this is the 'A List'. Then make a list of the people who influence them: this is the 'B List'. Then make a list of the people that would be good to have on side: you have probably guessed by now that this is the 'C List'.

It is important to acknowledge some of your line-management protocols at this point as we do not want to start this process by upsetting a whole bunch of people. It may be that on the 'A List' there are people who you would be expected to communicate with through other layers of management. You must make sure that you get to listen to these people appropriately.

Everyone on the first two lists must be allocated to people on the team who have to invite them for a short chat. We suggest that they contact them to invite them for a half-hour informal meeting by appointment, at a location where their guest will be able to relax most.

The invitation should include some information about the agenda. 'We have been talking to customers about … I would really appreciate it if you could spare a half-hour to give me your thoughts about …' In the gaps, put in the questions to which you had no answers when you first met your customers at the Breakthrough Zone event. Thus each of the people in your lists is about to be included in the inquiry.

The session with them is an opportunity to listen to influential people in your organization on the topic of your STOP Statement. You will collectively hear about where they are in relationship to your realizations and insights. Some of these people on your lists will share some of your insights. This will be doubly good news because they are already enrolled in part in where you are going. In the fullness of time these people will need to be acknowledged as joint sources for the insight they have expressed. Those people on your lists whose thinking is further away from you and your team will need to be connected by other means – their points of view linked to the bigger results of your insight work. Remember that it is important to include doubts as well as certainties.

In order for this to succeed, you will have to acknowledge the anxious resistance in your own Breakthrough Team. It is likely that some of your team will be terrified of some of the influential people on your 'A List' or even the 'B List'.

It is important now that you and your facilitators admit your own anxiety when meeting important and influential people. This gives permission to the group to be open too. You have been together for long enough now to be able to broach these subjects with increasing ease. To get beyond any anxiety, ask the group the following question, and give them ten minutes to talk it through.

> 'What kinds of resistance (corners of the Resistance Model) will we use to avoid doing the Listening Programme? What are we most anxious about in doing this and how could it affect our success?'

We then split the large group into four sub-groups. We divide the room into four corners. Each corner is labelled with one of the four resistances in the Four-Box Resistance Model. And has enough chairs for people to sit on. The room looks like the model itself. Each group is asked to sit in one of the four corners and to role-play a discussion about the Listening Programme in the style of the resistance marked on the flip-chart; in other words, the group in the blame corner blames, the group in the plotting corner plots etc. We urge them to really mean what they say, even if they *are* making it up. We give the groups four minutes in the corner and then instruct them to change corners, adopting the attitude dictated by the new type of resistance on the sign.

When each group has had four minutes in each corner we ask each group to feed back the results. How would the group tend to resist the Listening Programme?

There is only one way to overcome the behaviours and habits of resistance that we know, and that is to spot it fast and do the thing that we feel anxious about. Always take the action that will make the difference as opposed to indulging the resistance that will maintain the status quo. We recommend that you collectively agree to support each other by:

- buddying up – people are paired with someone else;
- agreeing a deadline for completion of the Listening Programme;
- by each person establishing a date by which they will have set up the meetings;

- scheduling a 'buddy' check-up, during which each pair can confirm that they are on track with their part of the programme; and

- ensuring that you don't deluge the same person on your lists with many requests for meetings. Don't duplicate, it will make them nervous! It will also send a poor message about your teamwork and coordination.

Although people in the team may have all sorts of great ideas based on their insights, it is important to hold back right now until the community has been listened to. To evangelize at this point would be guaranteed to reinforce existing resistance. Moreover, evangelizing is definitely *not* professional. In itself this style of behaviour will create new resistance. The intelligence that comes back from the Listening Programme will give you more valuable information about where the organization is, relative to your insights, and will enrol more people through the time you invest in listening than any amount of going forth preaching or presenting. Wait a little longer, and your patience will be rewarded.

The team will need to complete this Listening Programme within one month, after which they must meet one more time before the next stage begins. At this final Insight Meeting decisions will be made about what to champion. You will need your report and analysis as well as your edited version of the film that was shot in the Breakthrough Zone. The film needs to be punchy, and reflect the themes that have been surfaced through the Insight Workshop. The report needs to be authoritative, simple and above all easy to read. It is worth a short diversion into each of these.

Editing the video

There are no short cuts to the video that you need. We will outline what you need to know in order to get the best results. If you have hired the right film crew and editor your results will be enhanced.

Now is the time to inform the editors of the video of the themes and shape required for the final video. It should not be longer than 15 minutes unless absolutely necessary. Remember that this is going to be the best evidence of what customers told you. The people shown speaking need to be customers, and if you followed our instruction to urge customer guests to present all the feedback in the Breakthrough Zone, then you will have plenty of useable footage. As a rule, do not include the wilder games or anything that might humiliate colleagues. Those were the means by which we accessed the most important learning, not the learning itself. When you are presenting the video to your senior colleagues they could easily discredit what they see as meaningless fooling around – they were not there. Make this easy for them to understand and be inspired by. We have, however, found it advantageous to include some shots of people moving about and playing the warm up games behind the opening titles, music, or during any dividing titles as they help to communicate the energy and passion with which people attacked the process. We have found that senior teams are impressed that their customers should have both enjoyed the work and exhibited so much enthusiasm for helping the company.

Ask the film company to provide you with a written transcript of the Breakthrough Zone film complete with time codes. Time codes are just what you might expect; numbers that indicate the time of recording over the whole two days. They allow you to identify a piece of film exactly, to the fraction of a second. As well as this they indicate which roll of video is being referred to. When two cameras are filming simultaneously (recommended) the time codes help match the two different shots of the same moment. This is invaluable.

Editing video requires that someone looks through the transcript for relevant comments, finds them on the unedited video tape by viewing it and then decides where the chosen fragment should start (In-code) and where it should finish (Out-code).

If you look at the sample fragment of the editing sheet in Fig. 8.2, you will notice that in the column marked 'In-code' there is a series of four pairs of numbers, each divided by a colon. The first pair on the left hand side denotes hours. The next is minutes, and the third is seconds. The fourth is different. It denotes frames. Video is shot at 25 frames per second. You will notice that in this column the number never exceeds 24. In the 'Out-code' column the time code has moved on in time. The hour is the same (03) the minutes have not moved on either (15) but the seconds have moved from 21 to 22. The number of

Shot no.	In-code	Out-code	Comments and identifiers
6	03:15:21:01	03:15:22:24	Woman in yellow - 'Want to be able to choose product elements I want...'
22	03:21:24:02	03:21:25:07	Melvyn - 'Please don't be so bossy...'
36	04:01:03:00	04:02:12:15	Man in pink shirt - 'Slug in my salad...'

Fig. 8.2   Sample editing sheet.

frames has changed as well, from 1 to 24. The total time for the fragment you have identified is nearly one second or 23 frames. On the editing sheet always mark an extra five seconds on either side of the actual clip you want. This makes life easier for the editor. When recording Breakthrough Zone events we ensure that all the cameras are synchronized with the actual time of day. This makes it easy to switch from one camera to another as you search for the best pictures. Then when you come to making your editing decisions it will be easy to find all the different angles of the same shot. If one camera has missed a desirable shot, another may have caught it well.

This initial part of editing is called the 'paper edit'. Once you have identified the clips you want in your video, then it is important to put them in some sort of order. We usually arrange them into themes, and have a separate editing sheet for each of the themes. It is helpful for the editor if you write a story for the video. What kind of introduction do you want? What will be the *hors d'oeuvre*? What will be the order of themes that you want to communicate? How will you end? What kind of rhythm do you want it to have?

We sometimes have a series of up to eight people just saying the same word in a very fast sequence to reinforce a key theme. One shot is rarely allowed to be more than 20 seconds unless it has something powerful to contribute to the overall impact of the film. Remember that the whole breakthrough process is reliant on impact. You will want the video to have an impact especially on those important people who were not at the event itself.

The 'Shot No.' column is there so that you can enter the order of the shots as you want them in the final video.

The editor will first do what is called a 'rough cut' or an 'offline edit'. This means that they will put together a low quality version of your choice of clips on cheaper equipment at a relatively low resolution. This quite simply minimizes the cost of the process. This will take a couple of days. When this is done you will be able to get a good idea of whether or not the video sequence is right, whether or not you have too much or too little of anything, and whether anything is missing. This rough cut may also be shown to the team for its approval. Be careful here, most people have not had much experience in creating films for their colleagues to watch and tend to make them too long. You might consult your investor. Once you have established a more accurate idea of what you want and made any necessary corrections or additions, your editor can then add the final 'bells and whistles', titles, music, any effects you might need, other camera angles (called 'cut-aways'), etc. When that is approved, they will then create an 'online version'. This is the high-resolution, high-quality version of your video account of the Breakthrough Zone and its outputs. Changing shots in this will be expensive, so make sure that you get all the changes you need made at the 'Offline' stage of the process.

Many editors are brilliant, and know all sorts of tricks that will add style and nuance to your film. Listen to their suggestions and consider their advice. If they disagree with something you are absolutely certain you want, then it is advisable to question yourself. You are more likely to regret overriding the advice of a professional editor than to be proven right.

You will help both your budget and the editor no end if your paper edit is clearly and legibly written out and you communicate as many or all the major changes you want to the rough cut to them in one or two goes. Remember, they are artists, and praise will count for a great deal with them – acknowledgement is the best route to a win-win. You will be a rarity in the corporate video world if you praise them extensively for their good work prior to any critical feedback and requests for changes.

Writing the report

The report on the Breakthrough Zone event will form one of the most important reference points as the project moves forward. You will have a number of concrete outputs from the Zone and these are most likely to be:

- a transcript of the video of the event,
- notes taken on the feedback and during the working groups,
- artwork or constructions from the creative sessions,
- flip charts containing the outputs from the various groups,
- photos taken during the event,
- insights from the Insight Workshop, and
- verbatim reports and recall from the Breakthrough Team.

One of the difficulties with large-group work, as with small groups, is the sheer volume of outputs. There is always too much rather than too little. It is vital for the analyst/report writer to revisit all of this data systematically and thoroughly in the days following the Insight Workshop.

During this time watch out for themes and their echoes in the data. Make a note of these and build a set of insight platforms from them. If they were true and valid, what implications would they have for the brand, product or service? As you do this a shape for the report will almost certainly start to occur to you. The shapes that we use most frequently are these:

1 a chronological structure which follows the pattern of events in the Breakthrough Zone;
2 a structure dictated by the questions in the Breakthrough Zone; or

3   a structure that describes the events in the Zone and then pro-
ceeds to an analysis and interpretation of them.

Our advice is to create the main detail of the report first. Based on the primary data, create a commentary and slot in quotes, art, diagrams or key bullet
points.

Then, the system we use is to reflect on this structure for a few days. We
carry it about in our minds, mulling it over and playing it back to ourselves. We
notice what keeps coming to the surface, no matter how trivial. Then, when the
internal pressure has built up, as it does when revising for an exam, we commit
our entire top-of-the-mind thoughts at that point to paper. Usually this can be
done in one session and forms the basis of the summary and conclusions for
the report. Often it is right first time. Sometimes it comes in segments rather
than as a whole and you may need to take a break or two while new things
surface. You can see too how this follows the basic outline of our structure for
creativity described earlier.

1   *Reproduce* the essential experiences of the Breakthrough Zone by
revisiting the primary data.

2   *Generate from* the primary data by writing it up in a commentary,
either chronologically or thematically. At this stage we are still
anchored in the original texts.

3   After a period of incubation, *generate* a text which bursts forth
onto paper. This text is a creative event, sourced as it is in the
experiences and outputs from the Zone but generated in a spontaneous flow after a considerable period of cooking up the raw
ingredients. It is a bit like creative cooking and the analogy is a
good one. You have the raw materials, you have reviewed the
recipe and then you put them all away and start at a bare chop-
ping board.

9 | Winning the Power to Keep Moving

Follow up Insight Meeting

You are now a month beyond your Insight Workshop, and you are in your one-day workshop with as many of your original Breakthrough Team as you can muster. They have been listening to the community and will have an enormous amount to say about the impressions they have picked up and what they have heard.

The objectives for your meeting today are the following:

1 Establish how near or far away from your insights are the people you have been listening to?
2 What is the bottom-line request, need or desire to be met in order to satisfy customers, expressed in a single sentence? How could that be expressed as a proposition to customers?
3 What already exists within the organization that contributes to the satisfaction of the customer request, needs or desires?
4 What is stuck and/or missing that constitutes an obstacle?
5 'Imagibuilding' possibilities.

We always aim to start this second Insight Meeting by showing the video of the event. The longer the time from the Breakthrough Zone Event, the more the customers will have dropped out of consciousness of the team. We also display relevant artwork from the art-from-within process, and any photo stills that might help to recall the spirit of the Breakthrough Event. Without fail the team are viscerally reminded of the relationships they formed with real people over their weekend together, and anyone who is experiencing the dulling of their commitment gets a much needed 'shot in the arm'.

After some short feedback about the video it is time to get on with the agenda.

The questions to ask are as follows. What have people heard from the organization? How are the people your team listened to positioned relative to the learning we have distilled from the Breakthrough Zone? Are they aligned or not?

By sticking several sheets of flip-chart paper together end to end you can create a long enough piece of paper to mark out a bar graph. Along the horizontal axis name the people that have been listened to, and along the vertical axis mark out degrees of alignment to a maximum score of 20. Although not the most empirically reliable of exercises, it does give you a rough picture of the current attitudes of the movers and shakers in your business community. This is important information as you move forward into the next phases of this process. Like any good consumer research, if you want to influence people, you need to know what your starting point is. This will help you to develop a strategy that will engage them.

Take some time to look at the result. Does this indicate anything that you need to be aware of? Are there areas of the business that are particularly aligned or not aligned? This alignment graph data will be invaluable later. Do not lose it.

Now it is time to distil your insights thus far into one single customer-centred statement that sums up their bottom-line desires or needs. In other words, what are you striving to satisfy in your customers? At this point we are looking at all the themes, the inventions and the learning, as well as the emotional and psychological glue that hold them all together.

Working with a company in the sanitary protection market their customers pointed out that nearly every word used to describe menstruation had negative, even derisory overtones; 'the curse' being the most common. Customers pointed out that periods were actually a sign of health but were treated more like a symptom of illness. The company took this on board and launched a Well Woman Week which was supported by radio programmes and a touring bus which visited supermarkets and village greens providing advice and information for women on health issues. The company also instituted a 'Well Woman' helpline that received more than a million calls in six months.

Service staff in hotels pointed out that customers often arrived after long and difficult journeys. In this exhausted state they could be quite unreasonable and rude. We helped the hotel chain to create a support programme for its own staff to give them somewhere to share their difficulties and get help from peers and colleagues so that they didn't have to carry the wounds of service on their own. This was part of the backup to a customer proposition that coming to this hotel chain was like coming home.

Customers who bought new computers were longing for simple procedures and accessible support. They wanted jargon-free conversations and technical assistance that didn't make them feel even more like idiots than they already did. They wanted to be regarded as useful junior members of the 'club' of computer literates.

Working with airline passengers over time we have noticed that behind all of the requests for configurable seating, more choice of food, more entertainment, more flexibility, lies a desire for autonomy in an environment where people are confined and dependent on the crew for their very survival. Restoring autonomy at every opportunity became the sole aim of the project from that point onwards.

In the private healthcare market we noticed that people wanted to experience reliable care throughout the process and in every interaction. If they had to claim, they wanted to be emotionally supported and to experience a trouble-free service. They wanted to feel confident about putting their lives and the lives of their loved ones into the company's hands. Quite simply, they wanted to be taken care of at a personal level. This was the psychological and emotional glue that held all their requests together.

Inform the groups that they will know when they have found the bottom line because it will be simple, human, and recognizable. What is it that your learning calls for? Now express it in a single simple sentence.

We find that doing this exercise is particularly effective in groups of no more than four. Each group will create individual nuance that will enrich your final sentence. Remember this is not a mission statement or vision, it is simply an expression of what customers are calling for. Find that and you are cooking. Even if you end up with four different expressions of the same thing, you can still use each of them in the next stage after this workshop.

Now imagine an organization other than your own – an imaginary company – whose sole task is to deliver products and services that fulfil this statement of needs and desires on behalf of customers. What kind of proposition would it make to its customers? How would it feel to do business with such a company? What might it be called? What products/services would it have on its menu? What might a customer-facing interaction be like? How would it inspire loyalty in its staff and customers?

Ask your groups these questions. Give them some time to discuss them and then to develop their results on flip charts and present them back to the wider group. Now ask the groups to revisit the STOP Statement. Ask them to reacquaint themselves with it, and to examine how this new guiding proposition will impact on the problem that started the whole Breakthrough Zone inquiry. Does what you have discovered deal with the issues as expressed in the STOP Statement?

In our experience you are guaranteed to have results which will solve the problem expressed in the statement. Use your STOP Statement to guide some adjustments to the wording of the new proposition to ensure that it is effectively targeted at the key issues. This is now your guide for action, and this is why we call it the 'guiding proposition'. It is your template for any design work in the development phase you are about to enter.

Now display the Corporate Impact Map and ask the teams to specify, where possible, the likely effect this guiding proposition may have on it. Where the objective problem is having an impact on the business is where this process must been seen to have a positive impact – it is where your success will be most measurable. What does the team think are the likely benefits to each of these affected areas of the business? This information will provide you with invaluable aids to enrolling your colleagues into supporting your inventions.

Once this is complete, ask people to regroup according to their functions. Should there be functions missing from this meeting, this is not a problem as they will be represented in the design stage. For now, what you have is all you need. You are going to ask them to audit the company, by looking for aspects of the culture that are already in place that would support this new guiding proposition. Again, give them time to be as thorough as they can be. The group will tend to want to focus on what is not there, what is wrong with the company and why. Point this out to the groups, and reassure them that you want an inventory of positive and contributory aspects of current reality. This increases the sense of possibility in the group, and you are going to need as much evidence of this as possible. It inspires action, and it lowers costs!

Once the groups have presented their work, solicit feedback about their impressions. How possible does it seem for this organization to redirect itself towards the ends outlined in the guiding proposition?

You are now beginning to distinguish the journey that you need to take your organization on. What your customers want is already clearer to everyone, and some of the things that are in the way are now visible. Usually we find at this point that people start to have creative ideas that they can implement at no cost just by tweaking what they already do. These small shifts can have enormous and beneficial repercussions. They will contribute to everyone's confidence in your findings, and reassure your investor. They also provide opportunities for your insights to prove their worth where it matters.

Building further on the last session, ask groups to answer in some significant detail the question, 'What is stuck in the way we currently do things that will be an obstacle to delivering such a proposition?' What you are asking for is a list of facts. What are the same problems that keep showing up over and over again? Where do they show up? This is what we mean by 'stuck'. It's a bit like having your foot nailed to the ground when you're trying to move on. Caution the groups not to fall into the trap of problem-solving at this point. All you require them to do is to identify and make a note of anything that is stuck, not how it got to be that way, or whose fault it is. Once the list is done, ask them to highlight any stuck issues that would be easy to unstick immediately and at no cost or low cost.

When the group finishes their lists, ask them to present once more. What you have now is an emerging picture of how resourced your company is to support where your customers want you to go, and how existing reality both contributes to, and blocks, the way there. In any creative endeavour it is essential to see reality before you start to create anything at all.

Having generated all this data, now comes the fun part. We ask people to divide a flip-chart page into three columns. The column on the left is labelled 'run-of-the-mill', the middle column is labelled 'good fit', and the right-hand column 'out-of-the-box'. We now want people to invent new products and services for the imaginary company and its guiding proposition. We want these products and services to be as ordinary or outrageous as people can generate in the knowledge that we are not committing to anything particular yet. In order to create the ideas we will have to allow and value the worst ideas as well as the best.

None of the ideas at the moment has to fit inside the existing organization, but must reflect a company that is totally dedicated to the delivery of the guiding proposition you invented earlier. All the ideas must be represented in the list, however wacky or boring they may seem. What you are particularly interested in is the centre column. What ideas sit there? Which fall into a category that might fit your existing brand and cultural spirit, or stretch it in ways that would benefit both your business and your customers?

Now it is time to 'imagibuild' your favourite idea. The word explains exactly what we mean – imagine it as if it is already there, and now build it into an experiential representation or prototype that details as accurately as possible everything you imagined. Leaving nothing out, build it into a role-play if it is service-based, or build a physical prototype of the product. As a facilitator it is important to keep the instructions simple here. The more complex you make the task, the more of the groups' creative energy will be diverted from their 'imagibuilding' and invested in responding to the rules. Ask them to prepare something that will allow the whole group to experience the spirit of the product or service. Tell them to have fun too. This will free them to explore spontaneously and allow them to be more liberally creative.

Once these have been presented back to the group it is time to wind up. This Breakthrough Team have been through an extraordinary series of events. They will have given up an enormous amount of their own time. They will have taken risks, and formed relationships with each other, some of which will last a lifetime. It is important that they have a chance to finish well.

We always run some sort of ending ritual. Often this can be a simple as asking people to stand in front of the group as they did that on that first session in the Breakthrough Training, just to look and then to see if they have anything that they want to say in order to feel complete. Although this might feel non-essential when there is so much work to be done, in practice it can be an extremely powerful and significant experience for people who have invested their hearts, minds and creativity into this unusual process.

When summing up, be sure to ask them to support the whole process by speaking well of it to others in the organization and by being advocates for whatever is implemented in the future. Request that they keep listening to people in the business, that they implement whatever they can that will make a difference and that, above all, they identify successes and report them to you so that you can incorporate this information in communication with your investor

After appropriate thanks and acknowledgements, it is time to say goodbye and assure people that you will keep them informed as things progress.

The Breakthrough Team has fulfilled its function at this point. The research and discovery phase is now over and the process moves into development towards implementation. You have everything you need. You have:

- Your STOP Statement.
- A Corporate Impact Map and list of benefits.
- Outputs from the Breakthrough Zone.
- Insight-based learning evidenced in:
  - video format;
  - analytical report; and
  - physical outputs (art, photos etc.).
- An alignment graph indicating initial impressions of the current internal climate relative to your insights.
- A customer-led guiding proposition.
- Audit material – what already exists that supports or obstructs implementation.
- 'Imagibuilt' possibilities.
- An engaged team of advocates.

This is an impressive and powerful set of outputs. Well done for getting this far. The intelligence you have generated would be invaluable to your company

WINNING THE POWER TO KEEP MOVING   185

even if you went no further. Give yourself a pat on the back and take a deep breath before you move on. Stick with it, and follow the steps. We are going on to even greater heights together.

Now it is time to go with your results to your Internal Investor for permission to conduct the first stage in development – draft design.

Resources for the follow-up Insight Workshop

All the usual principles apply for space, comfort and accommodation:

- the space should be twice the size necessary for the number of people;
- flip charts – one for every four people;
- Sellotape or masking tape;
- plenty of notepaper and pens;
- the video and video player with a decent-sized television screen; and
- a good lunch.

Presenting to your investor

It is time to inform your investor how you spent their money and used the power they divested to you, and to make your recommendations about the next steps. Remember that they want you to return an increase in power to them – what is the return on their investment at this stage? What can you put into their hands to increase their potency? What political currency can you bestow through your learning thus far?

You will probably know best how your investor likes to receive their information. Some of them expect a PowerPoint presentation, some a relatively casual chat. Some like to invite peers along to be included in the decision about whether or not to continue and how. How far has your investor stuck their neck out? The further it is, the more vulnerable they will feel. Bear in mind what your best assessment of their personal agenda might be. Consider this as you prepare your presentation to them, and construct it to feed them what they most want whilst remaining true to the insights.

Show the video and then present your learning to them bearing in mind that they have not been part of the experience you have had. You do not want to present them with an impossible task, but walk-able avenues to greater success. The most powerful tool you have is your customers and what they have said. Make sure that any claim you make about what customers want can be

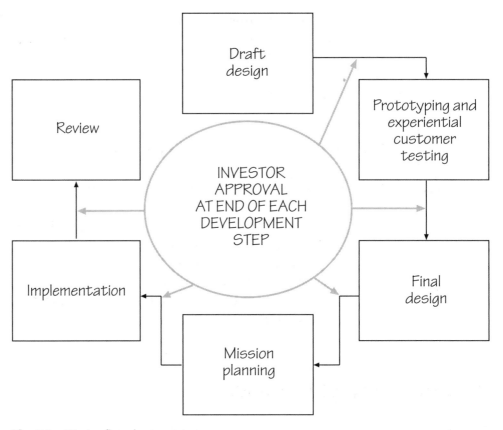

Fig. 9.1   Mission flow chart.

substantiated visually. Make sure that your seminal insights are clearly and simply supported by what you show them.

The underlying purpose of this presentation is to indicate that further investment in the process on which you have embarked is worthwhile.

Present them with an overall picture of the stages of this next phase (Fig. 9.1).

Each of the boxes in the flow chart indicates the activities of one development stage. Between each of the stages there is a presentation of results to the investor and a request for the power to continue to the next stage. The most reassuring aspect of this approach from the investor's perspective is that budget is released in stages too. There is an opportunity at each stage for the investor to pull out or continue. The agreement to continue is clear and costs are measurable. This means each time you consult your investor you are asking for the power to complete the next stage only. The process will not run out of control. Each step is outlined clearly and simply, the results informing the ensuing stage. This is a recipe for an increased sense of control for the investor and accountability for you and your team.

So, at this point, the next stage that you wish to finance and be empowered to complete is the *draft design process*. To accomplish this you will need a team of five people as well as yourself. This is your *Breakthrough Engagement Team*. One of the people on this new team will need to be someone who is trusted by your investor. Their job will be to report back to the investor independently of you. This will give your investor two sources of information about what is going on and its feasibility – you, and his appointee.

The remaining four will have very specific roles to fulfil which we will describe in the next chapter.

As well as this you will assemble a separate design team representing each of the company functions involved in delivering any new products or services emerging from your discoveries thus far. You will want them to have a substantial amount of time together to build a full picture of the products and services that your organization might choose to deliver to meet the desires and needs expressed by your customers. They will not be briefed to work out how they could be implemented, but simply what they might be. The amount of time they spend away together will depend on how far you want to go. The bigger the breakthrough your company requires, the more time this cross-functional design team will need. The team will need to be off-site, with their mobile phones switched off, released from their normal daily duties so that they can concentrate on this detailed task.

Your investor might need to know now what the further stages of this process will be, so we suggest that you finish reading this book before proceeding, so that you can explain this fully.

You are asking for the authority and budget to create a team consisting of five people plus you, as well as a cross-functional group of experts from relevant departments to work for a period of time exclusively on designing products and services that will meet the needs of your customers. When the draft design is complete, you will show it to your investor before proceeding any further.

It is a good idea to have this request for authority in written form and ask them to sign it. A signature signifies their commitment and represents a formal contract. The request for a signature encourages them to make sure that they are absolutely clear about what they are agreeing to and for you to do so too. It almost invariably surfaces all the objections and vulnerabilities so that they can be factored into the process as you go. Without this level of clarity you will be hampered by uncertainty as to the scope of your permission. All too often projects in business are fuzzy in their objectives, and either over-controlled by sponsors or liberally under-supervised. All of these factors lead to uncertain parameters for the team charged with the project, as well as varying degrees of paranoia and general anxiety for all concerned.

Using this method you will be aware of how much power you have, and what you have been given permission to use it for. We have often come across business cases to support developments that are based on pure guesswork, with numbers that have been pulled out of thin air merely to get budgets signed off. Aside from being dishonest, it creates stress for all concerned as people run around desperate to make the numbers work.

Knowing what is yours and what is not creates the best foundation for each stage in development to succeed by delivering on its promises.

Good luck. See you in the next chapter.

10 Beginning the Mission

Project or mission? – Building the new team

Congratulations on winning the next tranche of power to continue to the next steps in this exciting journey. The first thing to do, if you have not already, is to establish a physical home for your Breakthrough Mission.

In these days of 'hot-desking' and shared offices, fewer and fewer people in organizations have a space to call their own. Projects that do not have a geographical location or a territory, however small, struggle to exist. Once people throughout the business are in action they will need somewhere to refer to as home. Without it everything they do will get caught up and confused with everything else they are already doing. The boundaries will get fuzzy and all too quickly your precious efforts will become lost among routine activities. Rarely is a 'virtual office' sufficient for a real world mission. Real world space is almost certainly required.

Find somewhere and call it the Mission Centre. It should be big enough for you to have meetings in. Why 'Mission Centre' you may ask? The words that you use have a significant impact not just on the way others see you but also on your own relationship with your work. One of the reasons why the world of business has to keep reinventing its vocabulary is that words lose their power over time. Everyone gets used to them and they are integrated into everyday speech. As their use becomes more widespread, their impact is less singular. This is not an argument in favour of jargon, simply an argument for calling things by names that distinguish them and then using those names much as we do when we name children. Every few years or so, the favourite names for children change and it must be so if we are not to become engulfed in Kylies, Darrens or Sophies.

In business let's take the example of the word 'project'. In your organization there will be a metaphorical box inside which any and every thing called 'a project' will be put. Your company will have its own set of expectations of anything called a project. Personally the word inspires us with instant fatigue. It's a kind of business 'Kylie'.

A project usually means having to continue to meet the demands of your day job as well as a whole bunch of new stuff for the project. We have already mentioned the Australian company that spoke the word with a chuckle because no one believed that any project would go anywhere successful. We do not want our endeavours caught up with that kind of attitude before it has even got off the ground. It is a lightweight word.

We want to stand out from that crowd. Being on a mission has a different energy to it from running a project. Whether or not the name gets lampooned or taken seriously, it will be talked about. Lampooning is evidence that what you are up to has been noticed. Follow the process and it will prove its worth.

Most often, people name their projects after the product or service being invented, for example 'the Customer Delight Project'. In this example we would change 'project' to 'mission' – and Bob's your uncle.

So you have a mission and a home for it. Now you need a new team.

The Breakthrough Engagement Team

There are a number of essential roles that are required for the fulfilment of any innovation. The people who perform these roles will form the heart of the mission as your Breakthrough Engagement Team. They are:

- engagement manager;
- reality supervisor;
- design team leader;
- internal marketing manager;
- internal clients' consultant; and
- administrative assistant.

Engagement manager

One of the main barriers to the success of projects is poor definition of roles, and ineffective communication. The term 'project manager' suggests to us that the role involves the caretaking of processes, events and deadlines. The project is a thing and the manager manages it.

Well, unsurprisingly perhaps, we do not see it that way at all. Remember our principle *that relationships are the source of results*? It is relationships that need to be managed, cultivated and nourished. Someone needs to be in charge of this function. This is the optimum role for you as Mission Leader.

Your Breakthrough Innovation Mission needs someone who can hold all the relationships together. This is the best way to build the desired results and make sure they are focused on predefined objectives. The role of the engagement manager is the creation and maintenance of engagement. Everyone involved needs to remain engaged, not just with the necessary tasks, but with each other, the solutions, the customer, and contingent business realities. Keeping everyone engaged and pointed in the right direction is the primary task for our engagement manager.

Reality supervisor

Innovation can often lead to wishful thinking, and that can be the death of even the best-laid plans. Having someone on board with permission to ask the testy questions is your best insurance against this happening. The reality supervisor should be the person appointed by your Internal Investor(s). This may seem like a rather depressing idea at face value, but the benefits to your relationship with your Internal Investor will be manifold. The job is simply to keep a check on reality. Is that technology available? Can this product be distributed? Who might want to sell it? Will customers pay for this premium service?

As you get closer to implementation and the budgets increase, being able to prove that your project is feasible will be a key. Knowing what questions to ask and to answer will be the difference between confidence and anxious white knuckles. Although having someone around asking the questions as you go along will inevitably be awkward from time to time, you will be better prepared to meet and reassure your Internal Investor when you need to.

Design team leader

As the mission progresses there will be increasing demands for accuracy in design of whatever the Breakthrough Innovation will be. The design is for the finished article, i.e. the product or service that will be implemented. The design will develop from an initial thought, doodle or sketch, through to a prototype for customer testing, and ultimately to its finished form. This will then be incorporated in the Breakthrough Innovation Plan. No plan can be detailed until this final picture has been scoped out.

The design team leader needs to have facilitation skills as he or she is going to be metaphorically locked away with a cross-functional design team on two significant occasions in a catalytic role.

Internal marketing manager

Informing the wider community about the process as it gains momentum will be essential for success. All too often resistance in front-line staff and managers is created by ineffectual internal communication strategies. People who are running the core operations value efficiency and predictability and do not welcome surprises. Creating an effective communication strategy is of paramount importance. Without it, at the very least, you will appear discourteous.

Internal clients' consultant

This person is charged with preparing the staff who will deliver whatever the innovation is, collecting their advice and input and helping them assess and communicate their needs and requirements in terms of resources, training, etc. The internal clients' consultant and his team must be the sole consultants to the internal clients. They will present the designs at each stage to representative groups of internal staff for their feedback. This feedback will in turn be presented to the design team who will factor it in to their work.

Administrative assistant

Any venture of this nature will require administrative support, and this person is responsible for taking minutes, constructing reports, organizing the venues for meetings, communicating with the team and all administrative duties.

These roles are summarized in Fig. 10.1.

These are the people on your Breakthrough Engagement Team. Your collective job is engagement through all of the stages of the Breakthrough Mission. That is your primary task. Everyone else will be busy building the future – you will be in service to them in as many ways as are needed. Choose each one carefully, and take especially good care of your reality supervisor. He or she will be a crucial link between you and your Internal Investor.

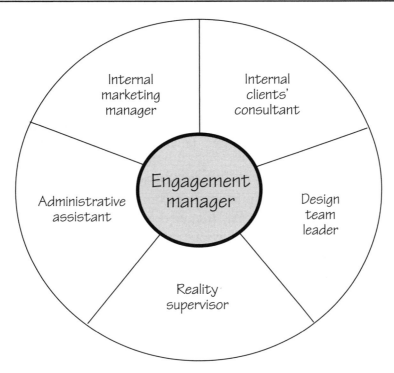

Fig. 10.1   The Breakthrough Engagement Team.

Getting started

You can be sure that what you have been up to will be being talked about. Several factors assure this. Firstly, this is an unusual approach to development and innovation. Unless you have worked with us before, your company will almost certainly have used normal market-research methods. To co-create with a group of customers and to take this amount of time in doing so will be unprecedented. The second factor is that you and your team have spent a great deal of time listening to people around your organization. The conversation has already started, so you are not starting from scratch.

You may need your investor's influence to assemble a team of experts who represent each element of the business on your Corporate Impact Map, as well as any other departments whose knowledge will be essential to the design and development of products and services that meet the requirements of your Guiding Proposition.

At this stage you do not need the people who will be charged with the actual delivery of outputs from this first development stage. This is your initial design team. It is made up of a group of expert people from within your company who have time together to design products or services that deliver things that satisfy the customer needs you have distinguished in the Breakthrough Zone.

How you implement it – the Mission Plan – comes later. The team needs to be taken out of mainstream activities for a significant period of time, off site, and comfortably housed. This time away is, of course, the major cost of this stage. Only once you have the team assembled will you be able to accurately quantify the cost.

Their most important instruction must be 'Make it possible'. If the customers want it, it is up to the team to deliver something that satisfies their desires and is profitable.

Dr Bruce Tuckman of Ohio State University distinguished a useful set of stages which every group trying to accomplish a task goes through.[1] Our experience has indicated clearly that work groups formed inside organizations tend to be limited by the behaviours associated with each of these stages unless they have a facilitator who can guide them through. The time allotted to the group needs to take this into account.

Forming

individuals who are not accustomed to working together as an established team tend to pair up and make associations as quickly as possible in order to feel safe when they first meet. Very often these associations break down speedily as they are usually cobbled together expeditiously rather than judiciously. This early stage is characterized by a 'buzz' in the air of nervous chatter and excitement, jokes and light interaction. In an endeavour where competing ideas, points of view and negotiation are going to prevail, this level of relationship will not get the job done. In this stage individuals demonstrate a high level of dependence on the facilitator, asking questions about the purpose, methodology, timing, task details, ground rules, etc. At a certain point, once enough direction has been received from the facilitator, the group tends to move into the most testing stage of all.

Storming

During this stage, hostilities of various kinds will break out. There will be arguments over details and principles, silent sulky faces, sudden changes of direction and a feeling of tension and chaos. The facilitator is likely to feel frustrated and anxious, and is likely to try to smooth over what might seem like animosity in the group. This may not work. Nobody wants to be powerless in a group, and at this point people are starting to carve out a place for themselves within it. They jockey for position, test the rules, question process and method, and disagree with each other and the facilitator apparently for the sake of it. Coming to agreement about anything is difficult. At this time the only stable point is the brief with which the team is charged. Whoever facilitates this process must remember that:

- Storming is necessary for the development of a fully functioning team.
- They personally are not the target of the challenges, although it may feel that way.
- This stage will pass, however unnerving it might be. Compromises might be necessary, but not at the expense of the objective of designing the product or service that most closely matched the insightful learning from the Breakthrough Zone. The group gradually settles into agreement about those things which can be agreed, and allows incongruities to remain without their preventing further progress. This marks the beginning of the next stage in the group's development.

Norming

Roles and responsibilities get clarified and starting points emerge. People begin to respond to facilitation. The energy and commitment of the group begins to rise. People relax and find that their sense of humour returns. Agreeing their process for working and their working style is now easier and necessary compromise comes without struggle. The facilitator will find that the group starts to take over some of the leadership requirements of the task. It is essential that the facilitator is not threatened by this, but allows it. It is a healthy sign that the group is taking ownership of the task. The facilitator's role now shifts into enabling the group and its sub-groups, maintaining an awareness of schedule and timekeeping, and reminding the group of its objectives should it stray too far from them. The group can now move into its next developmental phase.

Performing

Now the team can fulfil its purpose. It has accepted its task and developed some clarity in its operations. It has a shared purpose and has built the relationships which enable it to handle what it will take. It is possible that the group may slip back into storming over new issues when they arise, but it is likely that they will be resolved with increasing speed. The facilitator can expect to be required to delegate tasks to sub-groups. Keeping the team on task and moving in the required direction is his/her role as opposed to instructing or assisting.

Professor Tuckman has shown in his research that to deliver results both individuals and teams require what he calls 'attitude, strategy and drive'. Drive, he asserts, is increased by introducing and conducting tests.

The 'tests' that we have found to be most effective are those imposed by the Corporate Impact Map ('Does what you have designed alleviate or solve these issues?'), the STOP Statement ('Does what you have designed solve the objective problem?'), deadlines ('Can you get this done within the next 30 minutes?'), and conducting presentations, which inevitably pitch one sub-group competitively against another. Ongoing testing is essential. Without it the team will lose its drive and focus as sure as night follows day.

At the end of their time together they must present their designs to as senior a group as you can muster including your Internal Investor. This is a critical meeting, as implementation and success will depend on the approval of this senior group. As the engagement manager you should have spoken with all of the visiting members before this meeting and passed their interests and concerns onto the expert team.

The initial design must explain what the product or service is, how it works, some educated ballpark costs and the customer benefit. The expertise in the team needs to have its say through the design – what kind of marketing does this call for, sales style, customer relationship management, reward schemes, what should be on the menu, how should the support systems work, the administration be linked in, etc.?

The final process for implementation should not be the concern of this design team at this stage, although some initial impressions about how it might happen could be useful should time permit. Some issues will need to be examined for feasibility, others need to be left for future consideration.

On a Breakthrough Mission for an insurer the underwriting problems had to be addressed at this stage, as changes here were essential to make possible the substantial requests that customers had made. Redesigning the way risk was assessed and costs applied were crucial dependencies in the initial design process. Without it nothing else could work, and leaving it to be ironed out later was not an option. Conversely, whether or not the sales force would like the new products or not did not need to be talked about yet.

When completing the initial design process, as with your Breakthrough Team, it is vital for the maintenance of goodwill towards your mission that you end well.

Bad endings lead to bad feelings, and your mission needs as much goodwill as it can create, because when it gets to implementation, however much you try to avoid it, resistance will surface and can make or break your success. Have a party. Creating anything new is like giving birth – it takes effort beyond our normal output of energy. Celebrate what has been created. Charge your internal marketing manager with ensuring that the initial design team are kept up to date with progress reports as to how their new 'baby' is growing.

Once the design process is completed, it is time for your administrative assistant to collect in all of the outputs and record them all. Charts need to be reproduced electronically; products, services and menus recorded. A presentation of the product or service design needs to be created so that it can be shown and explained to other people whose enrolment you will need.

It is not quite time to return to your Internal Investor for anything more than a progress report, as there are two more things for your Engagement Team to do before you go to the next stage with confidence. It is time to do some communication and research.

Note

1   Tuckman, Bruce W. (2000) *Using Frequent Testing to Increase Students' Motivation to Achieve*, The Ohio State University Press.

11 | Internal Consultations and Final Design

Communicate, communicate, communicate

 Here are the three most important elements to your mission's success: communication, communication, and communication. Any change process requires more, not less communication. If your programme of events has occurred according to our recommendations there will already be rumours rumbling around the company.

Your communications strategy is now due. Rumours can become expensive, and although right now is not the time to unleash a full-blown internal marketing campaign, touching the parts of the business that are going to be touched by your mission is crucial.

We suggest that all missions develop a new method of reaching the community they will effect. Intranet or Web-based communication for general consumption is generally not enough. Most non-IT people use the Web for e-mail and very little else. Anything that requires effort beyond the call of their daily duties is liable to be ignored. There is no challenger to direct human contact at the top of the hierarchy of effective communication. Relationships are always the source of results. In all communication get as close to personal contact as you can. Always take the option that is closest, however far removed it might seem in practice.

Now it is time to activate your client consultant for an initial raft of internal consultation. There are two fundamentally important bits of research work to complete.

First, there will be areas of the business where people will be crucially affected by the type of developments that are emerging. They need to be given a chance to affect the invention process. The Engagement Team needs to prepare a compelling presentation that:

- informs internal staff about the Breakthrough Zone results,
- inspires them to participate, and
- allows them to contribute to the design before it is chiselled in stone. This will help them take ownership of the innovation. When people can see their part in the creation of something it makes it easier for them to accept the changes necessary to support it.

At this point it is important to say that the size of your organization will have some influence on the level at which you conduct such internal research. Smaller organizations will require less effort. The larger your company, the more extensive must be your consultations. Remember the key task for the Engagement Team is to engage the company in the development and implementation of things created in the mission. This is an 'engagement strategy'.

We would advocate that you create a series of half-day meetings to which people from all functions in the business that will touch the new product or service are invited. These meetings must pull in representatives of both the areas of the company included in the initial design process and especially those areas not included. They must be given the space to contribute too.

The sessions must inform, inspire and invite those who participate. The information needs to be complete, but easy to pass on to other people. Show them the video from the Breakthrough Zone. Give them simple handouts with six or seven bullet points that summarize the Breakthrough Zone learning. Take them through the initial design and share with them the implications that you are aware of. Invite their considered feedback.

Then use the most important tool in the tool kit – listening. Listen to what they have to say to you. Some of it will probably be resistance, which, as we have said before, is a manifestation of anxiety. They might storm for a while. Let that blow itself out. Listen out for key learning that will contribute towards the mission. As we described in Chapter 8, asking people to use their cynicism as a guide to the things that could go wrong so that they can be put right is extremely effective. Rather than resisting their scepticism, invite and include it. It's not only a great tool to get people into action on the job in hand, but it can expose potential obstacles before they have a chance to do any damage.

As well as informing, inspiring and inviting the community to get on board, you are also gathering invaluable data, all of which will need to be considered in the final design. Harnessing the expertise and experience of the wider community means that everyone wins – especially your investor and ultimately the most important person of all, your customer.

Second, your company will have its established preferences for research methods. However much you might be wary of conventional methods, a culture's appetite for research delivered in ways that it has learned to trust cannot be bypassed without causing enormous fallout. Resistance here is likely to undermine confidence and affect what you propose further down the line. Anyone you sideline will likely become an enemy; or at very best a bystander. Include everyone you can.

> Harnessing the expertise and experience of the wider community means that everyone wins – especially your investor and ultimately the most important person of all, your customer.

Already you have concepts, product and service ideas that you are championing. Give your market research department, if you have one, a role in testing some of the high level ideas using their most trusted methods. If you are worried about this, remember that customers helped you to surface the learning you have been developing. If what you have done thus far has remained faithful to what they told you, then your suggestions are likely to do well in research. Should they expose weaknesses, then now is the time you want to know what they are. Invite them to do their stuff, and again use your most powerful tool and listen to their results.

The last thing that you must do before you meet with your investor is to bottom out the performance targets for this innovation. What must it deliver and how will that be measured? The answers to this question must contain antidotes to the issues exposed on your Corporate Impact Map. They may be expressed in terms of customer satisfaction scores, sales volumes, revenue, profits, brand loyalty, or retention of staff and customers. The most appropriate criteria will emerge depending on the type of innovation involved. Until we have the final design there is not much point in a thorough cost-benefit analysis or finance/capital budgeting. Once you have specified the form and size of the result you can choose how you quantify costs. For now you must get permission to go ahead to the Final Design.

With the initial design, together with the data from your internal and external research and the performance criteria for the new product or service, you have enough to brief your investor fully and request that he empowers you to conduct the next piece of work. If things have not gone as you hoped, you also have another opportunity to stop and review the innovations at this stage.

Remember, as always in contractual matters, be clear about the agreement you are making. You only require the amount of budget necessary to produce a final authoritative design. You are not going to take it any further before you return to your investor with the results. Maintain their sense of control and you will keep their confidence. And especially remember, that a signature means business! Get one.

Final Design

This is it. This is the most authoritative 'imagibuild.' It will give your organization a blueprint for its forthcoming innovation. This is the launch design for the product or service. The idea is that the recommended result must be 'faultlessly buildable' from the design created here.

For this to work, the best expertise must be available to join the team. The Initial Design Team may have included enough of the right people for you to get them together again. Any expertise that you did not have at that stage must be included now. Go back to your three lists that you created in Chapter 8 for the Listening Programme. You have lists A, B and C compiled by your Breakthrough Team. On them is a hierarchy of people with influence over the mission. Check this resource for experts. Are they there? If not, then where else in the organization are they? You may have already involved design experts from external agencies in your design team, especially if there are technical complexities to the product. If the expertise is not available within existing resources, then you must buy it in. To exclude it now will leave holes in the design for which you may pay later.

The length of time that you devote to this will be dictated by the size of the outcome you need and technical difficulties inherent in the design. The bigger the innovation, the more time you will require. Suffice it to say that a large shift in products, sales, marketing, underwriting and support functions that changed the face of a financial services organization took two weeks of solid work by a top team. Often companies are overgenerous with time and thus development teams fill it! We would recommend two weeks as a maximum. It galvanizes action. This is an ideal and we are aware that in your area regulatory requirements may insist that the product undergoes a stringent set of tests for safety, legality or other reasons that may necessitate a series of steps and revisions in the design phase.

Authoritative events need a sense of being history in the making. This is theatrical, but effective. Occurrences of great moment are marked and validated by oratory from high-status speakers. Get someone high ranking to speak to the designers about the importance of what they are about to do. This will reassure the designers of the significance of their undertaking.

The principles are the same as those used in the initial design. They must be undistracted from the task in hand, comfortably housed off-site. These people will be designing the future of your company. There is nothing more important than that right now.

The overall instruction to the Final Design Team, as it was with the initial design team, must be 'Make it possible'.

This is not the opportunity to develop the Mission Plan, i.e. the implementation process for the Final Launch. This is a separate and essential piece of work that will need its own team with time to create when the time is right. Until we know the 'what' we can not reliably develop the 'how and when'.

Remember too, the work of Professor Tuckman. To maintain the team's drive there must be test points included in their time together. These are times when they must open their doors to related outsiders to whom they will present their work. It will focus their time together, and add pressure to perform.

The final presentation should be a prestigious affair. This is the theoretical unveiling of a future which is becoming more inevitable as you take each step.

The initial speaker should be there, board representatives, the CEO. The design team should be nervous and excited as they prepare to present to an auspicious and influential group. They should be ready to answer questions, and where unable to answer they should take note, for these will be areas that will need finessing and redesign.

There will be many unanswered questions, and these will form the basis for ongoing development work. The work this team has done will need to be praised, and thanks targeted at the contributors. Elements of the design will need to be taken back to the relevant departments for these answers, solutions, developments to be created.

A deadline for the final answers needs to be established at this point, and individuals charged with the task of resolving problems, creating solutions or adapting parts of the design. However, it is as well that the design team do not know this until the end so that they get as far as they can within their allotted time.

Pricing is always an issue where innovation is involved. If it is new then it is likely that it has never been sold before. Price tolerance in the market will be unknown, so some pricing research may be needed.

There will be an emerging view as to the feasibility of the design, but a final costing remains to be done. Legacy systems and processes will need to be audited and examined for compatibility, and mismatches resolved and priced. Training dependencies will need to be assessed and priced. Recruitment, reward and recognition processes will need to be scrutinized too as we have never seen a successful change in product, service or service style where new behaviours were not linked to pay or recognition or both!

Strangely, one of the last things to change in organizations, especially larger ones, is the recruitment specifications for a new service style. We have often seen companies continue recruiting the wrong people for new jobs, especially the jobs with lower status. This creates an immediate problem if the culture and style is not in place to deliver the innovation appropriately. There are two things that influence the taste of your cappuccino; the hard factors like the taste of the coffee and temperature of the milk and soft factors like the rapport established by your server and the ambience of the venue. Be sure to consider both what you do and how you do it.

Again, depending on the size of what has been designed, your innovation is going to make waves. Thoroughness now will set the tone for your launch. Speed and accuracy are the most needed qualities as the company audits itself against the Final Design. This information will be collected, collated and presented back to you by the internal client consultant.

Each department needs to cost against the design. They do this by imagining a situation in which they are already running the necessary processes to support the efficient delivery of the product or service that has been designed. The question to ask is:

'What would have to be in place to support this innovation?'

The answer to this question will indicate what needs to be changed, replaced or reinvented.

The next questions are:

'What will be one-off costs, and what will be ongoing?'
    'Do my ongoing departmental costs increase or decrease and by how much?'
    'What can I save through creative problem solving?'

This gives you four essential pieces of information:

1   How near or far are we from being able to support the design?
2   How much one-off investment will be needed?
3   Do our running costs increase or decrease?
4   Where are the areas of saving through creative solutions?

Furnished with your final design, and some information about costs, your business is now in a position to examine the feasibility of the design. What would the benefits be to the business if the design were already implemented? What revenue would it have to generate, or what would the value proposition to the business be? How would it add value? Would this be sufficient to justify the costs involved in maintaining it? If so, would it justify the costs involved in implementing it as far as can be assessed right now? Over what period might you expect to break even?

The mission is about to go into its most expensive phases. Without all this knowledge you are not going to be appropriately resourced to succeed, nor is your investor going to have what he/she needs to remain confident. Remember the time needed will be more or less dependent on the size and ambition of the changes you are advocating. Short cuts are costly. This is time well spent.

12 | Prototypes and Customer Experience Testing

Researching experience

Focus groups are useful for certain things. Good ones can be extremely useful, but their use is limited to what they are capable of delivering. They are not reliable for measuring experience. We have seen brilliant ideas killed off by the inappropriate use of focus groups. In Chapter 3 we advocated research using large groups as opposed to the accepted conventions of small group work. Now we want to go a bit further.

Let us take a moment to recap on what you have done.

1   You have participated in a discovery process with your customers. Together you mined for new learning that was not available through other means. It existed deep within all of you together, and when it had its impact you took the trouble to notice the fact.

2   You inquired into the nature and meaning of this impact, interpreting it until it made sense to you.

3   Out of this learning you created insightful possibilities for future products or services. They were built from experience at the personal and private level. What you have created will deliver both a functional benefit and an experience – the experience will be a big part of the value that will not only sell it, but make it unique.

Experience is what makes Starbucks coffee unique in a market that has coffee available on every street corner. We doubt that many of us could tell the difference between Starbucks and Costa coffee tasted blind. Nor would it matter much to most of us if we could. Separating the Starbucks experience for 'product and concept' testing using the standard approach of product test and qualitative groups is all very well. But we worry that with experience the whole is more than the sum of the parts. Experiences have process as well as components. These processes are key to the impression left by the experience. Having a decent cup of coffee is an entry level requirement in this market. Researching the product alone is to inquire into only a percentage of the value, and thus is only a fraction of the information you require. The other part is probably more important. How different do you imagine the seats in Economy Class on Singapore Airlines are from other economy seats? How much of the comfort of travelling with them is contributed by the charm, courtesy and sensitivity of their brilliant cabin crew? We remember Anita Roddick saying that if she had listened to focus groups she would not have done many of the groundbreaking things that she did with The Body Shop.

So how do you go about authentically researching a product or service that only exists as a design? As you can imagine, we favour an experiential approach, building as far as we can a 'real' engagement with the product or service you are developing. We want, if possible, to experiment with something that is authentic, something which is what we call 'dependably real'.

Based upon a combination of ethnography and prototyping we have developed a more theatrical process in which customers can get to experience your product or service as closely as possible to the reality represented by the final design.

In the world of the theatre there is a concept called the 'suspension of disbelief'. It describes what an audience does when it enters a theatre and the performance begins. Those of you who attend plays or something like the opera will know that watching people sing at each other is a totally unnatural experience. Yet we believe what is going on so completely that we feel emotional reactions to the situations depicted as if they were happening in life itself! We catch ourselves hoping that Macbeth will not kill Duncan even though we know that he must do so – Shakespeare wrote it that way, and it has happened innumerable times throughout the last five hundred years, more or less the same way. Knowing this does not seem to affect our willingness to suspend our disbelief and experience the story at a physiological and emotional level. It is not choosing to believe on our part, it is surrendering our disbelief. By leaving it on the backburner we get to experience events on stage as if they were real, as if we ourselves were up there in the situations being played out before us. This phenomenon is a researcher's gift, and yet is very seldom employed.

We have been willing to play 'let's pretend' since we were children. When children do this, they do not stay sitting down in the living room, they lend their whole person to the job. Their bodies get involved, their voices, gestures and expressions. Karaoke is a phenomenon that exemplifies this. Grown adults get to pretend for the duration of an entire song that they are a musical star of their choice. We have seen this across the world. Even in some of the most constrained cultures karaoke blossoms. People get to experience performing to an audience. Ask them what it was like and they will use words that reflect the feelings they had whilst doing it. We could intellectualize about the function that karaoke fulfils, but that would be guesswork. If you want to know how it feels you just have to do it and notice what happens inside the experience. To find out what the common themes of experience are, you need to have a decent sample of people try it out and tell you.

While this has some similarities to a product test, we attempt as far as possible to simulate the intended circumstances of the final offering. This is of particular importance if the experience will last for some time or has several stages. So we will fly on aeroplanes across the world with people, listening to their experiences in real time. We will accompany people through a sales process where a new product and sales style are on offer. We will check in with people at an hotel and suffer with them the congestion of the queue. The check-in staff may be wonderful but how long do you have to wait? We will accompany them to their room and compare first impressions. We will give people a prototype of a new household product, and call round when they've had it for a while to listen to them. The fact that they may not have much to say about it is as interesting as any other finding.

All through the book we have suggested that there is no substitute for live experiences with customers and that goes for this experiential testing phase too. If the ideas you have developed are innovative, they may be difficult to research by comparison with things that already exist. If it is a breakthrough then you will have to prototype it.

Without this, the people you are researching will merely fit what you are asking them about inside what they already know; familiar experiences that have a preset framework of associations for them. They will report back to you about the experience that they already know. They will not have any internal reference points to have it be in any way different. The first guys who landed on the moon could not have created the experience they had without going there. In fact, they all reported distressing difficulties in trying to describe the experience to people who had not been there – at that point the entire rest of humanity!

Your new ideas must be tasted, smelt, touched, heard and seen. In short, your research must offer an opportunity to experience the innovation as if it were already on offer to them. This is where the theatre comes in. Things like the number of people involved at the same time can be crucial too. An empty 747 cabin is a very different experience from a full one.

In pursuit of groundbreaking healthcare products we set up an experience for two sets of 30 people, each of whom was accompanied by a research buddy as they spent three hours experiencing the benefits and processes which they would undergo in 13 months of membership.

The experience had to include:

- *advertising* (direct mail, magazines, newspapers, inserts, and TV mock-ups);
- *a contact channel* that they were drawn to (Internet, snail mail, telephone);
- *a sales advisory experience* in the new style of the product (telephone sales, Internet assessment, face-to-face adviser);
- *a welcome experience* (follow-up mail and customer service telephone conversation);
- *ongoing benefits experience* (a mail out to reflect the customer profile);
- *service recovery* after a mistake; and
- *a renewal experience* at the end of the first year (a new set of prices for people continuing, a leaving experience for those who decided not to).

You can imagine the work that had to go into creating this. The information technology department wrote and delivered a miniature IT system; we installed telephone systems, trained telephone sales staff, trained advisors, trained customer service staff and underwriters. Marketing materials had to be written and printed on a short print run. The advertising agency produced a mock-up of the commercial for the television.

People walked through the different experiences with specific budgets to allocate to various parts of their desired products so they could trade off elements of the products and experience against others. They got to choose their own route through each aspect of the process, and were interviewed as they went. We followed their preferences as they went. The results were spectacular, and reflected extremely accurately how the product then performed in the market place.

The organization had been activated cross-functionally by the production of the mini-systems and processes that were necessary for the research. Holes in the processes were highlighted, and inadequacies were brought to the surface whence they could be fixed. The final design was edited and redesigned appropriately. The process galvanized the teams of people into action and forced them into a level of co-operative relationship they had never before achieved. By the time we implemented, people were already talking together – the job was enhanced beyond expectation, and implementation was easy.

We mentioned earlier the use of skilled actors to give sales staff a face-to-face experience of the effects of their script and sales style. This worked beautifully to give staff a level of feedback about their work they could not otherwise get. Don't we all want to know about the effects we have on others?

If what you are proposing is a new seat in an aircraft, then let customers sit in it. Give them time to play with the knobs and buttons without direction from you so that they can discover the seat – make it their own. They will discover ways to configure it that nobody has yet thought of. Put them together in a space equivalent to the one in which it will be put with other people. Brief them simply, and let them loose to discover what they feel and think.

If you have too many tightly scripted questions, people are likely to make up the answers to get rid of you. People need time to seek out answers to your questions. Immerse them in a mock-up of the experience, and then ask questions that give them room to report how it felt, what they noticed – even what questions they think are important to ask!

If the service you want to research is delivered within a personal interaction with a member of staff, then your personnel will need training and not just a pep talk on the day itself. They will need to learn how to deliver a new and different experience to these research customers. Otherwise they will snap back to the way they have always done their job, and your research responses will be based on something old and nothing new.

Producing the theatrical mock-up will teach you much about what will be needed when you implement for real. There is no substitute for customer experience testing. If what you produce is a good model, then your 'customers' will play.

13 | The Mission Plan

Mission planning made simple

Putting your mission where you can measure it is the only way to ensure that everyone can see the results of their labours relative to the final desired outcome. Churches do it with the big red thermometers indicating how near they are to being able finally to fix the roof! In Singapore, building sites have charts outside for the public to view, relating to the number and types of accidents that have been experienced on the site. Having visual representations of progress helps keep people focussed. Knowing where you are is the first and necessary piece of intelligence before choosing where to go next.

There are Gantt Charts and PERT charts, and any number of ways of visually representing your Mission Plan. They all have a great deal to offer. There are a number of extremely good computer programs for project planning that will help you. Unless project planning is your thing, our advice is to keep it as simple as you can.

Suffice it to say that whatever you create or decide to use to achieve the pictorial tool you need, you just have to make sure it tells you the stuff you need to know as easily as possible.

What do you need to know when implementing anything new?

- What does it have to look like when it is finished (final design)?
- Who must do what and when?
- How long will each task take?

- What can be done only when something else has been done?
- What resources are needed for each thing that must be done?
- What is the best path from start to finish?
- How is it going schedule-wise?

If you have ever set out to tidy your house and tried to do a bit of everything at the same time you might have noticed this is a recipe to get nothing completely finished. It takes longer to accomplish anything, it is inefficient, overwhelming and dreadfully demoralizing. You are in danger of having brooms, dustpans, Dyson, polish, bathroom cleanser, new toilet rolls and bin bags lying everywhere creating as much mess to clean up as you had before you started.

A mission needs clear steps to be taken, and an appreciation of what steps need to be done before next ones can be taken. Some steps are thus dependent on others and need to be completed in sequence, and others are independent and can be done whenever they are needed, in parallel with other activities. These are well-established terms in this work, and have become so because they are pretty important.

A sequential task or activity needs to be scheduled very carefully relative to both the preceding task and the proceeding tasks ahead. Parallel tasks or activities can be completed more flexibly. Having a meeting today to report on the results of an event that happens next week would be pointless. To fulfil its purpose the meeting needs to happen after the event – the one is dependent on the other.

There are hundreds of ways of assembling this information into a visual aid that will allow you to see all of this at a glance in a comprehensible form. There are innumerable software packages, there is the Gantt Chart, which can be done using simple graph paper and you may or may not have a preference. As far as we are concerned the easiest, and most fun way of collecting and organizing the information that you will need is what PostIt notes were made for!

Assemble a representative team, preferably people who have some part in the design process. Please note that it is very, very important to have your reality supervisor here because in the second part of this workshop/meeting you will be taking a look at the risks and vulnerabilities of your plan. Join together three or even four pieces of flip chart paper together, oriented in landscape (see Fig. 13.1).

Each function should have one of these huge assemblies of paper. Draw a timeline from now to a date six months after you would like your innovation launched. Life does not stop at launch, it goes on. How your product or service performs is something for which you will all share collective responsibility – it must not just float, but sail magnificently to the chosen destinations that you have outlined in your performance criteria. Each function should have

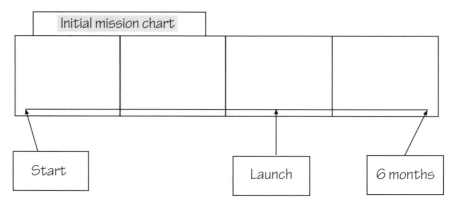

Fig. 13.1   The time line.

different colour PostIts to those of other functions. Each function will be distinguishable by the colour of its PostIt notes.

Along that timeline each function will have tasks that must be achieved in order to fulfil their part in the mission. One task per PostIt, with a list of resources needed.

When the tasks are exhausted they need to be sequenced where necessary – what tasks are dependent on others? Where the dependency crosses functions – in other words, where one department is dependent on the completion of something specific from another department – it is essential to go and check that the other department has identified this task. Deputize a representative to go and check.

Eventually each function will have the beginnings of a Mission Plan with all the tasks that will need to be completed to take the new product and/or service through to six months after launch, as well as a list of resources required for each task. They will also be in some sort of sequence. The beauty of the sticky notelet or PostIt is that it can be unstuck and re-stuck somewhere else without doing any damage.

Now it is time to put all the timelines together and to sequence the tasks across the functions. What is the sequence of dependent tasks and activities? Now what is the best place to put the parallel or non-dependent tasks and activities so that they do not interfere with the sequential ones? Are there any resource issues, savings that could be made by sequencing to maximize opportunities to share resources?

Now number them. This allows you to allocate a number to each task so that it can be identified easily, regardless of its place on the timeline. Once each task has a number, go through and identify the dependent actions – the 'sequential tasks' will need to have a second number on them. Each sequential task needs to have the number of the task or tasks on which it depends included on it (Fig. 13.2).

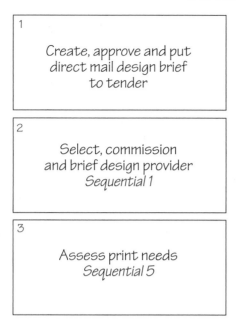

Fig. 13.2   Numbered tasks with dependencies identified.

Now we are motoring. The plan is beginning to emerge. Now, how long do you think each of the tasks is likely to take? Find a place on each PostIt to write the time you estimate it will take (Fig. 13.3).

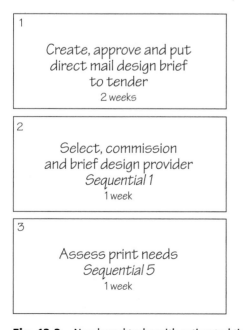

Fig. 13.3   Numbered tasks with estimated times.

Now look at all the information you have. You know what needs to be done, who needs to do it, how long it will take and what actions depend on the completion of other tasks before they can start. Each task has a number. Now you can draw a Mission Plan that makes all of that information available at a glance.

Some people like to plot out this information in an Excel style in columns. You can see a simple example here in Fig. 13.4. The parallel tasks are relatively moveable in comparison with the sequential ones, which are critical. Often a task might be dependent on several other tasks being completed, in which case each of the numbers for each of the tasks on which it depends must be in the relevant box. When all the information is entered into this table you are ready to convert all this information into an easy-to-read flow chart for the entire mission.

Number and task	Sequential or parallel	Start time	Time to complete	Dependent on which task numbers?
1. Create, approve and put direct mail design brief to tender	P	Wk 1	2 wks	
2. Select, commission and brief design provider	S	Wk 3	1 wk	1
3. Assess print needs	S	Wk 8	1 wk	5
4. Audit and select print suppliers	S	Wk 9	3 wks	3
5. Delivery of final direct mail design and text	S	Wk 4	4 wks	2
6. Merge and update databases	P	Wk 1	6 wks	
7. Legal checks on direct mail claims	S	Wk 5	3 wks	2
8. Alert mailshot company	S			5, 6
9. Telesales centre training audit	P	Wk 5	3 wks	
10. Training in new product	S	Wk 8	4 wks	9
11. Finalize mailing database	S	Wk 7	2 wks	6

Fig. 13.4   Mission chart.

You are merely two easy stages from having the Mission Plan that you will be proud to display at Mission Centre so that anyone and everyone who needs to can assess progress at any point in the process.

Firstly, summarize your mission by creating a table of contents as in Fig 13.4. In our simple example we have a list of 11 tasks just to give you an idea of how to lay out all the data.

Every task is numbered and defined, is sequential or parallel, has an estimate of start time and length of time it is likely to take. In the extreme right hand column are the tasks on which it is dependent, noted by number.

Next get some big graph paper and divide it into time-based columns. In the sample in Fig. 13.5 you can see a fragment with each column representing a week.

Observing the estimated start date now draw in each task as a horizontal line. The line length will vary according to the time the task is estimated to take. It is numbered and defined on the right, and on the line and above it are the numbers of the tasks on which the task is dependant.

Our example spans only the first 13 weeks. As far as charts go this may be all you need to do. You could do a Critical Path Analysis if you feel really bold. All this means is that as you connect the sequential tasks you begin to see the path that emerges as the dominant one, around which all the parallel activities

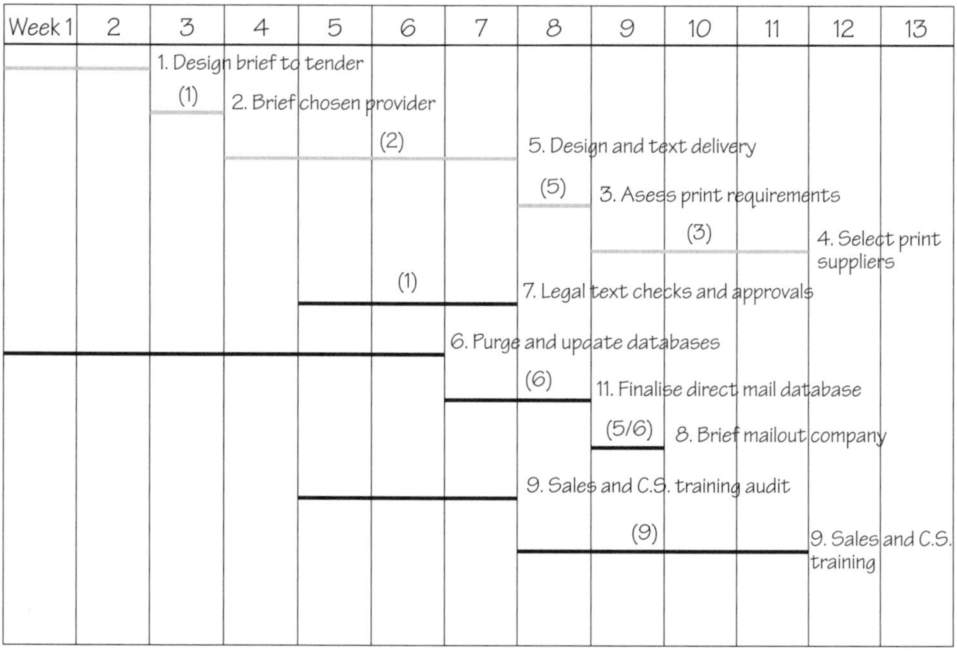

Fig. 13.5   Gantt chart.

start to form. In other words it is almost certainly the longest unbroken path of sequential tasks. In the diagram we have indicated it with the grey lines. A robust and detailed plan will save you both heartache and backache later down the line. Implementation can be the most tedious part of the process if the planning is done thoroughly and your preparation for inherent risks is sound.

Risk analysis

Irritating as it might be, no Mission Plan can be credible without some detailed analysis of the risks involved, and some good ideas about how to manage the most likely and potentially costly ones. When you begin risk analysis the process is up to you. In our opinion, innovation teams that get caught up in detailed analysis of risk before the plan has been created are trying to fix fog. It is rather like travelling towards a distant mountain. You see it well on clear days, you can head towards it accurately. However, when the fog descends, everyone is in danger of getting lost and walking in circles trying to fix the fog. You cannot fix fog because you cannot capture it. Every time you try to take a handful it just slips through your fingers. We can make up all sorts of risks to manage almost all of the time. Getting out of bed in the morning can be hazardous – you might twist your ankle, you might step onto a part of the floor that has mysteriously collapsed during the night or you could even step on a rattlesnake that has escaped form the local zoo and slipped through your letter box. We can have a riot using up all our best energies defeating the mission by generating catastrophic predictions.

Keeping our risk assessment grounded is essential. There will be risks and they have to be considered carefully, planned for and monitored, otherwise they could be costly.

The first step in risk assessment is to look at the plan and ask yourselves across the departmental functions *'what are the tasks that might i) use more resource than we plan for, adding to extra unexpected cost, ii) take more time than allocated thereby holding the mission up, iii) not meet the quality standard required for the ensuing sequential tasks, thereby threatening the performance of the final result?'*

You and your mission planning team need to brainstorm the risks. In terms of people that will need to deliver a completed task, where your relationships are strong you will have more certainty, and where they are weak less certainty. We repeat, relationships are the source of results. List all the risks and allow them to be wild and imaginative as well as feasible, as you can sift through them for reasonability later. These need to be recorded on a flip chart to create a 'risk register' after the session. However, while you are all together with as complete a list as you can collectively generate, ask people to rank the risks in order of a) likelihood, b) adverse impact.

Again, reining in the paranoid fantasies of the group will be important. If the world ends it will have a devastating impact on any mission, but we might rely on this being unlikely. To put the end of the world as a priority risk to manage just because its impact would be so huge would, we hope you agree, be more than a little misguided. We are looking to manage the most likely, highest-impact risks first, as well as to assess the others too.

Once this is complete, take the top ten risks with the highest likelihood and the highest impact, and ask yourselves a) who is the source of the risk, and b) who is best situated to manage it, or to 'bear' it. Knowing the answer to these questions is pretty important because with risk there are a number of ways to deal with it.

- You can *transfer* it to someone better positioned to deal with it than currently.
- You can *accept* the risk, and thereby hope for the best, or decide to respond should the need to arise.
- You can *eliminate* it, which is great if you can afford to do it or accomplish it easily as it makes it go away!
- You can *mitigate* the risk, which requires you to develop a strategy to decrease the likelihood of it happening at all and/or minimize the impact of it occurring.

You all need to decide which is best. A word of warning though, this is likely to be happening at the end of a busy day together and people may want to get home. Watch out for woolly planning. 'More communication' does not amount to a very secure mitigating strategy as it is virtually guaranteed not to occur. 'Daily progress update by phone immediately prior to close of business' starts to look more like an action that could be taken and measured. Make sure that where risk is to be transferred, the transferee knows and accepts it

When you have done this for as many risks as possible, but at least your top ten, it is time to take the flip charts away and record them. The information you have will dictate how you record it. It could be that you divide it up departmentally, or by risk-types (i.e. risks that threaten quality, cost or time). You should also record the decided strategy and the person to whom the risk has been transferred, where appropriate, because it is they who will be monitoring it and therefore will be the source of information relating to progress.

With a team of very exhausted people on your hands, you must praise and acknowledge them for their efforts, and let them know when they are going to next hear from you.

Now, one very important fact to consider is that all of your costs are based on assumptions right now. Even if you have experience of purchasing similar stuff recently, any number of factors may have affected prices. Your timescales are intelligent guesses too, and if you have got those significantly wrong, then you are more likely to be travelling red-faced to your investor to explain why the mission is delayed than the opposite.

Here are some figures for you. It is reckoned that any project costs without factual prices having been researched will vary plus or minus 20%. That famous law referred to when things go pear-shaped has a tendency to veer towards the plus rather like bread always falling butter-side down! Even with factual prices having been gathered there is an accepted plus or minus 10%. Every minute of every day the prices of some things are changing – someone we know observed that cost and schedule estimates can be 'like pushing treacle upstairs'.

The more complex and expensive your mission, the more you will need a risk model. This is the result of a computer running cost and time calculations based on some educated guesswork hundreds of times over. Each calculation is completed with a total. The totals that occur most frequently represent the most likely outcome with a best and a worst figure too. So, as an example, if you want to buy flowers from a garden centre for your garden, there are any number of price variables depending on the location of the nearest garden centre, the availability of the plants you require, the maturity of the plants and the price dictated by it. You also have the costs associated with going there and back, as well as the possibility that some may not survive and may have to be replaced. The soil quality you have may need improving, and your choice of product will have an influence.

By looking at each price element and doing some research you will be able to come up with three figures.

First, an advantageous one that you might get at best if you can factor in some discount for buying quantity, finding the cheapest available and with free delivery to your door.

Second, a worst-case price where they only have the most mature and expensive varieties, quantities of soil improver that exceed what you need but only available in larger sizes, and a double trip due to your being unable to manage the bulk of your purchases in one trip.

Third, you can then choose a price somewhere midway between the two figures that seems to be the likeliest price. If you look at Fig. 13.6 you will see

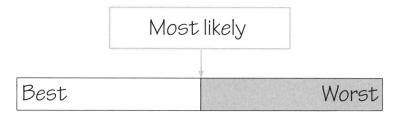

Fig. 13.6   Risk analysis output.

that it represents your optimum cost (ideal but unlikely), your worst case cost (possible but unlikely) and your likely cost.

By feeding this information for each element of spending into the appropriate risk management software and running what is known as a Monte Carlo simulation, the computer will calculate the likeliest costs with a plus or minus range. The objective of all the people who have been given risks to manage will be to deliver the likeliest cost or below.

Accurate time estimates are also difficult to generate without the same or similar mathematical tools. Going back to the garden centre again: look at the variables – travel time, possible break down, possible need to order and wait for delivery of plants, queues at the checkout (never go on a Saturday or Sunday!), stopping for petrol, breakdown of gardening tools etc. Appropriate software will allow you to run a similar process to calculate optimum, worst and most likely time estimates. Having these identified gives you and your implementation team times to meet or better. It also reassures your investor that you have all the angles covered, and you must never forget that their confidence matters crucially.

Every mission has milestones along its main critical path. These are your success or failure points, key events that mark progress. Once you have a best, worst and likely measure for each of these, you have measures in place that will stand you in good stead. Using Fig. 13.6 as a model you can represent your range of possible times in order to be prepared for the best or worst and to monitor progress accordingly.

As a general guide, if your mission is going to cost up to £125,000 you can quite justifiably keep your risk assessment to its simplest form. A risk register will usually suffice as long as risks are allocated and strategies clearly set. If you are handling a budget of up to a million, get an assistant to head it up, preferably someone with some experience of risk management. Above a million and under 50 million it is a good idea to get some consultants in and have a team member be responsible for running it.

Above that it is probably best to create a risk team to head it up.

Resources

Planning and risk assessment workshop

- A big enough venue for teams to work separately without getting in each other's way.
- Flip chart for each team.
- Sellotape or masking tape to join sheets of flip chart paper together.

Post workshop

- For budgets above £150,000, get risk assessment software (e.g. Monte Carlo from P3, or Suretrak from Primavera – please note we do not necessarily recommend these, but they are effective).

14 | Communication Strategy

Communication strategy and its importance

Suffice it to say that if you do not start to raise the level of communication at this time, you will regret it. It is now advisable to have your internal marketing manager and internal clients' consultant swing into action. This communication strategy must be part of your Mission Plan. It is at least as important as anything else that is being done to implement your innovations.

Whatever it is that you are doing, change will create anxiety. The greater the change, the more the anxiety. We have acknowledged this throughout the book, particularly in relation to the vulnerabilities of the most influential people in your company. Now you must deal with the sensibilities of the people who are going to have the most influence over the success or failure of your innovations. In fact, that means everyone who touches it or anything that supports it! The strategy you use to talk to them will depend largely on the size of your organisation. What you say will depend on:

- their questions; and
- your answers to those questions.

All too often the official communication consists of press releases designed for the financial markets. There is also a prevalent communication habit called 'cascading' information. Whether or not this is successful depends on the degree to which Chinese Whispers influences what is heard and then repeated.

Not all managers are good communicators. For the most part both cascading and press releases are one-way communications. Unless you invite a conversation in which the wider staff and the people heading up your mission are equal participants, all that will be going on is a great deal of telling with very little real feedback from those being told.

Countless corporate developments are hindered, hounded and confounded by companies refusing to deal with the real concerns of people who work for them. When people go to work in a new organisation in a new role they always feel nervous. Their heads are full of questions that they dare not ask. What should I be doing? What is expected of me? Will I be good enough? What will people think of me if I have to ask questions? Will they think I'm incompetent? Do they regret employing me already? Will I get the sack? Maybe this time they'll find me out! If you think back to your first day it will not be long before your pulse starts to increase and you feel echoes of the feelings generated by those day-one doubts. This is anxiety.

Here is our theory – *change means starting again*. The day you launch anything new everyone who is touched by the innovation has another 'first day' at work. To one degree or another everyone starts to generate the same kind of questions as their bygone first-day doubts. The sum total of this nervousness is massive when taken across the average business: unanswered, these questions persist and deepen. Let us remind you of the Four Corner resistance model that we outlined in Chapter 8. Unless you communicate what people need to know, their vulnerabilities will hamper the success of your innovations. You might even start to see an immediate downturn in productivity as people spend more and more time gossiping. When we were working on the breakthroughs which gave rise to the converter seat in the early 1990s – a seat which gave a much-wanted increase in space to passengers in the Euro-business cabin – there was much doubt that any product improvement could ever substantially improve the poor reputation of short-haul business products. Now that seat and its 2–3 pattern are a universal standard of business class in premium short-haul around the world. To listen to some of the early gossip you would have thought that it didn't stand a chance:

> 'There'll be a riot among those that have to sit in the threes. It's just not fair!'

None of us likes to have to live our daily lives without answers to questions that preoccupy us. Our minds like to have our world be as predictable as possible. Where there are no authoritative answers available, people will collectively fill in the knowledge gaps with rumour and gossip. Imagine a company in which the average hourly rate of pay is £10.00. Imagine 60 people spending 30 minutes per day gossiping about the future implications of impending change.

That costs £300 per day, £1500 per week, £6000 per month in lost productivity. Gossip is demoralising and expensive. The only way to inhibit it is to communicate effectively. The presence of rumours and gossip saps creativity and ties up thought even when we are not actively talking with others. Generating conspiracy theories and then 'selling' them to others is something that most of us will get up to in the face of uncertainty. This is a derivation of the Plotting corner in the Resistance Model. Your organisation will have some pet theories that get recycled from time to time. You will know what they are if you have been there for any length of time.

Often when things are changing, the first time people hear about it is when they are called to training. Sometimes we have seen organisations implement new products relying on a ten-minute pep-talk to staff on the morning they are expected to launch, sell and maintain it!

Once you have the authority you need to go ahead to implementation, you will need to start communicating relevant information as quickly and effectively as possible.

How to develop your strategy

Get together with your internal marketing manager and internal clients' consultant. The first thing to do is write a list of every area of the business that will need to receive communication from you. Make this comprehensive and detailed. You must ask yourselves if there are subdivisions of people within each area of your business who will require a separate communication in a different style. Different groups of people need to be spoken to in dissimilar ways. The more personal your communication, the better, providing you do not ignore basic protocols and boundaries that must be respected. This first step though requires that you merely make a list.

Once this is complete, have a look at the existing media available for communication throughout your business. Start off with one-to-one conversation, the most powerful communication medium of all, and work through every means you have at your disposal. List each one, for example Internet, intranet, staff magazine, memos, meetings, telephone, etc.

While it is important to pay due deference to people in the management lines, it is equally important for people to feel that they can have a meaningful conversation with the people at the centre of the mission. For it to be a conversation they need to be invited to speak. They also need to feel free to be honest about what is really on their minds. Remember what we have said about the professional and the personal agendas that proliferate in every community? This is apposite now. There may be some genuine professional concerns, and it is very important that you know what these are so that you can answer them.

However the biggest potential problems stem from personal agendas. As we have said, this one may be difficult to uncover, as it is habitually kept secret. It is often shared between friends and then fed into the gossip-mill. So one advantage of keeping your ear out for gossip is that you will soon learn what the main questions, doubts and concerns of the community are.

Before you start to answer people's questions, you need to know exactly what they are. As a rule of thumb if you really want people to own up to their personal agenda you have to create permission for them to do so. The most permissive thing you can do is to own up to your own. As engagement manager you will have experienced all sorts of anxiety. You will have worried for your future. You will have been worried that the mission would go sour. You will have worried that you didn't know the answers and everyone could see. So imagine, what kind of communication would allow you the space and permission to admit in writing the kinds of questions and doubts you have had during the entire process?

In order to be effective in inviting people to let you know what questions they have, you might have to include your best guesses as to the kind of questions that might be rumbling around in the background of their personal agendas. Here is a sample invitation that we have used in the past to great effect.

> 'You will have heard by now that we have conducted extensive research into a set of new products. Everyone who is involved in launching and promoting the new products is absolutely essential for its success. What we most need to know is what you need to know, not just about the product and how it will function, but anything that is important to you, about which you need answers. If you are a parent with children at school you may be concerned that your working hours might have to change. Are you worried that the new products won't need you to help them along? Have you found yourself worrying about your job security? You may wonder about training for the new products. These are the normal kind of questions that people have when changes occur.
>
> 'Whatever it is that may be concerning you right now about the new products, or about your own welfare, then please, please let us know by filling in this form. Once we have the questions will try to answer them all as quickly as possible. Those questions that we cannot answer right away either because of commercial sensitivity (we don't want the competition to know everything yet do we?) or because you have exposed something we have not thought through, we will let you know we cannot answer and why. We will then follow up with the answers when we have them, or secrecy is no longer an issue.
>
> 'Importantly you can send your questions to us directly and you need not say who you are. Through anonymity you can feel even freer to

let us know what you need. We want all questions in by _____ so that we can send you the first raft of answers by _____ three weeks later. This is really important so please help us. Thank you,

Andy Bright and team

You may be worried that you will create fears by inviting the doubts and insecurities people may have. You can be assured that they will be there already. They are default settings that we all have. They pre-exist and if they remain unidentified, unmanaged and unhindered they will create endless problems later. The innovations will end up swimming against a sea of resistance.

Once you have written your invitation to people, and you have chosen a style for each area of the business that you think suits them best, then decide which of your available media you will use. Could it be launched at a staff briefing? Maybe you need to create a special get-together for other departments. For sales staff who may be located regionally it may be best to telephone everyone individually and talk it through. Or arrange a visit to one of their regular meetings. The time you spend on this will save ten times as much time and money in the long run.

In order to keep track of progress you'll need another chart or plan. Again, keep it simple. All you need to create is a large graph. Your vertical axis will contain the list of people with whom you will be communicating, and your horizontal axis all available media. Depending on how expert you are, you may want to design differently worded and formatted communication for each department. If you do this, then give each version a number by which it can be identified. Now all you need to do is enter the number in the square that corresponds both to your chosen medium and to the department. When the invitation has been sent and the response has been received, all you need to do is colour in the square with a highlighter pen.

As soon as questions start coming in, the work must start in earnest. You will soon notice that some questions will be extremely common. Some may have a subversive quality with an unmistakably cynical ring. Regardless of their tone answer them all straightforwardly, with genuine information. This is the only way to win trust. Don't forget those questions that you cannot answer because of sensitivity or because you don't know the answer! Respond to these honestly and appropriately, too.

'The questions you ask about sales targets for the first year is too commercially sensitive for us to answer in a printed document just yet. The targets do exist, and you will be consulted about them two months prior to launch. Our research has suggested a level of demand, and it will be very valuable for us to check out your thoughts on the matter before we make a final goal.

'A number of people from customer services have asked what the strategy will be for customers to migrate from existing products to the new product. We can't answer this question for the moment because we haven't designed it. We are currently consulting people from customer services, underwriting, sales and finance to create a strategy with relevant incentives to make migration more attractive. As soon as we have a final design for the strategy it will be included in your training plan. If you think there is anything that this team should know, any ideas that you have or any considerations that you think should not be missed then e-mail them to jsmith@migstrat.co.uk as soon as you can.'

Plan out your responses in the same way as you did your invitations. Not every department will need the same questions answered. Make every effort to keep your replies relevant only to the inquiries you have received; if they are appropriate and targeted in this way, the more likely it is that your interlocutors will read what you send them.

Do not be dishonest, even and especially where bad news is involved.

Do not make promises that you cannot be sure you can keep. Do not be dishonest, even and especially where bad news is involved. If jobs are threatened then it is important that you are honest about it, and that the answers are delivered using the most appropriate and sensitive media, i.e. as close to one-to-one as possible. If you have to avoid the difficult conversations now, you will hit them harder later. Where people have to be 'let go', the popular euphemism for making redundancies, then your strategy must include the best method for doing so. Dishonesty does not work.

Internal marketing makes all the difference!

Again depending on the size of your organisation, publicly identifying people with success is one of the most motivating things you can do. It may be that you have an internal newspaper or newsletter that is already popular and widely read. If that is so, then use it. Negotiate with the publisher a special page for every edition that is exclusively about your mission and its progress. Sensational news goes a long way. It sells newspapers, and it will sell your mission. Look for the people and the departments that are really making a difference and feature them. Include pictures, however embarrassed the subjects might be; people are only embarrassed by genuine praise because they receive it so infrequently. This page can also become like the thermometer outside the church we described in the previous chapter.

Be creative in your ideas for recognition – cards, flowers, a pat on the back, a telephone call, a shake of the hand, a printed t-shirt that says 'My boss thinks

I'm CEO material!' on the front and 'He'd better watch his step!' written on the back. Trophies mean someone won something. Be bold.

In a particular South East Asian airline with whom we have worked extensively over the past year, customer focus is reinforced by posters that have been created for internal consumption. One has the image of a mum with two small children struggling with cabin baggage as she approaches the entrance to the plane. Her hair is in disarray, and tired lines are etched in her face. On the poster is written a question that reads something like this; 'This woman is on her own with children. What can you do for her that will give her a break?'

If your innovation will require a shift in your cultural attitude towards customers, which is often the case, then you may want to include catalytic marketing materials in a similar vein. When we worked with a major British airline on breakthrough training for cabin staff, the cabin staff themselves made a video that included footage of their interaction with passengers in the new breakthrough style. The rock band Queen provided a background track, a song called 'Breakthrough'. When people saw that video, short as it was, they were left in no doubt at all that something new and significant had arrived.

Whether or not you have the budget or will to pay royalties to a rock band is neither here nor there. Communicating about what you are up to, canvassing your staff about how they feel about it, and using marketing techniques creatively to inspire, inform and enrol your community at a similar level to that which you use to win new customers will pay enormous dividends. If people aren't talking about it, it doesn't exist. If people aren't excited about it, then it is at risk. If people are scared of it, it will be resisted. As the engagement team you are responsible for making sure that people are both excited by the mission and speaking well of it.

15 | Implementation and Review

Implementing the mission plan

We are not sure who first said it but its truth is absolutely beyond doubt – whatever is not measured does not get done. By now you will have measures for all of your milestones. Monitoring quality, cost and time as you go will keep you on top of progress or the lack of it. Quality is a relative term. It means different things to different people. In the case of the mission it does not mean 'the character of excellence', which is often a stick with which teams beat themselves. It merely means 'meeting and supporting the performance needs of the final product or service(s) to be implemented'. Is the task going to ensure the required performance? This is your quality standard. Cost and time are much more easily measured.

Where any of the tasks fall short they will have to be remedied unless you are willing to sacrifice quality, cost or time. This will be a decision that needs to involve those who are dependent on the task that might fall short. You will have to be aware of the impact of compromises that you make in any of these areas as there are likely to be implications as you work through your plan. Remember too, that as the engagement manager you will be the key to keeping things on track and people engaged with the mission and their parts in it.

Where the planning has been thorough and communication good, you will find yourself more often than not worried about why things are going so well. Nevertheless, no two plans, even if they were identical in all respects, could ever be implemented exactly the same way. The unexpected will happen without a shadow of a doubt. Something outside of anyone's control will occur. How can you plan for a virulent 'flu outbreak, or a devastating fire at a key supplier's warehouse? The answer is that you can only do so much and then you have to let go and trust the people on whom the mission depends. Always communicate with them from a sense of your own certainty that they can and will deliver.

However, should it transpire that a task is going to take longer, cost more or deliver lower quality than necessary, call a meeting immediately with people who are dependent on the task in question up to five tasks down the line. If you are going to sacrifice time, money or quality at this point, how is ground going to be regained further down the line. This will demand understanding, engagement and creativity on everyone's part. Open communication about problems and sharing the responsibility as widely as possible for the creation and implementation of solutions will turn potential disasters into rallying and team-reinforcing opportunities. Getting into blame, plotting, avoidance or pleasing (remember the four corner resistances to change in Chapter 8?) will exacerbate the issues and you will all too soon be playing catch up as people get increasingly frustrated, angry and disappointed.

What you must do is keep your engagement team on the ball. Your internal marketing manager should be looking for successes to publish, communicating and selling the mission and its results to the organisation at every opportunity – if it is not being talked about then it is not a priority. Your internal client consultant should be testing and measuring the staff climate and reporting back to you. Your design team leader needs to be overseeing the quality and accuracy of what is being implemented and reporting back regularly. Your reality supervisor will need to be kept abreast of all eventualities regarding the successes and failure of the risk planning. As engagement manager for the whole mission, you must keep your diary as clear or as flexible as possible throughout the implementation period. If something unexpected happens, it will need your swift intervention. It is not your job to do anything *to* people; it is your job to do things *with* them.

In short – act quickly. When things are going well remember the rule 'if it ain't broke don't fix it'. Knowing when to leave things well alone and when to intervene is the art. If you have to intervene be decisive about it – get all the parties together as soon as you can.

When the plan changes then change the plan! Laborious as it might seem, your road map to success is the mission chart hanging up in the Mission Centre. It is the bible for the whole team. If it gets rewritten, then make sure the rewritten version is displayed. Circulate smaller reproductions of it to people who need it. The last thing you want is either people deliberately going 'off-plan' or observing an old one when it has become obsolete. Unless something goes wrong, meet or better all the measures.

Launch

First, prepare to be very generous indeed. However you launch your innovations, remember that your investor is the person who needs to feel a return on their investment in terms of power. Launches are a great time to set this in motion.

Alongside the product or service you are announcing, the start of the show must be your investor. Without them nothing else could have happened – no Breakthrough Zone, no Insight Zone, no Engagement Team, etc. Although you and your team will have borne an enormous weight of responsibilities, the person with it all to lose is the person who entrusted enough power to you for you to proceed. Your investor may have preferences, and by now you will know him or her extremely well. Make much of them. You have done a great job, but they have always owned the mission!

Second, be careful how you thank those who have created the parts of the whole. There is another great piece of advice, the source of which we cannot trace:

> 'He who thanks everybody thanks nobody.'

The e-mail that says 'Well done everyone' is tantamount to disregard and in all honesty pretty rude. When people do their best they deserve recognition. In other words they need to be identified and the necessary plaudits addressed to them personally. If your internal marketing manager has been effective, they will have been collecting evidence of individuals' successes, acts of heroism, going the extra mile, creating solutions out of thin air. Now is the time to thank the individuals who have contributed to the mission this far. Leave no one out – you will need them again, and let's face it – the thing may be launched but it has yet to pay its way!

Launches can sometimes have a euphoric effect. There is a temptation to breathe a sigh of relief then relax. By all means take a short break and give yourselves a big hand, but we need you back on the job in a day or two. We want everyone to keep applying their best energies for the next six months – the Mission Plan will not have been completed until then.

Whatever the performance criteria, remember that the evidence of success lies in the Corporate Impact Map. Where was the evidence of the objective problem across the departments? How will you know when those symptoms start to change? You will need to monitor those and collect evidence of their alleviation and cure. Without that, how else will your investor benefit from being the person behind the solution to all those ills? These will ensure the appropriate payback.

Reviewing the mission

Six months after the launch, or when you have some quantifiable results from the innovation, it is not time to move on. Do not move on, move back. Doing something as new as this deserves to be reviewed and documented so that you the company can do it even better next time. We have noticed that launches are the sexy part of the innovation process for people in organizations. Rushing headlong into the next thing wastes a whole lot of experiential learning. This needs collecting and managing.

How you do this is dependent on your preferences and the size of your organization.

Creating a questionnaire that asks people who were involved in your mission to share what they learned is one way to do this, but, as you know well enough by now, relationships are the source of results.

The purposeful get-together is much more effective. Whatever you decide, you really need to collect responses to several questions:

- What worked?
- What did not work?
- What should we do differently next time?

Once you get this information, then it is time to say good bye. Finish well. You all deserve it. Now is the time to celebrate your achievement – oh yes … and then start the whole process all over again!

Index